Oracle SQL Developer

Learn Database design, development,
and administration using the feature-rich
SQL Developer 4.1 interface

Ajith Narayanan, Oracle ACE Associate

BIRMINGHAM - MUMBAI

Oracle SQL Developer

First published: January 2016

Production reference: 1250116

Published by Packt Publishing Ltd.
Livery Place
35 Livery Street
Birmingham B3 2PB, UK.

ISBN 978-1-78528-127-3

www.packtpub.com

Credits

Author

Ajith Narayanan

Reviewer

Lewis Cunningham

Acquisition Editors

Ruchita Bhansali

Sonali Vernekar

Content Development Editor

Anish Dhurat

Technical Editor

Ryan Kochery

Copy Editors

Akshata Lobo

Angad Singh

Merilyn Pereira

Stuti Srivastava

Vikrant Phadke

Project Coordinator

Bijal Patel

Proofreader

Safis Editing

Indexer

Rekha Nair

Production Coordinator

Aparna Bhagat

Cover Work

Aparna Bhagat

About the Author

Ajith Narayanan is the chief technology officer (CTO) of InfraStack-Labs in Bangalore, India, and has more than 11 years of work experience as an Oracle [apps] DBA and platform architect with expertise in infrastructure architecture, capacity planning, and performance tuning of medium to large e-business suite environments.

He holds a postgraduate degree with PGDBA (finance) from Symbiosis, Pune, an M.S. (software systems) from BITS Pilani, a BE (electronics and communication) from Amrita Institute of Technology, and a diploma (computer technology) from Sree Narayana Guru Institute of Technology.

He has worked in different technical positions as an Oracle DBA, APPS DBA, Oracle apps platform architect, and configuration management technical leader in companies such as GE, Dell, JP MorganChase, Oracle, and TCS. Ajith was at GE before joining InfraStack-Labs.

He is also a regular speaker at national and international Oracle user group conferences such as SANGAM, NZOUG, DOAG, UKOUG, OTN APAC Tour, AIOUG Tech Days, and so on. His white papers have been published on the Oracle Technology Network in English, Portuguese, and Spanish. Ajith is currently serving the ORACLERACSIG board as the web seminar chair (from October 2015), and has previously served the board as the website chair (September 2011 to September 2013).

I would like to thank my entire family, including my wife, Anjali, daughter, Akshara, and my father, mother, and sister, who always gave me continuous support. Also, thanks to Packt for giving me an opportunity to write a book.

I would also like to thank Lewis Cunningham for carefully reviewing the chapters and making the necessary recommendations and comments to make the chapters technically error-free and more informative.

About the Reviewer

Lewis Cunningham is an Oracle ACE and the author of multiple database-related books. He has multiple certifications (Oracle Certified Professional being one of them). Lewis works in the financial industry as a database architect and application developer and has been doing so for over 20 years.

He enjoys reading, writing, gardening, woodworking, programming, and playing FPS and RPG games. He lives in Tampa, Florida, USA, with his wife, two sons, three dogs, and one cat.

www.PacktPub.com

Support files, eBooks, discount offers, and more

For support files and downloads related to your book, please visit www.PacktPub.com.

Did you know that Packt offers eBook versions of every book published, with PDF and ePub files available? You can upgrade to the eBook version at www.PacktPub.com and as a print book customer, you are entitled to a discount on the eBook copy. Get in touch with us at service@packtpub.com for more details.

At www.PacktPub.com, you can also read a collection of free technical articles, sign up for a range of free newsletters and receive exclusive discounts and offers on Packt books and eBooks.

https://www2.packtpub.com/books/subscription/packtlib

Do you need instant solutions to your IT questions? PacktLib is Packt's online digital book library. Here, you can search, access, and read Packt's entire library of books.

Why subscribe?

- Fully searchable across every book published by Packt
- Copy and paste, print, and bookmark content
- On demand and accessible via a web browser

Free access for Packt account holders

If you have an account with Packt at www.PacktPub.com, you can use this to access PacktLib today and view 9 entirely free books. Simply use your login credentials for immediate access.

Instant updates on new Packt books

Get notified! Find out when new books are published by following @PacktEnterprise on Twitter or the Packt Enterprise Facebook page.

Table of Contents

Preface

The book dives into the details of Oracle SQL Developer 4.1, which is a graphical version of SQL*Plus. Oracle SQL Developer has been continuously evolving and reaching maturity with the capability to give database developers and DBAs a convenient way to perform basic and advanced database tasks. Oracle Developers and DBAs can browse, create, edit, and delete (drop); run SQL statements and scripts; edit and debug PL/SQL code; manipulate and export (unload) data; and view and create custom reports.

After reading this book, Oracle developers and DBAs will learn to install Oracle SQL Developer and learn to navigate through all its advanced features that have been introduced in version 4.1. You will be competent enough to use all the advanced features available, helping them perform basic and advanced database tasks with ease.

What this book covers

Chapter 1, *Getting Started with SQL Developer 4.1*, covers how to prepare the SQL Developer environment on your laptop, including the download, installation, installation options, creating database connections, and so on.

Chapter 2, *Database Connections and SQL Worksheet*, covers how to make database connections and create, update, or delete database objects using the SQL worksheet.

Chapter 3, *The Power of SQL Reports*, guides a DBA or an application developer to use reports for running a set of queries that are frequently executed. This chapter will explain how to categorize a group of these SQL queries (reports). The first section will discuss the reports navigator in general, how to run and use reports, and any errors you might encounter.

Chapter 4, Working with PL/SQL, shows you how to create, edit, compile, and debug PL/SQL blocks efficiently in the first section, followed by the use of SQL and PL/SQL tuning tools provided by SQL Developer.

Chapter 5, SQL Developer for DBAs, shows you how a DBA can leverage SQL Developer's features to efficiently work with multiple databases in the areas of manageability, monitoring, performance tuning, and so on.

Chapter 6, SQL Developer Accessibility, provides information about the accessibility features of Oracle SQL Developer. It includes using a screen reader and Java access bridge with Oracle SQL Developer, Oracle SQL Developer features that support accessibility, recommendations for customizing Oracle SQL Developer, and highly visual features of Oracle SQL Developer.

Chapter 7, Importing, Exporting, and Working with Data, uses SQL Developer features such as the export/import feature using which we can easily and quickly export and import data from within a database or across a database, and also compare all the data after the activity.

Chapter 8, Database Connections and JDBC Drivers, uses alternative Oracle connections such as tnsnames.ora, LDAP, JDBC URLs, and also shows you how to create non-Oracle database connections.

Chapter 9, Introducing SQL Developer Data Modeler, uses data modeler features such as diagrams, components, entity relationship diagrams, relational and physical data models, and some forward/reverse engineering possibilities using SQL developer.

Chapter 10, Extending SQL Developer, helps you learn the range of support available for adding XML extensions, a task that is easily within the reach of any database developer with SQL and PL/SQL skills. The nature of these extensions can range from including a single XML report to adding complex Java extensions bundled as JAR files.

Chapter 11, Working with Application Express, shows you how to connect to Application Express, browse your applications, review some of the administration utilities, and use the SQL Worksheet to refactor PL/SQL code.

Chapter 12, Working with SQL Developer Migrations, reviews the tool support for a migration without discussing the additional work required when planning and preparing for a migration.

Chapter 13, Oracle Data Miner 4.1, teaches you about the new Data Miner features in SQL Developer 4.1 and the general enhancements to Oracle Data Miner 4.1. In response to the growing popularity of JSON data and its use in big data configurations, Data Miner now provides an easy-to-use JSON query node.

Chapter 14, REST Data Services and REST Development, shows you how Oracle REST Data Services (a JEE-based alternative to Oracle HTTP Server (OHS) and mod_plsql) can be administered. The second session will be a detailed discussion of how we can use SQL Developer to create, maintain, and use RESTful services.

What you need for this book

This book was written on the SQL Developer 4.1 tool and the new features provided by Oracle. Though the name has "Developer" in it, the book should be equally useful for developers, DBAs, and architects. All the examples and features should work with version 4.1, which can be downloaded for free from the OTN website. We need minimum JDK 1.8 to use the SQL Developer 4.1 version.

Who this book is for

Oracle database developers and DBAs who seek a convenient way to perform basic and advanced database tasks are the audience of this book.

Conventions

In this book, you will find a number of text styles that distinguish between different kinds of information. Here are some examples of these styles and an explanation of their meaning.

Code words in text, database table names, folder names, filenames, file extensions, pathnames, dummy URLs, user input, and Twitter handles are shown as follows: "We can include other contexts through the use of the `include` directive."

A block of code is set as follows:

```
<queries>
  <query>
    <sql> </sql>
  </query>
  <columns>
  </columns>
</queries>
```

Any command-line input or output is written as follows:

```
FROM DEPARTMENTS WHERE DEPARTMENT_NAME = &DNAME;
```

New terms and **important words** are shown in bold. Words that you see on the screen, for example, in menus or dialog boxes, appear in the text like this: "If you want to use these extensions, then invoke the wizard, select **Search Update Centers**, and include the **Third Party SQL Developer Extensions**."

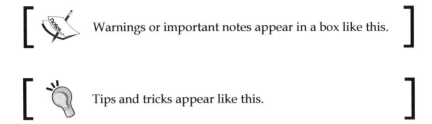

Warnings or important notes appear in a box like this.

Tips and tricks appear like this.

Reader feedback

Feedback from our readers is always welcome. Let us know what you think about this book—what you liked or disliked. Reader feedback is important for us as it helps us develop titles that you will really get the most out of.

To send us general feedback, simply e-mail feedback@packtpub.com, and mention the book's title in the subject of your message.

If there is a topic that you have expertise in and you are interested in either writing or contributing to a book, see our author guide at www.packtpub.com/authors.

Customer support

Now that you are the proud owner of a Packt book, we have a number of things to help you to get the most from your purchase.

Downloading the example code

You can download the example code files from your account at http://www.packtpub.com for all the Packt Publishing books you have purchased. If you purchased this book elsewhere, you can visit http://www.packtpub.com/support and register to have the files e-mailed directly to you.

Downloading the color images of this book

We also provide you with a PDF file that has color images of the screenshots/ diagrams used in this book. The color images will help you better understand the changes in the output. You can download this file from `https://www.packtpub. com/sites/default/files/downloads/B04512_ColorImages.pdf`.

Errata

Although we have taken every care to ensure the accuracy of our content, mistakes do happen. If you find a mistake in one of our books—maybe a mistake in the text or the code—we would be grateful if you could report this to us. By doing so, you can save other readers from frustration and help us improve subsequent versions of this book. If you find any errata, please report them by visiting `http://www.packtpub. com/submit-errata`, selecting your book, clicking on the **Errata Submission Form** link, and entering the details of your errata. Once your errata are verified, your submission will be accepted and the errata will be uploaded to our website or added to any list of existing errata under the Errata section of that title.

To view the previously submitted errata, go to `https://www.packtpub.com/books/ content/support` and enter the name of the book in the search field. The required information will appear under the **Errata** section.

Piracy

Piracy of copyrighted material on the Internet is an ongoing problem across all media. At Packt, we take the protection of our copyright and licenses very seriously. If you come across any illegal copies of our works in any form on the Internet, please provide us with the location address or website name immediately so that we can pursue a remedy.

Please contact us at `copyright@packtpub.com` with a link to the suspected pirated material.

We appreciate your help in protecting our authors and our ability to bring you valuable content.

Questions

If you have a problem with any aspect of this book, you can contact us at `questions@packtpub.com`, and we will do our best to address the problem.

1
Getting Started with SQL Developer 4.1

This book is divided into chapters that focus on the different areas or functionality in the recently released SQL Developer 4.1. The progression through the chapters is from the more frequently-used features to those less-frequently used. This initial chapter is all about preparing your environment, installing SQL Developer 4.1, and getting started.

SQL Developer 4.1 is easy to set up and use, so there is very little setup required to follow the examples in this book. The best way to learn is by practice, and for that you'll need a computer with access to an Oracle database and SQL Developer. This chapter, and indeed the rest of the book, is written with the assumption that you have a computer with Microsoft Windows, Linux, or Mac OS X installed, and that you have access to an Oracle database. It focuses on the alternative installations available for SQL Developer, where to find the product, and how to install it. Once your environment is set up, you can follow a quick product walk-through to familiarize yourself with the landscape. You'll create a few connections, touch on the various areas available (such as the SQL Worksheet and Reports navigator), and learn about the control of the windows and general product layout.

Preparing your environment

Preparing your environment depends on a few factors, including the platform you are working on and whether you have an earlier edition of SQL Developer previously installed. First, you need to locate the software, download it, and install it.

Finding and downloading the software

SQL Developer 4.1 is available through a variety of sources both as a standalone download and as part of the Oracle Database and Oracle JDeveloper installations.

SQL Developer is a free product, and you can download it from the Oracle Technology Network.

Here's the link:

```
http://www.oracle.com/technetwork/developer-tools/sql-developer/
overview/index.html
```

Use this link to visit the page that will allow you to download the latest standalone production release. It also includes details of the release and is regularly updated with news of preview releases and new articles. While SQL Developer is free to download and use, you are required to read and agree to the license before you can proceed with the download. The product also falls under Oracle Support contracts; if you have a Support contract for the database, then you can log in to Oracle Support tickets.

Downloading and installing the Java Development Kit

SQL Developer 4.1 requires the **Java SE Development Kit 8 (JDK8)** or later. This includes the **Java Runtime Environment (JRE)** and other tools, which are used by SQL Developer utilities such as the PL/SL Debugger.

For Microsoft Windows, you can download and install SQL Developer with the JDK already installed. This means that you'll download and unzip the product and will be ready to start, as there are no extra steps required. For other operating systems, you'll need to download the JDK and direct SQL Developer to the path yourself. Indeed, as many other products require a JDK to be installed, you may already have one in your system. In this case, just direct the product to use an existing JDK installation. For Microsoft Windows, ensure that you download SQL Developer without the JDK to make use of an existing JDK installation.

The SQL Developer 4.1 download site offers a selection of download choices, which are as follows:

- Microsoft Windows (with or without the JDK)
- Linux RPM (without the JDK)
- Mac OS X (without the JDK)

- Other platforms (without the JDK)
- Command Line: `sqlcli`

In each case, make your selection and download the required file.

JDK 8 can be downloaded using the following link:

```
http://www.oracle.com/technetwork/java/javase/downloads/jdk8-
downloads-2133151.html
```

 SQL Developer is shipped with the minimum JDK required for each release. You can download and use the latest updates to the JDK and should be aware that some updates to the JDK are not supported. This detail is posted on the SQL Developer Downloads page for each release. Starting from SQL Developer 4.1, JDK 1.8 is the minimum JDK supported.

Once you have installed the JDK, you can start SQL Developer.

Installing and starting SQL Developer

SQL Developer does not use an installer. All you need to do is unzip the given file into an empty folder, locate it, and run the executable.

 Do not unzip SQL Developer into an `$Oracle_Home` folder or an existing SQL Developer installation.

Unzipping the file creates a `sqldeveloper` folder, which includes a selection of sub-folders and files, including the `sqldeveloper.exe` executable.

If your download does not include the JDK, then you'll be prompted for the full path of the JDK folder. Browse to the location of the JDK folder and select it. The path should include the absolute path, as shown in the following screenshot:

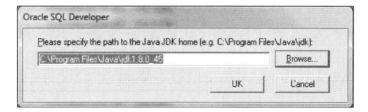

Working with different platforms

Whether you are accessing SQL Developer as part of the Oracle Database 11g installation or as a standalone installation, there is a selection of executables available to you. These are either platform-specific or provide additional detail while running the product.

Microsoft Windows

The first executable you'll find is in the `\sqldeveloper` root folder. This is the executable more generally used. If you navigate down to `\sqldeveloper\bin`, there are two additional executables, `sqldeveloper.exe` and `sqldeveloperW.exe`. The latter is the same as the executable in the root folder. Use either of these for running SQL Developer.

The additional executable is often used for debugging purposes. Use `\sqldeveloper\bin\sqldeveloper.exe` to invoke SQL Developer and a separate console window will open, which displays additional Java messages. You can use these messages when encountering errors in the product and if you want to log an issue with Oracle Support.

The three steps to getting started on Microsoft Windows are as follows:

- **Download**: Download the full file, with JDK, from the Oracle Technology Network web site
- **Unzip**: Unzip the file to an empty directory
- **Double-click**: Double-click on the `\sqldeveloper\sqldeveloper.exe` file

Alternative platforms

Microsoft Windows is the predominant platform used by SQL Developer users. There is a steadily growing audience for Linux and Max OS X. As neither of these platform downloads include the JDK, you need to first access, download, and install the JDK. On starting either Linux or the Mac OS, you'll be prompted with the full path of the JDK as described.

Mac OS X

Download the file specific to Mac OS X and double-click to unzip the file. This creates an icon for SQL Developer on your desktop. Double-click to run the application.

Linux

Use the Linux `rpm` command to install SQL Developer. For example, your command might look like the following:

```
rpm -Uhv sqldeveloper-4.1.0.19.07-1.noarch.rpm
```

In the same way that unzip creates a `sqldeveloper` folder, with sub-folders and files, the rpm command creates a `sqldeveloper` folder, complete with files and sub-folders. Switch to this new folder and run the `sqldeveloper.sh` executable.

Migrating settings from a previous release

In the initial startup of any release of SQL Developer, you may be asked one or two questions. The first is the location of the Java executable of the JDK as discussed. If you have installed the full release with the JDK, this question is skipped. The second question is if you want to migrate any preferences from a previous release. Regardless of whether this is the first SQL Developer installation on the machine or not, the first time you invoke SQL Developer, you are offered the choice of migrating your settings. You can migrate settings of any previous release to the current release from SQL Developer 1.5 version and above. By default, the utility looks for the latest version installed of the software.

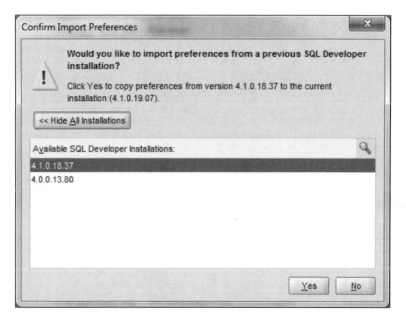

If you want to migrate from a different installation, select the **Show All Installations** button (as shown in the preceding screenshot). This displays a list of all SQL Developer installations that have the system folder in the Documents and Settings system folder (e.g. `C:\Documents and Settings\<your_user>\Application Data\SQL Developer\system4.1.0.19.07-1`) and includes releases from SQL Developer 1.5 and above. For releases prior to SQL Developer 1.5, the system folder was created within the SQL Developer installation (for example, `D:\SQLDeveloper\Builds\1.2.1\1.2.1.3213\sqldeveloper\sqldeveloper\system`).

Maintaining your environment

Once you have SQL Developer installed, it is helpful to know about the environmental settings and some of the files that are created when you start the product. Knowing about the version you have installed is important if only to be able to identify this when asking questions on the forum, or when contacting Oracle Support.

Verifying the current release

To verify the SQL Developer release you have, go to **Help | About** once you start SQL Developer or JDeveloper. In the dialog invoked, select the **Extensions** tab and find the Oracle SQL Developer extension, as shown in the next screenshot. This will match the build number on the download site if you have the latest release. The screenshot shows a number of the extensions that make up SQL Developer. If your dialog does not show the **Version** or **Status** columns, you can select the column headers to resize the visible columns and bring the others into focus.

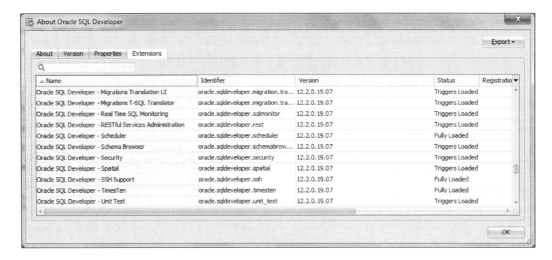

Using Check for Updates

SQL Developer offers a built-in patching and extensions utility, known as **Check for Updates**. Check for Updates is used to release the following:

- SQL Developer extensions
- General Oracle extensions
- Minor patches

- Third-party tools required by SQL Developer, such as the non-Oracle database drivers
- Third-party extensions

For all extensions, you need to start **Check for Updates** to see what's available. To do this, go to **Help | Features**. Just follow the dialog to find the updates that you require.

You can initially elect to see just the third-party updates, or all updates available, by selecting all options, as shown in the following screenshot:

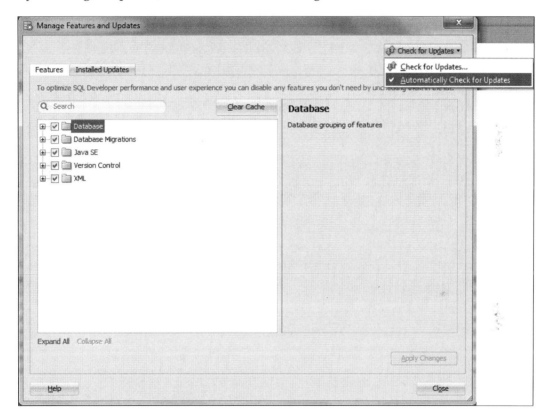

The database drivers for some of the non-Oracle databases are located in **Third Party SQL Developer Extensions**. The Third Party update center also includes a selection of customer developed SQL Developer extensions. The customer extensions are developed, supported, and updated by the customer involved; they are not tested, certified, or supported by Oracle.

As with all software downloads from the Internet, you are required to read and accept the license agreements. The **Check for Updates** utility directs you to the appropriate licenses before downloading the software. If the updates are from Oracle, you will need to provide your Oracle Technology Network sign-on details.

Managing the system folder and other files

SQL Developer stores user-related information in several places, with the specific location depending on the operating system and certain environment specifications. User-related information includes user-defined reports, user-defined snippets, SQL Worksheet history, code templates, and SQL Developer user preferences. In most cases, your user-related information is stored outside the SQL Developer installation directory hierarchy so that it is preserved if you delete that directory and install a new version.

The user-related information is stored in or under the IDE_USER_DIR environment variable location, if defined, otherwise as indicated in the following table, which shows the typical default locations (under a directory or in a file) for specific types of resources on different operating systems. (Note the period in the name of any directory named .sqldeveloper.)

Default Locations for user-related information resource type system are mentioned as follows (Windows, Linux, or Mac OS X):

User-defined reports	• Windows: `C:\Documents and Settings\<user-name>\ Application Data\SQL Developer\UserReports.xml` • Linux or Mac OS X: `~/.sqldeveloper/UserReports.xml`
User-defined snippets	• Windows: `C:\Documents and Settings\<user-name>\ Application Data\SQL Developer\UserSnippets.xml` • Linux: `~/.sqldeveloper/UserSnippets.xml` • Mac OS X: `/Users/<Your user>/Library/Application Support/ SQLDeveloper/UserSnippets.xml`
SQL history	• Windows: `C:\Documents and Settings\<user-name>\ Application Data\SQL Developer\SqlHistory.xml` • Linux: `~/.sqldeveloper/SqlHistory.xml` • Mac OS X: `/Users/<Your user>/Library/Application Support/ SQLDeveloper/ SqlHistory.xml`

Code templates	• Windows: `C:\Documents and Settings\<user-name>\ Application Data\SQL Developer\ CodeTemplate.xml` • Linux: `~/.sqldeveloper/CodeTemplate.xml` • Mac OS X: `/Users/<Your user>/Library/Application Support/ SQLDeveloper/ CodeTemplate.xml`
SQL Developer user preferences	• Windows: `C:\Documents and Settings\<user-name>\ Application Data\SQL Developer\systemn.n.n.n` • Linux or Mac OS X: `~/.sqldeveloper/systemn.n.n.n`

If you want to prevent other users from accessing your user-specific SQL Developer information, you must ensure that appropriate permissions are set on the directory where that information is stored or on a directory above it in the path hierarchy. For example, in a Windows system you may want to ensure that the `SQL Developer` folder and the `\<user-name>\Application Data\SQL Developer` folder under **Documents and Settings** are not sharable, whereas on a Linux or Mac OS X system you may want to ensure that the `~/.sqldeveloper` directory is not world-readable. **Sharing preferences**.

Preferences are set for your local environment and are therefore not shared globally between teams. However, you can export the **SQL Formatter** preferences set. This allows you to share the settings between team members and ensure that you all code to the same settings. To export your SQL Formatter settings, go to **Tools | Preferences** and expand the **Database** node in the tree. Select **SQL Formatter**, and you can now export or import previous saved settings.

Alternative installations of SQL Developer

We have been discussing the installation and management of the independent release of SQL Developer available on the Oracle Technology Network. SQL Developer is also available as part of the Oracle Database and Oracle JDeveloper installations.

Oracle JDeveloper

Most of SQL Developer is integrated into Oracle JDeveloper, which means you need to install JDeveloper to access and use the SQL Developer components. Having SQL Developer as part of JDeveloper means that if you are building Java applications and working with the **Fusion Middleware** platform, you can access and work with the Oracle Database without an additional install of SQL Developer. JDeveloper does not consume all of the extensions for SQL Developer (for example, extensions like Migrations and Versioning are not included).

Oracle JDeveloper 12c includes SQL Developer 4.0

Oracle Database 12c

SQL Developer is also shipped with the Oracle Database. Initially, Oracle Database 11g Release 1. SQL Developer is installed by default when you install the database. Once the installation is complete, locate the `sqldeveloper` directory (for example, `\product\11.1.0\db_1\sqldeveloper\sqldeveloper.exe`) to start SQL Developer. This was continued in 11g R2 and 12c as well.

Be aware that Oracle database releases are less frequent than those of SQL Developer, which, by its nature and size, allows for more frequent updates. This means the version of SQL Developer shipped with the database may not be the most current release. Oracle Database 12c is shipped with SQL Developer 3.2.20.09. All examples in this text are using SQL Developer 4.1. You may also update your database version less frequently than a client tool.

To upgrade the SQL Developer installation in Oracle Database 12c, you need to do a full new installation. As with other installations, create a new folder and unzip the latest download.

 Oracle Database 11g Release 1 ships with SQL Developer 1.1.3
Oracle Database 11g Release 2 ships with SQL Developer 1.5.5

Oracle Database 12c ships with SQL Developer 3.2.20.09 to work with 12c features like Multitenant stuff, Redaction, SQL Translation Framework, and Identity Columns.

Troubleshooting

It seems ominous to provide a section on troubleshooting at the start of a book! If you accept the fact that software can get in a tangle sometimes, either if you use the product as it's not designed, or perhaps include extensions that you'd prefer not to have and the product is no longer behaving as expected, then a few hints on how to escape that tangle can be useful.

Removing extensions

If you have created your own extensions, or have downloaded and installed other extensions that you no longer require, then go to **Tools** | **Features** and select **Extensions** from the tree. Here, you see that SQL Developer includes a number of default extensions, such as the Oracle TimesTen extension. In addition, any extension that you have included is listed here. You can deselect extensions here and the product will no longer have access to them. This does not delete the files installed for the extension. You will need to manually delete any files downloaded for that to happen. However, it does mean that you can restart the product and see if the extension is the root of the problem.

Resetting shortcut keys

Some users find that their keyboard shortcuts no longer work as expected. In this circumstance, you can navigate to **Tools** | **Preferences** and then select **Shortcut Keys** from the tree. Click on the **Load Keyboard Scheme** folder icon on the top-right extreme end, as shown in the following screenshot:

Select **Default** from the dialog to reset the keyboard accelerators to the shipped settings. This also replaces any settings you have added.

 In releases prior to SQL Developer 2.1, the **Shortcut Keys** are called **Accelerators**. In releases post 2.1, to reset the keys, select **Load Preset**.

Reset the environment, do not reinstall the product

When things go wrong, users sometimes resort to deleting and reinstalling a product. This may even require downloading the files again. This is time consuming, and in the case of SQL Developer, not necessary. Assuming you have not edited any of the .jar files (it's been known to happen and not legally permitted), you can reset the product to the shipped factory settings by deleting the system folder. Before you delete the system folder, export your connections and shut down SQL Developer.

To export your connections, select **Connections**, right-click and select **Export Connections**. Save the file to a new location.

When troubleshooting, deleting the system folder is useful. However, by deleting this folder you are also deleting all of the changes made to the preferences, your connections, and any layout changes you have made. Therefore, it is recommended that you delete the folder as a last resort, and not as a standard approach to troubleshooting.

Reset to factory settings

For Microsoft Windows, delete the `\Documents and Settings\<your_user>\Application Data\SQL Developer` folder to reset SQL Developer to the shipped factory settings.

For Linux, remove the `~.sqldeveloper` folder and on the Mac, remove the `~/Library/Application Support/SQL Developer` folder.

In addition to deleting all of the preferences set and connections created, this action also deletes user-defined reports, your SQL history, and any code templates and snippets you have created. In general, delete the lower level system folder for a less drastic reset.

A quick overview

Let's start with a walk-through of the product. This book is all about SQL Developer 4.1, using the product, and getting to know it. You may well ask yourself why there is a need for a book if we can walk through the product in twenty minutes or less. Generally only 10% of the SQL Developer features are used by people on average, but their sweet spots are probably different. By spending a little time delving into a number of areas of the product, you can start laying down a map of how the pieces connect and provide a base that you can drill down into later and become more productive.

Sample schemas

To follow the examples in the book, you need access to SYSTEM schema of a database and some of the shipped sample schemas, **HR, OE, SH, PM**, and **IX** available in Oracle Database *9i, 10g, 11g*, or *12c*. Specifically, this book uses the sample schemas shipped with Oracle Database 11g R2 & 12c.

There are two ways to install the sample schema. The first way is when you install the database. You can elect to have the sample schema installed at that point.

Second, if you have not installed these, then you can locate the sample schema in the `$ORACLE_HOME/demo/schema` folder and follow the instructions on installing them using the Oracle online documentation. Not all of these schemas are available for Oracle Express Edition. In this chapter, we use SYSTEM to verify that the HR schema is unlocked, and then we use the HR sample schema, which is available in Oracle Express Edition.

Creating your first connection

To complete this quick walk-through, you need to know the username and password of the SYSTEM user. You also need to know the location of the database, whether this is the machine name or the IP address, and the database SID.

To begin, start SQL Developer. The very first time you start SQL Developer, you'll be asked if you want to migrate from a previous version. Select **No** and allow the tool to start up.

The first thing you need to do after you have started SQL Developer for the first time is to create your initial connections.

To create a connection for SYSTEM, follow these steps:

1. Select **Connections**, right-click and select **New Connection**. This invokes the **New Database Connection** dialog. You can edit and control all of the connection details using this dialog.

2. Complete the details, as shown in the following screenshot, relevant to your environment.

3. Click on **Test** to ensure that you have the connection details correct and click on **Connect**.

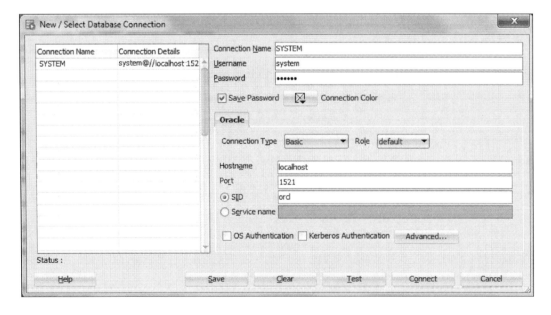

You are now connected as SYSTEM. Use this connection to verify your other users, by continuing with following steps.

4. Select the new connection you have created, expand the node, and scroll down to **Other Users**.

5. Expand **Other Users** and find the user **HR**. Right-click on it and select **Edit User**. Verify that the account for HR is unlocked and the **Password** has not expired, that is, the properties **Account is Locked** and **Password Expired** are deselected. If either of these is selected, deselect them. You can change the password for HR at this point too. It's good practice to modify the passwords of the shipped sample schemas once you have unlocked them.

Now you are really ready to begin.

1. Once again, select **Connections**, right-click and select **New Connection**.

2. Give the connection a name (for example, HR_11g).

3. Provide the **Username** (HR) and a **Password**. If you are working on Oracle Database 11g, be aware that passwords are now case sensitive.

4. Select the **Save Password** checkbox. This makes life easy while you are working with SQL Developer. Passwords are stored in an encrypted file. However, you should always be aware of saving passwords and possible security implications this may have.

5. Use the **Basic** connection. This requires no more detail than the location of the database and the **SID**, details you have.

6. Click on **Test** to test the connection.

7. Click on **Connect**.

Using basic commands in the SQL Worksheet

As soon as you connect to a user, SQL Developer opens an SQL Worksheet. You may have started working with Oracle using the SQL*Plus command line, or even the GUI window. Either way, you'd start with a selection of SQL*Plus and SQL commands.

Enter the following into the SQL Worksheet:

```
DESC DEPARTMENTS

SELECT * FROM DEPARTMENTS;
```

Press the *F5* key (or use the **Run Script** button).

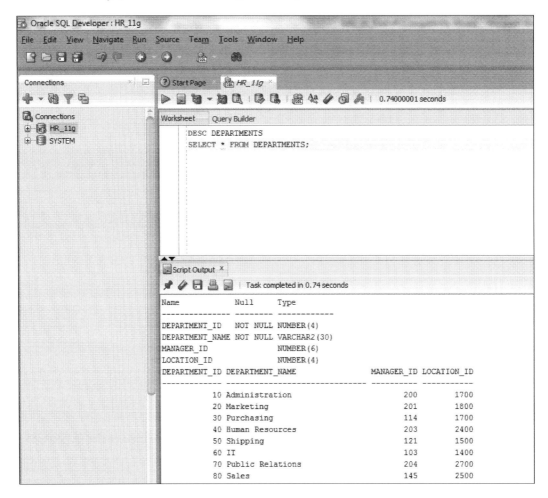

The output of both commands appears in the **Script Output** tab, which appears below the SQL Worksheet (as seen in the previous screenshot). Both commands are handled by a few simple clicks of the mouse in SQL Developer.

Select and expand the **HR_11g** connection in the **Connections** navigator. Expand the **Tables** node and select **DEPARTMENTS**.

The **DEPARTMENTS** tab now opens, displaying a list of the column names and details. These are the same details as given by the DESC (describe) SQL*Plus command that you entered in the SQL Worksheet. It also provides additional detail, such as the Primary Key and column comments.

Select the **Data** tab and notice that you now see the output from your second command. These two tabs are included with a number of other tabs, each with additional details about the **DEPARTMENTS** table. You would need to write a number of SQL queries in order to get the additional detail from the data dictionary if you were working in SQL*Plus.

Select the **EMPLOYEES** table. Notice that the new table, **EMPLOYEES**, immediately replaces the previous **DEPARTMENTS** table with its details. Select the **Triggers** tab, and select one of the triggers. The trigger and related trigger detail is displayed in a master-detail window, as shown in the following screenshot:

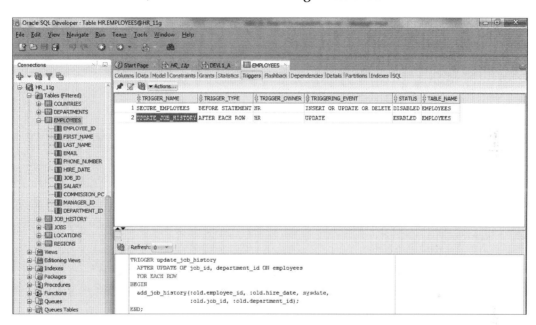

Browsing and updating data

Return to the **EMPLOYEES** data by again selecting the **Data** tab. The data grid that is displayed provides a variety of options. To get started with the data grid, double-click on an item or field, such as the name of one of the employees, and change it. Tab out of the field and notice that the change is applied to the data grid and an asterisk (*) flags the record. **Commit** and **Rollback** buttons are available to send the change to the database, or to undo your action. Roll back the changes.

Once again, you get feedback, this time in the **Messages Log,** as shown in the following screenshot:

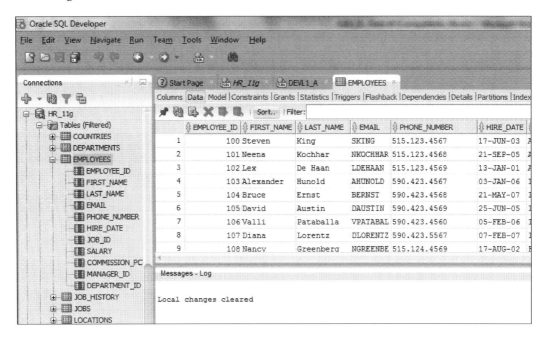

Running reports

To run your report, perform the following steps:

1. Select the **Reports** navigator and expand the **Data Dictionary Reports** node. Expand the **Table** node and review the available reports. Expand **Constraints** and select the **Unique Constraints** report.

2. As you select the report, a dialog displays requesting the **Connection** name. Select the connection you created, **HR_11g,** and click on **OK.**

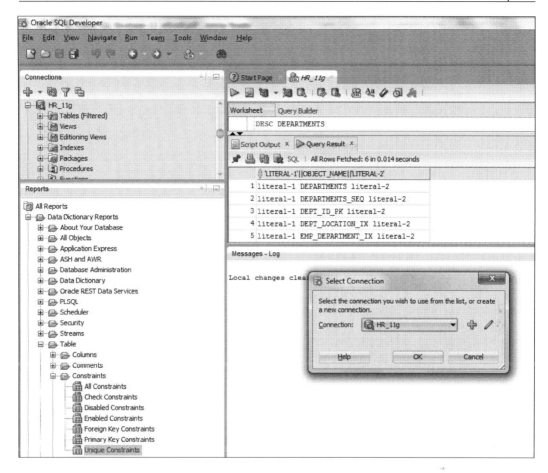

3. An **Enter Bind Values** dialog now appears, requesting the table name as an input parameter. Click on **Apply** to accept the default, which in this case, means all tables:

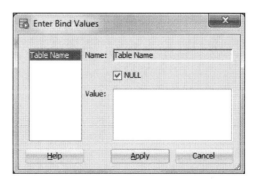

Run the same report for any user by selecting the **Connections** drop-down list on the right-hand side.

Navigating around SQL Developer

SQL Developer has a selection of windows, navigators, and tabs. On start-up, you are presented with the main navigator toolbars and menus, as shown in the following screenshot:

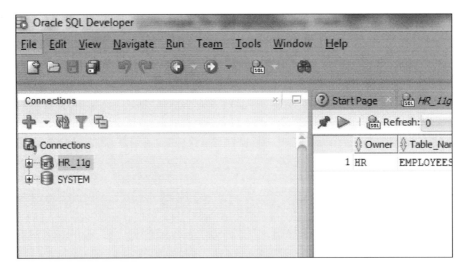

The two main navigators, **Connections** and **Reports**, are presented in a tabbed window. These and other navigators, such as the **Versioning Navigator**, are available through the main **View** menu. You can also open windows such as **Snippets**, **Recent Objects**, and **Find DB Objects** using the **View** menu.

 Any navigators that you open during a session, and that are still open when you close the product, are automatically opened when you restart the product.

Managing SQL Developer windows

With the exception of the SQL Worksheet and its associated tabs, all of the main
tabbed dialogs can be minimized or maximized and accessed while docked or
undocked. These menu controls are available through context menus in the tabs,
as shown in the following screenshot:

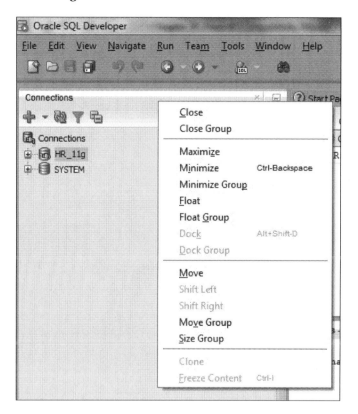

You can rearrange tabbed windows by selecting and dragging the tab into place.
Once any window is minimized, roll your mouse over the minimized tab to display
a floating window that stays active while your mouse lies over it and rolls back
into place when you move off. This is very useful when working with temporary
windows such as **Snippets** and **Find DB Object**. The following screenshot shows
the floating window for the **Snippets** dialog. If you roll the mouse over the area, you
can work in the window (for example, navigating about until you have located the
snippet of code you are after, and then dragging the code onto the worksheet). The
window will minimize out of the way once you have moved off it.

You can undock the floating window, move it off to one side, and keep it undocked while you work with the SQL Worksheet. In a dual-monitor setup, you can drag the floating window onto one monitor, while working with the SQL Worksheet on the other monitor.

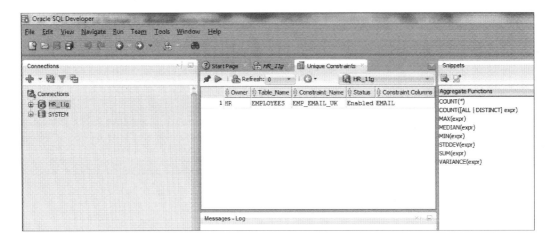

Tiling windows

Once you start working with connections, you will have more windows and tabs to deal with, especially if you have more than one connection created.

1. Select the **HR_11g** connection created in the previous section, expand the connection and **Tables** node, and select **EMPLOYEES**.

2. In the table definition window, select the pin button (**Freeze View**), as shown in the following screenshot, to freeze the view.

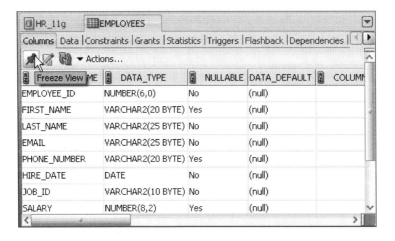

3. Now, select the **DEPARTMENTS** table. A second table definition window opens to display the details from the new table.

4. Select the **DEPARTMENTS** tab and drag it down to the lower portion of the screen. Notice the shape of the dragged object change as you drag it slightly to the left, to the center, and the lower portion of the window.

5. Each of the shapes represent a different layout position. Release the mouse to secure the new position. The screenshots that follow display two of the available positions:

   ○ Vertically:

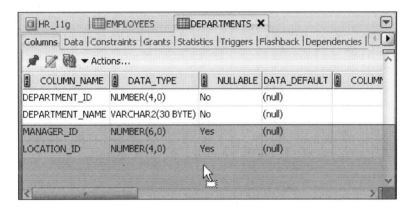

   ○ Horizontally:

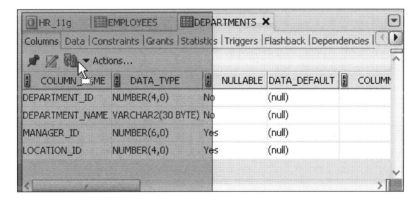

Splitting documents

When you tile windows, you can compare the details of two tables. However, as each table has a selection of tabs, it's useful to be able to review details in the tabs without having to switch back and forth between tabs. As is true for other layout features, you can split the document using a menu or by drag-and-drop. Each of the object definitions tabbed displays has a drag bar on the top and bottom right that you can select and drag to split the window horizontally, or vertically, as shown in the following screenshot:

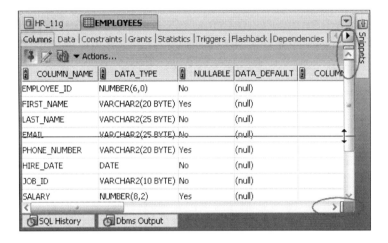

Maximizing detail

Almost all of the tabs in SQL Developer will maximize when double-clicked. There are a few that do not follow this rule, such as the tabs related to the SQL Worksheet. In general, this works for top-level tabs, which is any tab you can undock and move about, and not for secondary tabs. To maximize a tab, double-click on the tab. A second double-click will reverse the process.

 Double-click on the tab to maximize a top-level tab. Double-click again to revert to the previous layout.

Resetting the window layout

If you move your windows about a great deal, you may find that you want to get things back to the default settings.

The example in the following screenshot displays the standard docked **Connections** and **Reports** windows to the left. The **Reports** window, by default, docks below the connections. We have also docked the **Snippets** window to the right. These windows fill the columns to the left and right, leaving a central window for the editors and log files.

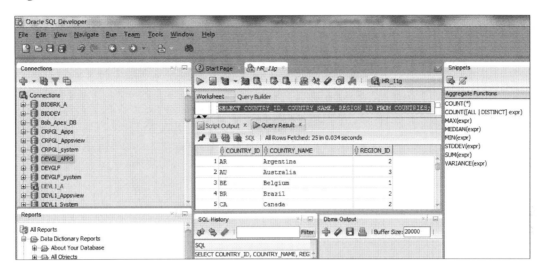

The layout is controlled by the window layout set in the preferences. Go to **Tools | Preferences** under the **Environment** node in the tree select **Dockable Windows**. The default layout, and the one that matches the example in the previous screenshot, is shown in the following screenshot:

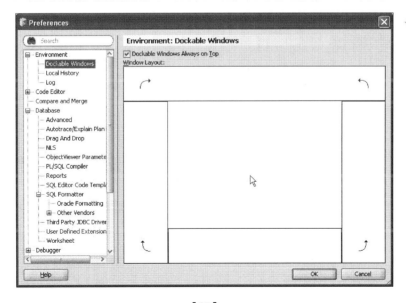

Each of the little curved arrows on the diagram is clickable, and as such controls the positioning of the windows. Clicking on the arrow extends or contracts the area taken up by the docked window.

In our example, and in the default SQL Developer environment, there is no full-docked window across the top of the screen. However, if you drag a window into the docked position below the main tool bar, it would stretch across the screen.

If you find your windows are in a muddle, first verify that the **Dockable Windows** layout is what you want, and then drag the various dockable windows back into place. Some suggestions on the SQL Developer forum are to remove the system folder (it works, but that's an extreme solution).

Database certification matrix (Oracle & Third-Party)

This section is just to give an introduction on the information on the databases and their versions that are certified for the usage of SQL Developer 4.1. Though this book only deals with examples of Oracle databases, the intention of adding this section is to inform you about the databases that SQL Developer can work with, thus projecting the actual capability of this tool (SQL Developer 4.1).

Oracle Database Certification for SQL Developer	
Product	**Releases**
Oracle Database	Oracle10g
	Oracle11g
	Oracle12c
Oracle Database Express Edition	Release 11.2

Non-Oracle (Third-Party) Database Certification for SQL Developer	
Database	**Releases**
IBM DB2	DB2 UDB
	DB2 7.x
	DB2 8.x
	DB2 9.x
Microsoft SQL Server	SQL Server 7
	SQL Server 2000
	SQL Server 2005
	SQL Server 2008
MySQL	MySQL 3.x
	MySQL 4.x
	MySQL 5.x
Sybase Adaptive Server	Sybase 12
	Sybase 15
Teradata	Teradata 12
	Teradata 13

Finding more help

SQL Developer has a site on the **Oracle Technology Network** (`http://www.oracle.com/technology/products/database/sql_developer/index.html`). This provides us with links to current and past magazine articles, white papers, and team blogs. It also has links to brief product demonstrations and longer hands-on exercises.

There is an active user forum on OTN, which can be found at `http://forums.oracle.com/forums/forum.jspa?forumID=260`. This forum is monitored by the development team and end users.

The SQL Developer Exchange, found at `http://sqldeveloper.oracle.com`, is a site where anyone using SQL Developer can log feature requests and vote on other requests already posted. In addition to posting feature requests, the site hosts reports and code snippets.

Summary

You've started and should now have SQL Developer installed. You should have a few connections created and an initial idea of how to navigate around the product. You are now set to learn a lot more about SQL Developer. From here, you can delve into different chapters, focusing on the areas you're most interested in.

In the next chapter, you will learn how to browse different types of objects and use SQL Developer to look at them in greater detail. We'll review the different editors and dialogs available and you'll learn how to manage what you see using preferences. You will also discover the different ways in which you can create objects and learn how to manipulate the data.

2
Database Connections and SQL Worksheet

In SQL Developer, one of the most important navigation windows is the Connections window pane. This is the window where we have all our predefined database connections. Once we have added the required connection definitions to the databases, we can quickly launch the connections to the databases and start working. Another important fixed window after making database connections is the SQL Worksheet window. The SQL Worksheet provides a scratch pad for all SQL, PL/SQL, and SQL*Plus statements and commands. You can run individual statements or a collection of commands. You can also run scripts and execute PL/SQL. In essence, you can do all you might do in a command-line interface like SQL*Plus. The SQL Worksheet provides more; it offers code templates, code snippets, assists with code insight and completion, and maintains a history of commands. In this chapter, we will look at the connections window and other features offered in the SQL Worksheet and how to use them. We will use SQL and SQL*Plus commands to illustrate features, using PL/SQL only where needed specifically for a feature.

Working with the Connections navigator

The **Connections** navigator lists all our database connections created by us. A double-click on each of those database connections will open the database connection for us using the saved credentials for that particular database. Objects are grouped into nodes in the **Connections** navigator to reflect their types. They are ordered by most commonly used with **Tables**, **Views**, and **Indexes** at the top of the list. You can refer to the following screenshot to see the grouping, order, and some of the currently available types displayed in the **Connections** navigator. The selection of browsable object types available increases with each release as the SQL Developer team adds support for more features. SQL Developer allows you to explore the contents of your database using the connection tree.

A complete list of supported database object types can be seen in the following screenshot:

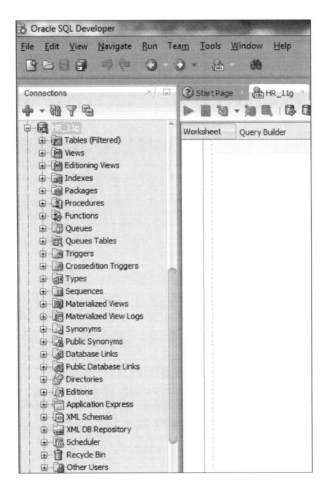

Opening connections

To open a connection in the navigator, follow these steps:

1. Under the **Connections** navigator, expand any of the existing database connection nodes to establish the database connection.

2. The second option is to right-click on any of the database connection nodes under the **Connections** navigator and select **Connect** from the context menu.

The first time you connect to a database schema, whether you open an existing connection or click on **Connect** in the **New Database Connections** dialog, SQL Developer automatically expands the connection in the **Connections** navigator and opens a SQL Worksheet. This automatic opening of the SQL Worksheet is controlled by a preference: Open a **Worksheet** on connect. Go to **Tools | Preferences**, expand the **Database** node, and select **Worksheet**.

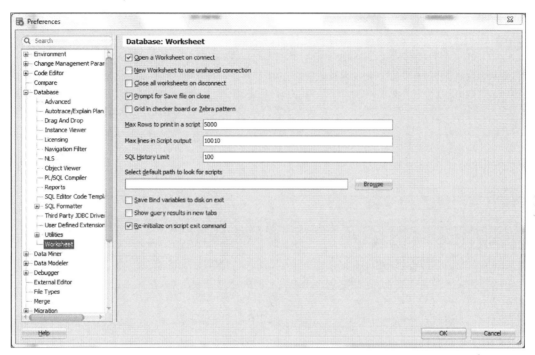

Reconnecting users

When doing administrative work with users, it can help to disconnect the user you are working with before making the changes and reconnect them afterwards. Some actions, such as dropping users or renaming connections, will not be possible without first disconnecting the connection.

Database schema or user?

The Oracle Concepts Guide states: *A schema is a collection of database objects. A schema is owned by a database user and has the same name as that user.*

Throughout the text, we use schema and user interchangeably. For the most part, we refer to the SYSTEM and HR schemas, meaning the collection of database objects. When closely or directly related to an activity we use "user", as the code does this. For example, consider DROP user HR cascade. It is a piece of code that drops all of the objects in the schema and the user itself.

Working with database objects

To work with any object, select and expand the respective object node. The most common node you'll work with is the **Tables** node. This displays all of the tables the user owns (all of the tables in the schema). Each of the object nodes is identified by an icon, and the **Tables** node highlights some of the main table types using these icons. Not all are singled out, but the more commonly used ones are. If you expand the **HR Tables** node, then the **COUNTRIES** table, which in the sample is an index-organized table, is identified by the slightly different table icon used. Partitioned tables are also distinguished from regular, simple tables using icons. The following screenshot displays the index organized, regular, external, partitioned, and temporary icons:

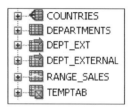

Display editors

Once you have expanded an object type node in the **Connections** navigator, selecting any object in that node opens a window of tabs, called display editors, which define the object. Each editor displays a data grid of details describing the selected object. These are based on queries against the data dictionary and you can get the same results by writing the SQL yourself.

The number and types of editors displayed will vary depending on the object or database that you are connected to. If you are connected to Oracle Database 11g or above, then an additional **Flashback** editor displays with the other table display editors.

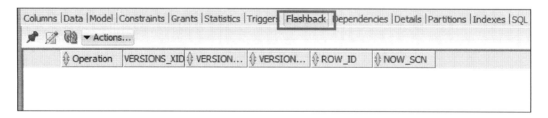

 The **Partitions** tab is permanently displayed from SQL Developer 2.1.

General display editors

Instead of itemizing each of the object types and the different collections of display editors, we'll use the **Tables** node to review some of the display editor details. Using the **HR** connection, select **EMPLOYEES** in the **Tables** node to see the general display editors, as shown in the following screenshot:

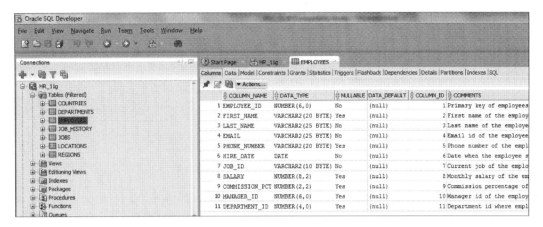

The **Columns** editor displays all of the column detail, including column comments. To get a feel for queries that run behind the editors, run the following query in the SQL Worksheet:

```
SELECT COLUMN_NAME,DATA_TYPE
FROM ALL_TAB_COLUMNS
WHERE TABLE_NAME ='EMPLOYEES'
AND OWNER = 'HR';
```

The output from the query matches the first two columns of the **Columns** display editor (this is a simplified example). If you need to find out more information about any object in the database without a GUI tool, you need to start by querying the data dictionary to determine which tables hold the metadata about your objects. From there, you must decide what detail you need from these tables, in our example it was the single **ALL_TAB_COLUMNS** table, and then write the join clause to query all of the selected tables.

There is a set of editors for each of the object types. For tables, these include **Constraints**, **Grants**, **Statistics**, **Triggers**, and **Partitions**. The data in each data grid is a result of a query joining a number of data dictionary tables. SQL Developer provides a framework for you to create and add your own display editors. You can do this with user extensions.

Some of the editors display master-detail output. To see the detail result set, you need to select an individual record in the master result set. The following screenshot shows the **EMP_NAME_IX** for the **EMPLOYEES** table. By selecting the index, you can quickly see that this index is made up of two columns, as shown in the following screenshot:

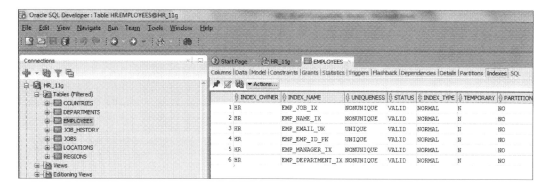

To create the index using SQL, use the following query:

```
CREATE INDEX "EMP_NAME_IX" ON "EMPLOYEES" ("LAST_NAME", "FIRST_NAME");
```

Working with the display editors

Each new object selected in the navigator replaces the last, regardless of object type or connection, unless you click on the **Freeze View** pin button ( ) on the object display. This locks the window and a new window opens with a new set of editors.

> **Freezing the Object Viewer**
>
> You can control whether each new object select opens a new set of editors. Select **Tools | Preferences** in the tree display, expand **Database**. Next, click on **ObjectViewer** and select **Automatically Freeze Object Viewer Windows**.

To see this feature in action, expand the **HR Tables** node. Select the **EMPLOYEES** table and note the set of display editors. Now select the **DEPARTMENTS** table, and note that it replaces the details of the **EMPLOYEES** table. Expand the **Sequences** node and click through each of the sequences available. These now replace the tables which were previously displayed. This replacing feature is very useful as it saves screen real estate and keeps the screen and work area uncluttered. However, it is also very useful to be able to compare two sets of data, side by side. Therefore, by selecting the **Freeze View** pin, each new object selected opens in a new window and you can then tile the windows.

SQL Developer automatically opens the display editors as you click on the object, or if you navigate down through the objects using the keyboard. You can control this by changing the default **Open Object on Single Click** behavior. Go to **Tools** | **Preferences** in the tree displayed, expand **Database**, select **ObjectViewer**, and deselect **Open Object on Single Click**.

Using the SQL display editor

The **SQL** editor is displayed at the end of the set of shipped display editors and is available for most object types (any editors you create are added after the **SQL** editor). The **SQL** editor displays the query required to recreate the object selected. When you select the **SQL** editor, SQL Developer uses the DBMS_METADATA package to query the database and return the SQL required for recreating the object selected. So, clicking on the editor with a table selected displays the SQL (DDL) for that table.

Select the **COUNTRIES** table in the **Connections** navigator. The default display provides the full CREATE TABLE SQL in a single statement, as shown in the following screenshot:

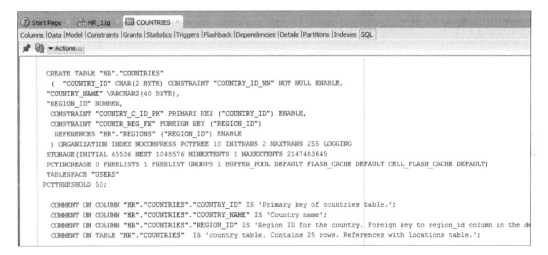

Working with the data grids

The contents of each display editor are displayed in data grids, which typically have three or more columns of data within the grid. A few are two column name-value pair data grids, such as the **Details** editor. The data in these grids is not editable and merely reflects the details about the object or structure selected. There are two exceptions. The first exception is the **Data** editor included with the set of display editors for certain objects, such as tables and views. The **Data** editor displays the *instance* data for a table and, depending on the object, this data can be edited and the changes can be committed to the database. The second exception is the **Code** editor for PL/SQL objects, where you are placed into a PL/SQL editor when you select the object.

Data grids throughout SQL Developer have context menus on the column's headings and the data grid itself. You can control the layout and what data is displayed by using these two context menus. For the remaining portion of this section we'll review the various options on these context menus.

The following screenshot shows the customizable columns capability of the data grids:

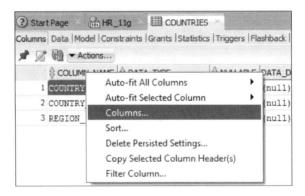

The next screenshot shows the sorting capability of the data grids:

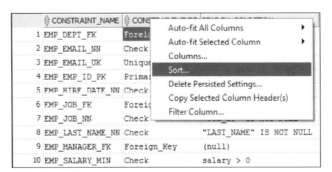

The following screenshot shows the data filtering capability of the data grids:

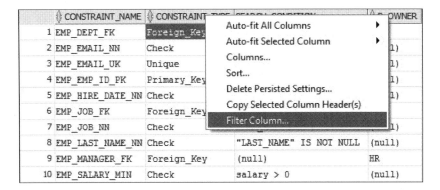

The next screenshot shows the data find/highlighting capability of the data grids:

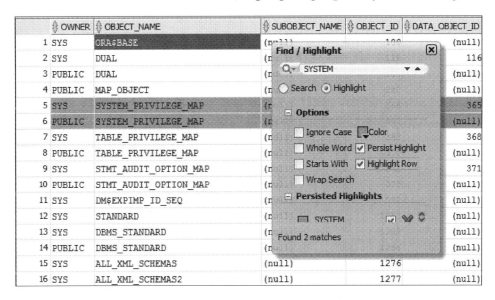

Reviewing other database object nodes

As you select each of the other database objects, you'll notice that the set of display editors varies considerably.

It would be tedious to single out each of the object nodes and describe them here. The display editors and data grids behave the same for each of them.

Working with PL/SQL objects

Triggers, functions, procedures, and packages all have their own separate nodes in the **Connections** navigator. A single-click on any object in these PL/SQL nodes opens as editable PL/SQL code, as shown here:

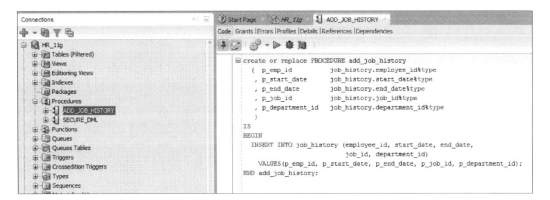

In the preceding screenshot, the initial **Code** editor is the editable PL/SQL code editor. This **Code** editor is included in the set of display editors for the selected procedure.

Unlike with other database objects, each new selected PL/SQL object opens a new window. In other words, the windows are automatically pinned for the PL/SQL windows. For more information, see the *Chapter 4, Working with PL/SQL*.

Accessing objects you don't own

Very often, you may have the connection details for one schema that has access to objects in another schema. One of the most frequently asked questions on the SQL Developer forum is about viewing objects that the schema does not own.

Other users

As discussed, the objects under your connection are objects created or owned by the schema defined in the connection. To view any other objects that your connection (schema) has access to, use the **Other Users** node. When you expand **Other Users**, for your current connection, you are executing the equivalent SQL query SELECT * FROM ALL_USERS;. This query returns all of the users in the current database. However, it does not mean that you have access to the objects in each of those schemas.

To review the objects the HR schema has access to, expand the **Other Users** node for the HR connection. Select and expand the user OE, and then expand the **Tables** node. You should see the selection of OE tables displayed. Not only does HR have access to these objects, the HR schema can query the data. You can select each table and display the set of editors available. HR is not a privileged user, but is granted the SELECT ANY TABLE system privilege.

The user SCOTT/TIGER is another of the Oracle database shipped schemas. SCOTT was the original sample user and is not a privileged user. If you have access to SCOTT, create a new database connection for SCOTT and repeat the exercise. If you expand the OE or HR tables nodes under SCOTT's **Other Users** node, the nodes are empty. SCOTT does not have access to these objects.

Synonyms and filters

You can expand and work with objects you have access to in the **Other Users** node. You can also create synonyms for these objects and then, using **Filters**, display the objects within each respective object type node in your connection.

Consider the following example: the HR schema has access to query the OE's **CUSTOMERS** table. HR can query the table, using SELECT * from OE.CUSTOMERS;. Now, create a synonym using CREATE SYNONYM CUSTOMERS FOR OE.CUSTOMERS;. This means the HR schema can write the queries without having to refer to the OE schema.

In SQL Developer, the synonym definition appears in the **Synonyms** node. The CUSTOMERS object will appear in the **Tables** node by setting the **Include Synonyms** option in the **Filter** dialog.

Recycle Bin

The **Recycle Bin** was introduced to Oracle databases in Oracle Database 10g. SQL Developer displays the contents of the Recycle Bin in the **Recycle Bin** node. For supported databases, the Recycle Bin provides a listing of all objects deleted from the schema. The information displayed about dropped objects includes the date the object was created and dropped and whether the object can be un-dropped (reinstated) or purged. SQL Developer displays the original name of the object in the **Connections** navigator for ease of use. However, once dropped, the object will have a new name. This allows you to drop objects and create new ones without the dropped object name blocking the action. In SQL Developer, displaying the old name makes it easier to decide what object you are dealing with, unless of course you repeatedly recreate and drop the object.

Creating new database objects

In the first section of the chapter, we looked at browsing objects and data in the database. You may, if you are an application developer and working with a completed database design, spend most of your time doing just that. It is more likely, though, that you'll need to make changes such as adding or modifying structures and data. SQL Developer provides the dialogs to assist you.

In the same way that you can write SQL queries to extract information about the objects you have access to, you can write the SQL **Data Definition Language (DDL)** to create, edit, and modify these objects. Almost all of the object nodes in the **Connections** navigator provide a context menu to create a new object. To invoke a dialog that creates any new object, select the object in the navigator and invoke the context menu.

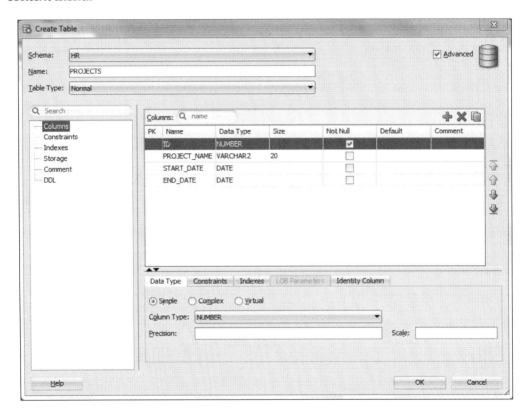

The following list is an exception for creating new objects using context menus:

- Editioning Views
- Queues
- Queue Tables
- Cross Edition Triggers
- Directories
- Editions
- Application Express
- XML DB Repository
- Recycle Bin

A right-click on the previously listed objects nodes under **Connections** navigator will not provide us with the **Create New** option.

Editing database objects – putting context menus to work

Each object in the **Connections** navigator has a context menu associated with it. Each context menu invokes a dialog that supports SQL commands that range from a single, simple command (such as DROP TABLE HR.COUNTRIES) to a collection of basic and complex commands. Throughout the chapter, we have stated that any of the activities that we're performing uses a UI as an interface for the underlying SQL command. Certainly, typing the drop table command is faster than selecting the items and invoking the dialog, assuming of course that you know the syntax. In this section, we'll briefly single out a few of these context menus.

Editing objects

Each of the **Create** dialogs has a matching **Edit** dialog. Most of the **Edit** dialogs directly match the object's **Create** dialog. If you invoke any **Edit** dialog, the **DDL** tab or node is initially empty, as it was when you first invoked the **Create** dialog. As soon as you change any of the properties, the **DDL** tab or node is populated with the SQL to reflect the changes. For many objects, such as triggers or views, editing the object results in a **Create or Replace...** command. For other objects, such as **Sequences** or **Tables**, editing the objects results in an **Alter...** command.

Consider the **Edit Table** dialog as shown in the following screenshot. The dialog is in the form of the advanced **Create** table dialog. Notice that you can no longer switch the table type nor create partitions. While you can certainly add or delete columns, you cannot reorder them (unless you drop and recreate them). You'll find that other database rules, such as reducing the column width, are also enforced if the column already contains data.

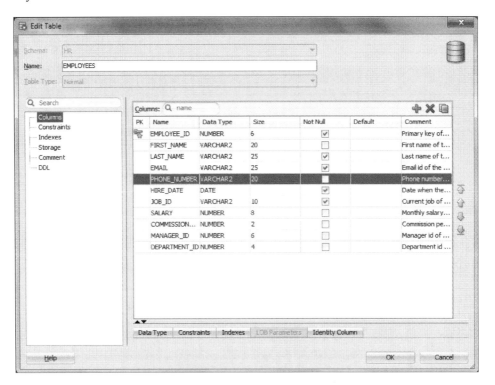

Script Runner/Running scripts

Possibly, one of the most commonly used group of SQL*Plus commands are those that run scripts: @, @@, and start. The script runner emulates a limited set of SQL*Plus features. You can often enter SQL and SQL*Plus statements and execute them by clicking the **Run Script** icon, which is shown in the next screenshot. The **Script Output** pane displays the output.

You need to use @@ when running one script that calls a second or third script. In this case, it is necessary to set the path for the top-level file.

For either, set the path navigating to **Database | Worksheet**. Press *F5* to run the script.

Set the default path for executing SQL scripts

To set the default path for scripts, invoke the **Preferences** dialog and set the path by navigating to **Database | Worksheet**. Click on **Browse** to locate or enter the path.

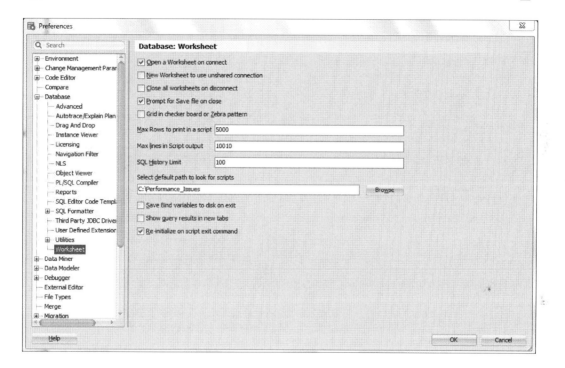

As with SQL*Plus, if you use @ or start to run a single SQL script file, you can either enter the full path (for example @C:\Performance_Issues\MyScript.sql) or you can set the path in the **Preferences** dialog, as shown in the following screenshot:

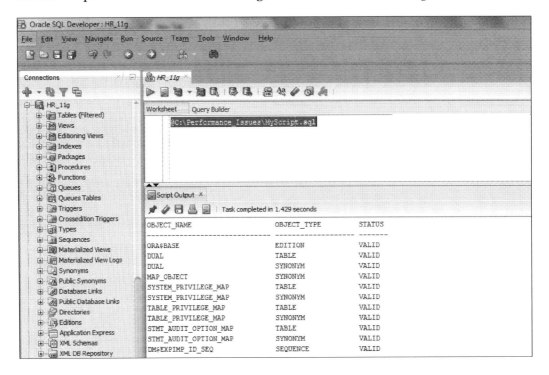

Few exceptions apply in SQL Developer script runner. For example, use of bind variables is not supported. (Bind variables of type VARCHAR2, NUMBER, and DATE.)

For substitution variables, the syntax &&variable assigns a permanent variable value, and the syntax &variable assigns a temporary (not stored) variable value.

For EXIT and QUIT, commit is the default behavior, but you can specify rollback. In either case, the context is reset: for example, the WHENEVER command information and substitution variable values are cleared.

DESCRIBE works for most, but not all, object types for which it is supported in SQL*Plus.

Execution plan

The execute **Explain Plan** icon, as shown in the next screenshot, generates the execution plan for a given query in a single click. The execution plan shows us the sequence of operations that will be performed to execute the SQL statement.

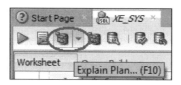

An execution plan shows a row source tree with the hierarchy of operations that make up the statement. For each operation the ordering of the tables referenced by the statement, access method for each table in the statement, join method for tables, and data operations such as filter, sort, or aggregation. The following is a screenshot of an explain plan feature:

The plan table also displays information about optimization (such as the cost and cardinality of each operation), partitioning (such as the set of accessed partitions), and parallel execution (such as the distribution method of join inputs). However, in future chapters, we will be discussing more on this feature.

Autotrace pane

The **Autotrace** pane displays trace-related information when you execute the SQL statement by clicking on the **Autotrace** icon. Most of the specific information displayed is determined by the SQL Developer preferences for database: **Autotrace/Explain Plan**, as shown in the following screenshot:

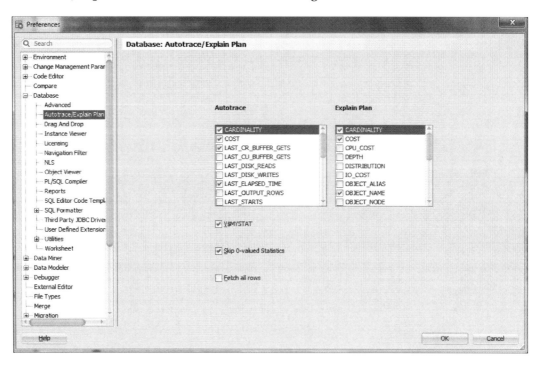

This information can help you to identify SQL statements that will benefit from tuning. For example, you may be able to optimize predicate handling by transitively adding predicates, rewriting predicates using Boolean algebra principles, moving predicates around in the execution plan, and so on. To use the **Autotrace** feature, the database user for the connection must have the **SELECT_CATALOG_ROLE** and **SELECT ANY DICTIONARY** privileges, If these privileges are not available to the user who is running the auto-trace, a pop-up message will be displayed, as shown in the following screenshot:

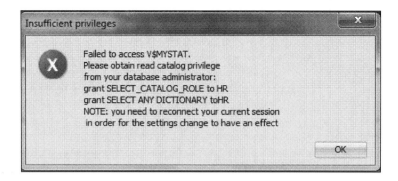

Once the required grants are given to the user, you will be able to do an auto-trace for your session, as shown in the following screenshot:

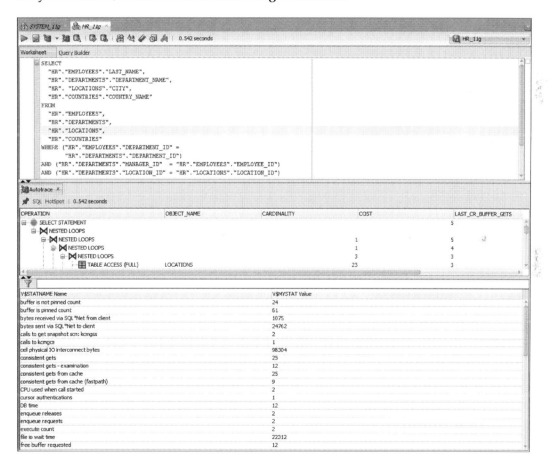

DBMS Output pane

If you execute any PL/SQL in a worksheet that contains DBMS_OUTPUT commands, whether an anonymous block or a compiled procedure, the output is sent to the **Dbms Output** window. Click on the **Dbms Output** option under the **View** menu for the **Dbms Output** window. Next, click on the connection add icon to open a tab for the connection. This also runs the set server output on command.

If you switch to another schema to execute PL/SQL for the new schema, the **Dbms Output** window is not affected. To see the output from this new user, you need to click the Add new **Dbms Output** tab button to open a tab for the new schema's connection.

In the example, PL/SQL was executed for both the HR and SYSTEM schemas. In both cases, the output was sent to the **Dbms Output** window. To see the results, select the appropriate schema using the connection tabs.

Some of the options seen in the **Dbms Output** window are explained in the following list:

- **Add New DBMS Output Tab**: This prompts you to specify a database connection, after which a tab is opened within the Dbms Output pane for that connection, and the SET SERVEROUTPUT setting is turned on so that any output is displayed in that tab. (To stop displaying output for that connection, close the tab.)

- **Clear**: This erases the contents of the pane.

- **Save**: This saves the contents of the pane to a file that you specify.

- **Print**: This prints the contents of the pane.

- **Buffer Size**: For databases before Oracle Database 10.2, this limits the amount of data that can be stored in the DBMS_OUTPUT buffer. The buffer size can be between 1 and 1000000 (1 million).

- **Poll**: This is the interval (in seconds) at which SQL Developer checks the DBMS_OUTPUT buffer to see if there is data to print. The poll rate can be between 1 and 15.

OWA output pane

Oracle Web Agent (OWA) or MOD_PLSQL is an Apache (Web Server) extension module that enables you to create dynamic web pages from PL/SQL packages and stored procedures. The **OWA Output** pane enables you to see the HTML output of MOD_PLSQL actions that have been executed in the SQL Worksheet. To enable **OWA Output** window, click the **OWA Output** option under **View**. Next, click on the connection add icon to open a tab for the connection:

Some of the options seen in the **OWA Output** window are explained here:

- **Add New OWA Output Tab**: This prompts you to specify a database connection, after which a tab is opened within the **OWA Output** pane for that connection, and entries written to the **OWA Output** buffer are displayed in that tab. (To stop displaying output for that connection, close the tab.)

- **Clear**: This erases the contents of the pane.

- **Save**: This saves the contents of the pane to a file that you specify.

- **Print**: This prints the contents of the pane.

Query Builder

The **Query Builder** tab in the SQL Worksheet enables you to display and build SQL queries graphically. You can create a SELECT statement by dragging and dropping the table and view names and by graphically specifying columns and other elements of the query. While you are building the query, you can click on the **Worksheet** tab to see the SELECT statement reflecting current specifications, and then click on the **Query Builder** tab to continue building the query if you want.

In the area below the graphical display of tables and views, you can specify one or more lines with the following information:

- **Output**: This specifies whether to include the expression in the statement output.

- **Expression**: This is the column name or expression.

- **Aggregate**: This denotes the aggregation function to be used (Avg, Avg Distinct, Count, and so on).

- **Alias**: This refers to the column alias to be used.

- **Sort Type**: This refers to the type of sorting of results, whether in an ascending order or in a descending order.

- **Sort Order**: This is the order to use in sorting results if multiple columns or expressions are to be used (for example, sorting first by department and then by salary within each department).

- **Grouping**: This specifies whether to insert a GROUP BY clause.

- **Criteria**: This is an expression with one or more criteria that must be satisfied for a result to be returned. You can specify any WHERE clause (without the WHERE keyword). Consider this example: for employees, SALARY, specifying > 10000 limits the results to employees with salaries greater than $10,000.

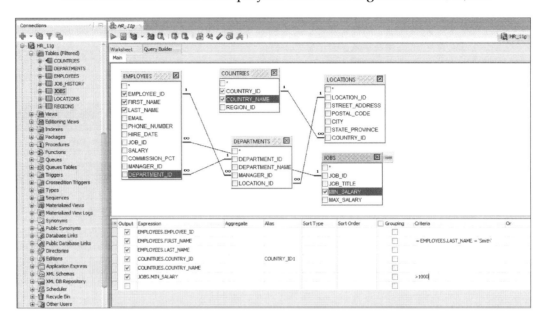

Command-line interface for SQL formatting

As an alternative to using the SQL Developer graphical interface for formatting, put an .sql file or all .sql files in a directory or folder.

Before invoking the command-line interface for SQL formatting, start the SQL Developer graphical interface so that the database, that is SQL Formatter preferences (which are used for the formatting), is loaded and available.

The following example takes the SQL code in C:\Performance_Issues\MyScript.sql and creates C:\Performance_Issues\MyScript_Out.sql containing the formatted code. (Enter the command in one command line.):

```
C:\sqldeveloper\sqldeveloper\bin>sdcli format input= C:\Performance_
Issues\MyScript.sql output= C:\Performance_Issues\MyScript_Out.sql
```

SQL Worksheet "hints" for formatting output

You can use special SQL Worksheet "hints" to generate output in several formats, such as CSV and SQL INSERT statements. (These hints do not work in SQL*Plus but do work in SQLcli.) You must use **Run Script** (*F5*), not **Execute Statement**, to see the formatted output. The hints must be in lowercase. Some example statements showing the available special SQL Worksheet hints are as follows:

SELECT /*ansiconsole*/ * FROM EMPLOYEES; — Best appearance for ANSI terminal.

SELECT /*csv*/ * FROM EMPLOYEES; — Comma-separated values

SELECT /*delimited*/ * FROM EMPLOYEES; — (Same as csv)

SELECT /*fixed*/ * FROM EMPLOYEES; — Fixed-width fields with trailing blanks

SELECT /*html*/ * FROM EMPLOYEES; — Marked-up HTML table

SELECT /*insert*/ * FROM EMPLOYEES; — SQL INSERT statements

SELECT /*json*/ * FROM EMPLOYEES; — JSON object format

SELECT /*loader*/ * FROM EMPLOYEES; — Pipe-delimited format for SQL*Loader

SELECT /*text*/ * FROM EMPLOYEES; — Plain text

SELECT /*xml*/ * FROM EMPLOYEES; — Tagged XML

The following example shows the output generated by the first statement (SELECT /*csv*/ * FROM EMPLOYEES;):

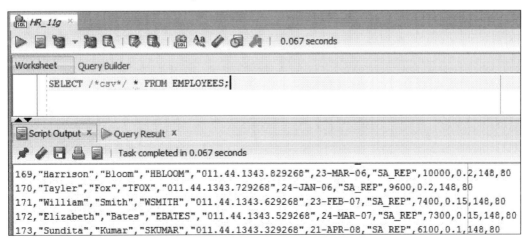

Summary

In this chapter, we reviewed the **Connection** navigator pane and then proceeded with SQL Worksheet and all its features that can assist in your daily tasks.

In the next chapter, we will introduce all of the shipped SQL Developer reports and show you how to create and run your own. You do not need to have completed this chapter to complete the chapter on reports. However, having an understanding of building SQL scripts will be useful.

The Power of SQL Reports

3

In addition to browsing objects and writing your own ad hoc queries against the database, Oracle SQL Developer has a separate **Reports** navigator with a set of predefined SQL queries known as reports. The main focus is the set of predefined data dictionary reports that range from providing basic details about your database to database administration, security, and quality assurance. Having these predefined reports means that you can quickly run a variety of SQL queries to analyze and assess the health and status of your database, saving you from needing to write the queries yourself.

The **Reports** navigator provides shipped reports to review the results of any non-Oracle database migrations that have been run, the details of any **Database Data Dictionary** and **Data Modeler** designs that have been exported, and any available Oracle Application Express applications. The output of any of these reports is controlled by the database connection used while executing a report.

You can extend the set of shipped, predefined reports by adding your own local or shared reports. While creating your own reports, not only can you add to the existing data dictionary reports, but you can also build up a set of reports to review and analyze the instance data in any application under development.

In this chapter, we will review the **Reports** navigator entirely. You will learn more about the shipped reports and how to run them. We'll look briefly at the Migration, Oracle APEX, and Data Modeler reports. These are also covered in the chapters on each of these topics. We'll review the various report styles available and show how you can make use of these different styles while creating your own reports.

Introducing SQL Developer reports

Whether you are a DBA or an application developer, running SQL queries against the data dictionary is a useful source of information. It provides you with details about the objects various schemas own, the health of a system, and the integrity of the data in the applications. If you work with the Oracle database regularly, you almost certainly already have a set of queries that you frequently run. For example, you might have a query to determine the tables that have no **Primary Keys** or, if you are a DBA, you might have a query to find out the currently connected sessions. Over the years, you may gather these queries in a file and have them at hand no matter what project you are working on, and they can play a significant role in your daily tasks.

SQL Developer has a categorized group of these SQL queries (reports) and it also provides the tools to create and save your essential queries as reports.

In this first section, we'll discuss the **Reports** navigator in general, how to run and use the reports, and any errors you might encounter.

To run any report in SQL Developer, you need a connection to the database.

Who can run reports?

Anyone can run or create reports in SQL Developer, from the least to the most privileged user. What you see depends on your security access, which is true throughout SQL Developer. It is not the product that enforces security, but the database itself. So, if you are presented with an error while running a report, consider the privileges you have and whether you'd be able to run this query in any other environment or circumstance, such as in SQL*Plus or the SQL Worksheet. Invariably, the error message displayed does explain the problem at hand and more often than not, it is a security level access issue.

When do you use reports?

You can use the reports on a daily basis throughout a project to track the details about your system. Reports provide high-level details about your database and can be used to drill down to the finest detail.

Tree layout for ease of navigation

The following screenshot shows the broad categories of the shipped reports that are available:

Use the shipped reports to determine the details about your system, which include:

- Finding the version and parameters' details of the database that you are connected to
- Learning more about the data dictionary
- Reviewing the tables and related details for a particular schema
- Finding the objects in a schema
- Reviewing the valid and invalid PL/SQL in a system
- Searching for PL/SQL text

Running a report

To run a report, expand any of the nodes in the **Reports** navigator and select the report. The first time you select a report, the **Select Connection** dialog will be invoked to offer a choice of connections, as shown in the following screenshot:

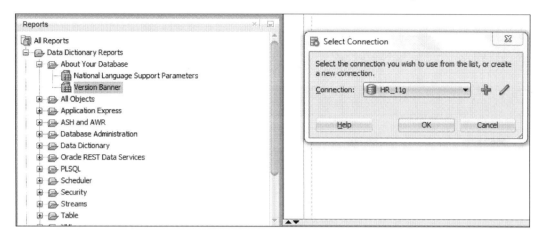

Some reports are parameter-driven as shown in the following screenshot:

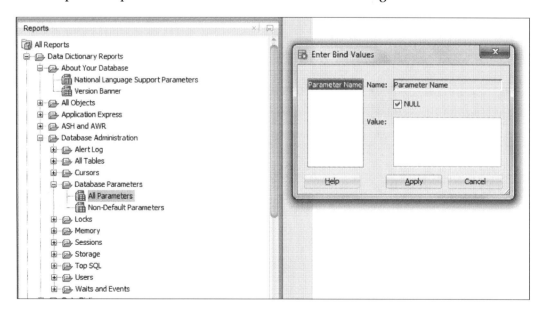

Privileges required for running reports

Most users can successfully run most of the shipped reports, needing only the database connection to start. Even users with the most limited connection privileges can run many of the reports, such as those in the **About Your Database** category. However, they will have limited or no access to the reports in the **Database Administration** category, as **SYSTEM** or DBA privileges are required to run these.

If you do not have access to the underlying tables being queried, you will get the standard Oracle error message, **"table or view does not exist"**. This is a common security access error message and you will need to switch to another more privileged user to run the report.

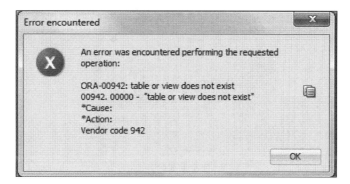

In the same way, you also need access to the underlying tables in a project to run user-defined report, where you might create a report for the instance data.

 Instance data, in this context, is the data in the application. In our examples, instance data is the data in the HR tables.

Running data dictionary reports

The first major category of the reports shipped with SQL Developer is the **Data Dictionary Reports** node. These are, by definition, about the data dictionary, and therefore, do not include any instance data reports, which you can define in the **User Defined Reports** section.

Getting to know the data dictionary

Once you have learned to write a select statement, getting to know the data dictionary is an important and useful progression to make. This is the data dictionary that holds the metadata about your database. Knowing how to query the data dictionary means that you can determine which dictionary view holds the information about the tables, columns, constraints, and privileges you can access. Therefore, you can find details about the project or the application that you are working on. As mentioned earlier, many people who are familiar with the data dictionary have SQL scripts and queries, which they frequently run. This is exactly what the shipped reports provide.

We have said that SQL Developer provides a long list of reports that query the data dictionary, but these do not cover every possibility. Starting with the two reports under the **Data Dictionary** node will help you become familiar with this environment.

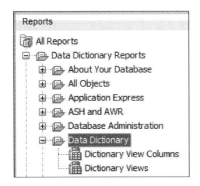

If the reports SQL Developer provides are sufficient for all your query purposes, then you may never use them. However, if you want to know something about your database that is not available through any report provided, then you can start with these two dictionary views and build a query based on your findings.

For example, SQL Developer does not provide any report on dimensions. If you want to learn about any dimension you have, you can write an SQL query, but you first need to know which dictionary views to query. This is where the **Data Dictionary | Dictionary Views** report can help. Select the report and run it. Provide the bind variable input parameter "dimension" when prompted. You do not need to add any wild cards (%), as the report does this for you.

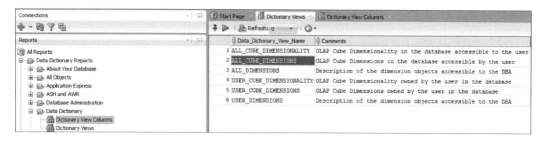

The report returns the set of records that relate to dimensions, listing the view names and the descriptions about the views. Once you have determined which view to use, use the **Data Dictionary | Dictionary View Columns** report (as shown in the following screenshot) to determine the columns in the view. You can now use the detail to write the query in the SQL Worksheet.

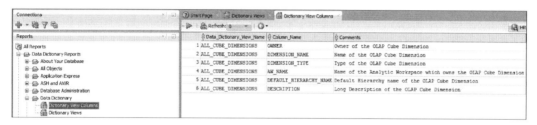

Both the reports are shown in the previous screenshots, illustrating the detail you need to be able to write your own query.

About the database

If you work with a number of different databases, then there are a few reports that are very useful to determine the version of the database you're connected to and the database parameters that are set. These reports fall under two categories:

- **About Your Database**
- **Database Parameters** — found in the **Database Administration** section

In the example that we have just seen, the **All Parameters** report has been run with a bind variable of "cursors" to list all of the parameters related to cursors. By using the connections drop-down list on the right-hand side, you can switch between database connections and compare these cursor parameters between databases.

Reviewing privileges and security reports

SQL Developer provides a number of reports that are related to security issues, including the **Auditing** and **Encryption** reports. If you are new to the database and are getting to know your environment, you are more likely to frequently run a group of security-related reports in the Grants and Privileges folder. If you are unable to access certain objects or find that you have no ability to create, edit, or update objects, then reviewing the **Role Privileges** and **System Privileges** reports is a good place to start.

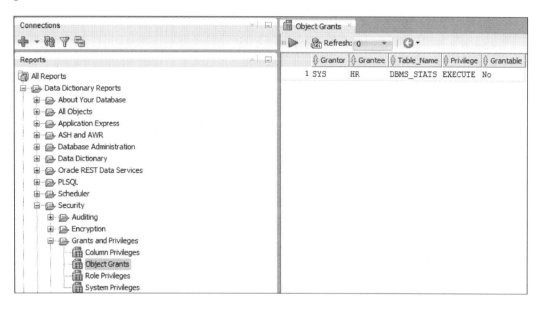

In the example shown in the previous screenshot, we have selected the **Object Grants** report for **HR**. Here, we see that the HR schema has an **EXECUTE** privilege on the **DBMS_STATS** procedure owned by the **SYS** user.

Assisting with quality assurance

The selection of **Quality Assurance** reports in the **Table** node is useful while working on a project or application development. This is not a comprehensive list (as shown in the following screenshot), but a good indication of the type of reports you might create to keep a check on the status of an application:

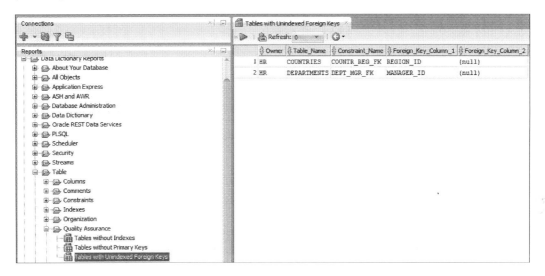

It's also worth noting that these are just reports and not suggestions of the best practice. While it is advisable to have indexes on your tables, there may be a good reason why some tables are not indexed. For example, if you were adding bulk sets of data, you would want to add the indexes after the fact. Having the report indicates where there are gaps. You'll need to make the decisions based on the results.

Using PL/SQL reports

There are a few reports in the PLSQL node. Possibly, the most useful one is the **Search Source Code** report. SQL Developer provides a number of search facilities, not just in the reports area, which help you find:

- Parameters in the PL/SQL code
- Objects in a schema
- Words and text in the current editor

If you use a command-line tool, such as SQL*Plus to access the database, then you will need to write an SQL query to search for specific strings in the SQL or PL/SQL code. The **PLSQL | Search Source Code** report allows you to look for either the PL/SQL object by name, or a string or piece of text in the code, as shown in the following screenshot:

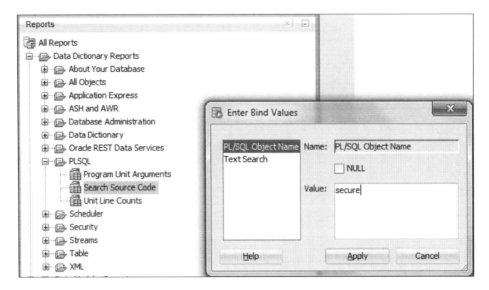

Once you have found the source code, you can move to the code using the context menu on the object name, or by double-clicking on the object name.

Running ASH and AWR reports

There are a growing number of **Oracle Active Session History (ASH)** and **Automatic Workload Repository (AWR)** reports provided by SQL Developer. AWR captures workload-related performance data at user and system levels. ASH provides the history of the activities in the recent active sessions. The following report is a chart of **Daily ASH Statistics**:

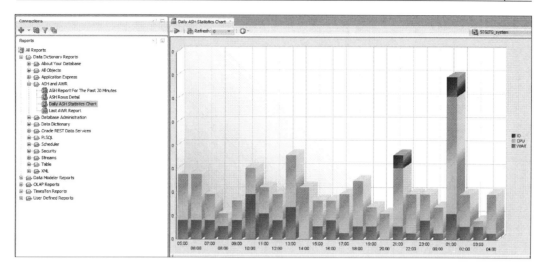

These reports are database-specific and require the **Oracle Diagnostics Pack** to be licensed for the databases you run the reports against. You are warned before you run these reports that the underlying reports require the license.

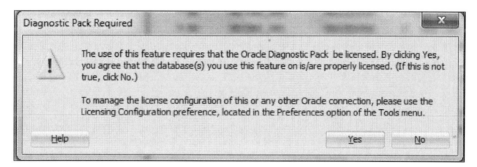

Migration reports

SQL Developer provides a selection of reports that are useful if you are involved in migrations from non-Oracle databases. As for the other reports, if you do not have access to the underlying structures, the reports will deny you access. You'd typically run these reports as the migrations repository owner or as a migrations user with similar privileges.

Application Express reports

SQL Developer provides a selection of **Application Express** reports. These are listed in the **Application Express** node under **Data Dictionary Reports**. These reports provide details about the applications you have access to. The **Applications** and **Pages** reports provide the same details that are available in the **Connection** navigator. For more information on this and all the Application Express support in SQL Developer, see the chapter on *Chapter 11, Working with Application Express.*

Data Modeler reports

A new category of reports was added in SQL Developer 2.1. This is the **Data Modeler Reports** node. The tables that these reports run against are first created and populated when you export your design from Oracle SQL Developer **Data Modeler**. Subsequent records are added each time you export a design in the **Data Modeler**. The reporting repository and the **Data Modeler** are discussed in the chapter on *Chapter 9, Introducing SQL Developer Data Modeler.*

More report categories

A new category of reports or additional reports in the existing categories is always added in the latest releases of SQL Developer. Since SQL Developer version 2.1, there has been many additional categories of reports added. For example, the **OLAP Reports** and **TimesTen Reports** nodes. We can easily explore all the reports by just clicking on the reports followed by the selection of the databases you want to run the report on.

Running reports from other menus

A report available from a top-level menu saves having to navigate to the report in the correct category. These reports are **Monitor Sessions** and **Monitor SQL**, which are both available on the main **Tools** menu, and **Manage Database**, which is available in the **Connections** main context menu. We'll now review each of these reports.

The Monitor Sessions report

The **Monitor Sessions** report displays the connected SQL Developer sessions and is available:

* In the **Sessions** category in the **Database Administration** section

The context menu for the report includes two additional items, **Trace Session** and **Kill Session** (as shown in the following screenshot). If you run this report as **SYSTEM** or a DBA, you can terminate these SQL Developer sessions using the menu. This is particularly useful if a session has not been terminated in a clean manner and needs to specifically be terminated.

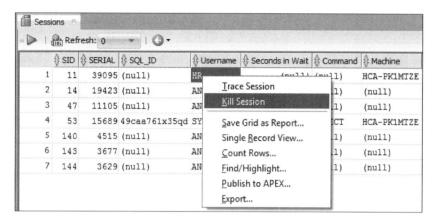

* On the main **Tools** menu

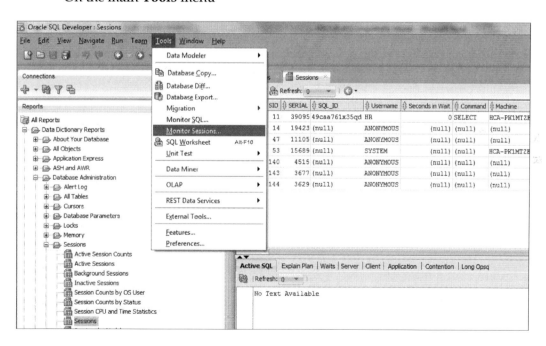

Managing the database

You can run the **Manage Database** report using the context menu for any connection in the **Connections** navigator. This report displays the tablespaces and the associated details. If you run the report as **SYS**, you can also shut down the database from this report, as the report provides an additional **Shutdown** button.

STGITG_system

	Target	Current
Maximum System Global Area (SGA) Size	2048	2,039
Program Global Area (PGA) Aggregate Target	1024	491
Current Configuration: (SGA + PGA)	3072	

Refresh

	TABLESPACE_NAME	PERCENT_USED	PCT_USED	ALLOCATED	USED	FREE	DATAFILES
1	APPS_UNDOTS1		97.41	1705	1660.88	44.13	1
2	APPS_TS_TX_DATA		94.52	6108.25	5773.38	334.88	4
3	SYSTEM		93.5	12085	11299.27	785.73	11
4	APPS_TS_TX_IDX		89.4	8940.875	7992.88	948	5
5	CTXD		88.59	23	20.38	2.63	1
6	APPS_TS_SEED		87.67	3036	2661.75	374.25	2
7	APPS_TS_SUMMARY		87.36	1051	918.13	132.88	1
8	APPS_TS_MEDIA		86.19	1373	1183.38	189.63	1
9	APPS_TS_INTERFACE		71.65	1100	788.13	311.88	1
10	APPS_TS_ARCHIVE		66.53	750	499	251	1
11	APPS_TS_NOLOGGING		64.58	60	38.75	21.25	1
12	SYSAUX		63.68	1000	636.75	363.25	1
13	USERS		61.25	10	6.13	3.88	1
14	OLAP		30.75	100	30.75	69.25	1
15	CLM_TBS_INDX		25.63	30	7.69	22.31	1
16	ODM		14.5	100	14.5	85.5	1
17	HPPPM_TS_TX_802_IDX		12.52	5000.0625	626.06	4374	1
18	HPPPM_TS_TX_802_DATA		8.62	5000.0625	431.06	4569	1
19	APPS_TS_QUEUES		8.19	1000	81.88	918.13	2
20	CLM_TBS_INTF		7.81	60	4.69	55.31	1
21	CLM_TBS_ARCH		1.67	60	1	59	1
22	PORTAL		1.38	100	1.38	98.63	1
23	OWAPUB		1.25	10	0.13	9.88	1
24	HPPPM_TS_TX_802_LOB		1.08	5000.0625	54.06	4946	1

Real-time SQL monitoring

Oracle Database 11g introduced real-time SQL monitoring, a feature now also exposed in the SQL Developer releases. Tuning is often considered the domain of DBAs, and this feature is typically used for monitoring performance and finding problem areas (for example, what point a query has reached in the explained plan and where the time is being spent). Having a report you can run easily brings tuning closer to the developer. Real-time SQL monitoring is useful for long running queries and comes into play by default when:

- The STATISTICS_LEVEL initialization parameter is set to ALL or TYPICAL (the default value)
- SQL statements consume more than 5 seconds
- SQL queries run in parallel

In SQL Developer, the report is **Monitor SQL** under the **Tools** menu. When you run it, it will display a grid of all the monitored statements.

In the following example, we used the shipped reports via **All Objects | Object Count by Type**. You can write your own long-running query or do the same. Once the report has started running, switch to or invoke the **Monitor SQL** report. A data grid of records will be displayed, as shown in the following screenshot:

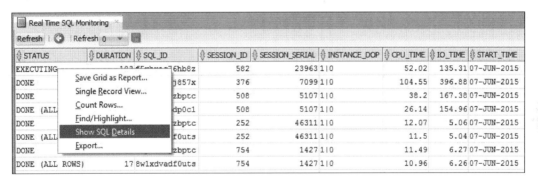

We have run a number of reports, so we have a record for each of the queries that fit the earlier mentioned criteria. To see the details of the report, invoke the context menu and select **Show Sql Details**.

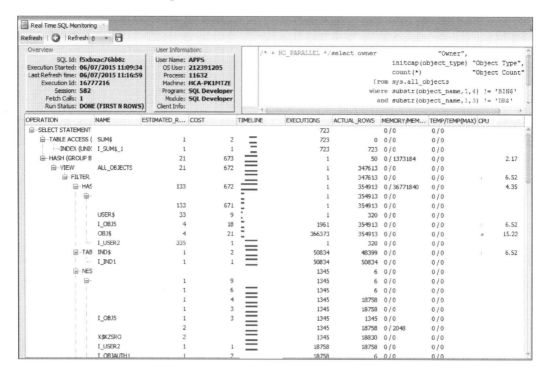

This query is still in progress, so the statements with the green arrows are still being executed.

 The real-time SQL monitoring feature is a part of the **Oracle Tuning Pack**, an Oracle Database 11g Cost Option, and as such, you are warned of this detail when you invoke the report.

Creating your own reports

You can create any of the reports described earlier under **User Defined Reports**, either by copying them and then making modifications, or by starting from scratch. Defining your own reports also means that you can query instance data in your application or project. If you run certain queries regularly, they are well-suited to be stored as reports.

User-defined report styles include basic tabular reports, charting, and master-detail reports. In this section, we will use the HR sample schema to demonstrate how to build your own reports. You can use the techniques described to build more complex reports.

Getting started

The first time you use the SQL Developer **Reports** navigator, the **User Defined Reports** folder will be available and initially empty. You can populate the folder using a number of approaches, for example:

- Importing existing reports that were previously created
- Copying a report
- Creating a report from scratch

Regardless of the approach used, it is advisable to categorize your reports. You can do this using folders.

Creating folders

Storing reports in folders serves a number of purposes in SQL Developer. Folders help you categorize reports that belong to a particular project or have a similar theme. This in turn helps you quickly find a category of reports, whether instance data or data dictionary reports. In addition, having folders of reports means that you can export, and therefore, later import the folders to reuse and share. You can create nested folders to further organize your reports.

To create a folder, select the **User Defined Reports** node in the **Reports** navigator and select **New Folder** from the context menu, as follows:

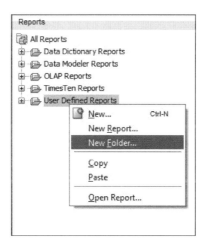

This invokes a simple dialog as shown in the following screenshot, which you can then populate with the details about the folder. This folder dialog only requires the **Name** field to be filled. However, if you provide more detail, it is useful to share reports later.

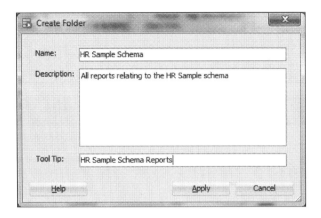

Storing reports

As soon as you create an initial folder or report, a new `UserReports.xml` file will be created in the `C:\Documents and Settings\<user>\Application Data\SQL Developer` folder.

The other change to be aware of is that reports created prior to SQL Developer 1.5 were created in `UserReports.xml` and stored in the `C:\Documents and Settings\<user>\.sqldeveloper` folder. In SQL Developer 1.5, this location was changed to the `Application Data` folder as described.

The initial code created using the earlier mentioned folder example looks as follows:

```
<?xml version="1.0" encoding="UTF-8" ?><displays><folder>
  <name><![CDATA[HR Sample Schema]]></name>
  <tooltip><![CDATA[HR Sample Schema reports]]></tooltip>
  <description><![CDATA[All reports relating to the HR Sample
              Schema]]></description>
  </folder>
</displays>
```

This is the file that your new reports are added to, which you share with other users. We'll discuss sharing reports later.

As soon as you add reports to a folder or edit reports in the folder, the folder will be rendered in italics. Saving the new updates using the **Save All** button updates the folder definition and the `UserReports.xml` file.

Creating general reports

To create a report, select the **User Defined Reports** node or a subfolder under the node, and invoke the **Create Report** dialog using **New Report** from the context menu. The initial dialog is the same for all the reports. At this point, you can enter all of the details about the report, including the **SQL**, **Bind Variables**, **Child Reports**, and so on. Once all the required report building requirements are entered, the **Test Report** icon will run the test report on the database selected from the connections list we already have (on the right-hand side of the **Test Report** icon, as shown in the following screenshot):

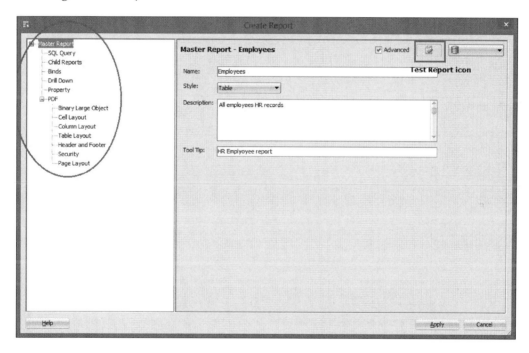

In the example that we have just seen, notice the report **Style** drop-down list. This allows you to control the visual output of the report (for example, a table or chart).

The **Test** button allows you to test the SQL script for validity, so it's often easier to leave the report's style unchanged. The default **Style** is **Table**. Test the SQL and then change the style as required.

Building general tabular reports

This is the most common form of reporting used and, with the exception of a few charts provided, all the shipped reports follow this style. Tabular reports are also used in drill-down and master-detail reports. Regardless of the report you're about to create, you need to start with the initial SQL query. Consider the following query:

```
SELECT B.DEPARTMENT_ID,
    B.DEPARTMENT_NAME,
    A.FIRST_NAME,
    A.LAST_NAME,
    A.PHONE_NUMBER,
    A.HIRE_DATE,
    A.SALARY,
    C.JOB_TITLE
FROM HR.DEPARTMENTS B,
    HR.EMPLOYEES A,
    HR.JOBS C
WHERE A.EMPLOYEE_ID  = B.MANAGER_ID
AND B.DEPARTMENT_ID = A.DEPARTMENT_ID
AND C.JOB_ID        = A.JOB_ID;
```

When this query is used in a tabular report, the output will appear, as shown in the following screenshot:

Adding bind variables

If you work with large sets of data, restricting the records returned using a WHERE clause makes the result set more manageable. Writing the query to support input values or a bind variable means that you can rerun the query using different values. This kind of a query makes a good report, because you can pass in values to restrict the result set.

It is important to know that while writing a query with bind variables, unless otherwise handled, the data is stored in the database in the uppercase. If you have data in mixed case in the database, you'll need to code for this.

For example, you can add `AND C.JOB_TITLE LIKE :JOB_NAME` to the previous query. This is fine, except you need to know what you are searching for and that, in this case, is Job Titles stored in mixed case. So, entering "sales" or "manager" would not return any records. In this example, it's safer to enter the code `AND UPPER (C.JOB_TITLE) LIKE UPPER (:JOB_NAME)`. Then, the user does not need to know the composition of the data.

Once you have set up the binds in your report, you can run the report. You will be prompted for the value that you can add, as shown in the following screenshot:

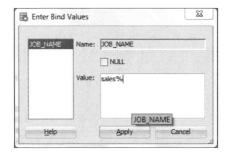

The **Create Report** dialog also provides the opportunity to add more meaningful detail to the binds in your reports.

Below the SQL script region is a set of tabs, one of which is the **Binds** tab, as shown in the following screenshot. This allows you to add more detail to the bind variables declared, which is useful and especially true if you pass a number of parameters.

```
FROM HR.DEPARTMENTS B,
HR.EMPLOYEES A,
HR.JOBS C
WHERE A.EMPLOYEE_ID = B.MANAGER_ID
AND B.DEPARTMENT_ID = A.DEPARTMENT_ID
AND C.JOB_ID = A.JOB_ID
AND UPPER (C.JOB_TITLE) LIKE UPPER (:JOB_NAME)
```

In the example shown in the following screenshot, we have provided a **Default** search value, **Prompt**, and **ToolTip**. All of these provide added information to other users running the report.

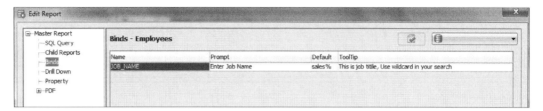

 To invoke the **Create Report** dialog after it has been closed, select **Edit Report** from the context menu while highlighting the report.

Drilling down through reports

You can create a report that steps from one report to the next. You can also navigate to the definition of an object. Therefore, a report that returns a list of tables has an additional context menu that you can use to navigate to the table in question. The shipped reports also support drill-down reports. Consider the **All Constraints** report in the **Tables | Constraints** node. In addition to returning the **Constraint** details, the report displays a list of tables. Here, the context menu displays an extra menu option to navigate to the table in question:

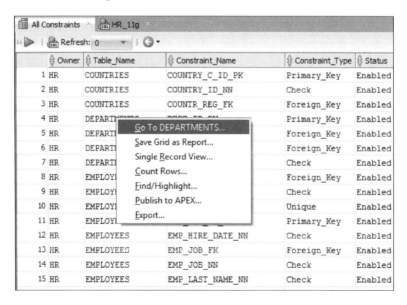

Creating a drill-down report

To create a drill-down report, create the initial master report, as you would do for any other tabular report. By way of an example, we'll create a master or top-level report using the same query that we used before:

```
SELECT DEPARTMENT_ID,
       DEPARTMENT_NAME,
       LOCATION_ID
FROM DEPARTMENTS
```

Create a second report using a query that will provide the results of the detail records (following the drill-down action from the first):

```
SELECT EMPLOYEE_ID,FIRST_NAME,LAST_NAME,EMAIL,DEPARTMENT_ID
FROM EMPLOYEES
WHERE department_id =:DEPARTMENT_ID
```

Give the report a descriptive name (for example, **Employee Details**); you'll need to access this later. Notice, for this report, we included a bind variable. Therefore, the report either requires a value to be entered using the Bind Variable dialog, or it has a value passed from the top-level or master report.

Now, return to the top-level report and select the **Advanced** tab.

Select **Add Report** and enter the **Name** of the detail report. This is the value that is displayed in the context menu. In the **Report** field, there is a drop-down list of all the reports available, whether shipped or user-defined. Find and select the detail report you created, as shown in the following screenshot. Clicking on **Apply** saves the changes and runs the report.

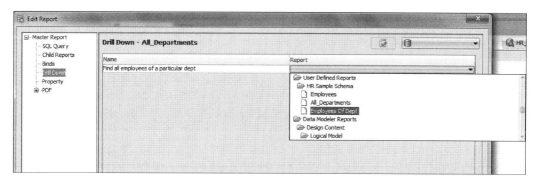

Running the top-level report is no different from any other tabular report. The context menu now displays an addition menu called **Reports**. All of the reports that you can navigate to from this report are displayed in the submenu. In the following example, the value that you have selected is passed to the called detail report as a bind parameter:

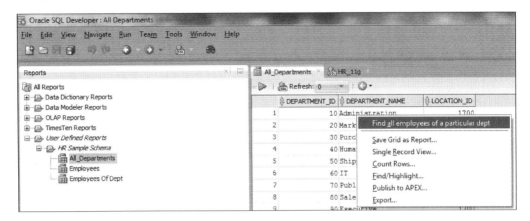

While drilling down through the reports, a new button becomes available to allow you to traverse back up through the reports, as shown in the following screenshot:

Case-sensitive bind variables

Bind variable values are case-sensitive. For bind variables that access a column name in the database, use the case of the column, as it is stored. The default is uppercase.

Master-detail reports

Master-detail reports are useful to review related data on a single screen. Initially, when you run a master-detail report, only the master records are displayed. Once you select one of the master records, the details for that master are displayed. Consider one of the shipped **Data Dictionary** reports, **Active Sessions**, shown in the following screenshot (this can be found under **Database Administration | Sessions**). The report has a number of sibling details that are displayed in a set of tabs below the master record.

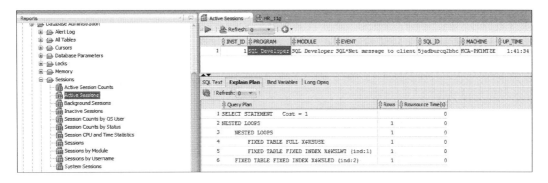

Creating master-detail reports

Initially, you create a regular tabular report as the master report. In the following example, we will use the same query as before:

```sql
SELECT DEPARTMENT_ID,
       DEPARTMENT_NAME,
       LOCATION_ID
FROM DEPARTMENTS
```

You can create, test, and even run the report as you would in any tabular report. This will ensure that the master records and reports are correct. In the example shown in the following screenshot, we have run **Report Test**:

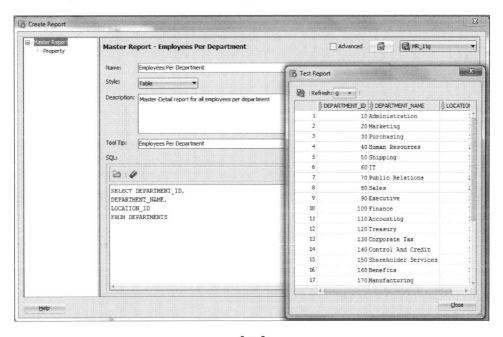

To add the detail, click on the **Add Child** button on the main report. This invokes a new panel in the dialog and allows you to add the detail records.

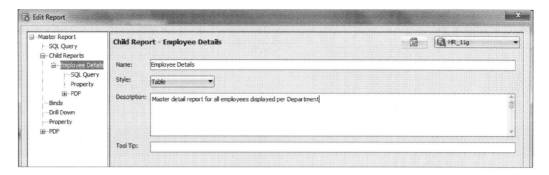

The example in the following screenshot displays the full set of employees for any record in the master report. In order to have a meaningful set of records for each department, you need to link the master to the detail. For example:

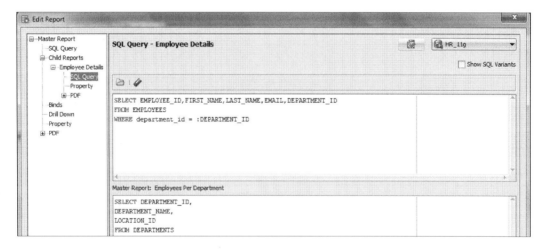

```
SELECT EMPLOYEE_ID,FIRST_NAME,LAST_NAME,EMAIL,DEPARTMENT_ID
FROM    EMPLOYEES
WHERE   department_id = :DEPARTMENT_ID
```

The two key elements here are first that the `department_id` bind variable is in uppercase (or the case of the column name in the database) as the report is looking for this "variable" in the database, and the second is that you have the join value in the master report.

Once you have created the report, you can tab through the master records to display each set of related detail records.

Notice that it is the name of the report that is displayed in the master and detail tabs.

Adding charts

You can create reports and display them as charts instead of as a tabular output. The basic premise of a chart is that you need values for the *x*- and *y*-axis and the central value. Therefore, a report query is structured as follows:

```
SELECT <group>,<series>,<value>
FROM <table(s)>
```

The query SELECT DEPARTMENT_ID, LAST_NAME, SALARY FROM EMPLOYEES is an easy example to start with.

Once you have entered the query, switch the display style to **Chart** and select the **Chart Details** tab.

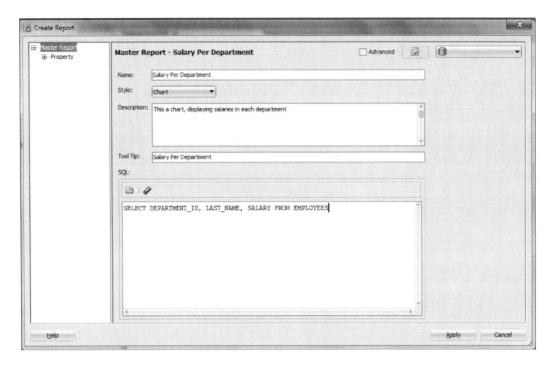

The **Property** node under **Master Report** in the left navigation pane provides you with more control on the style of chart you are going to display. The choices of chart styles are as follows:

- Pie
- Bar stacked (vertical or horizontal)
- Bar cluster (vertical or horizontal)

The number of records returned should drive the choice of the chart style you make. For example, the **PIE_MULTI** choice for **Chart Type** produces a pie chart for each record and is therefore better suited for fewer records or a query different from the one displayed earlier.

There are a number of other settings, which you can adjust, that control the appearance of the final chart. In the example we are using, **Legend** has been switched off as this displays each **LAST_NAME** and makes the report very busy.

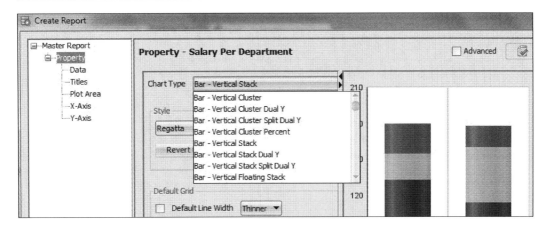

The final output for the chart is shown in the following screenshot:

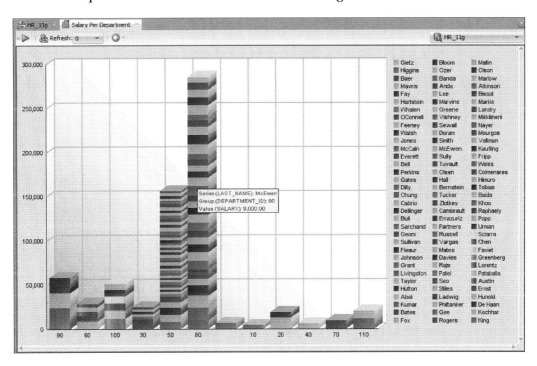

Notice that as you roll the mouse pointer on the various regions in the chart, the values are displayed. You can now incorporate these charts as details in a master-detail report.

SQL Developer offers a limited choice of graphical reports. The product is not a graphical reporting tool, so while these reports may seem limited, they do provide a visual report of the data being queried. Other graphical chart options can be pie charts and gauge charts.

Importing and exporting

Once you have a selection of reports created, you can export and save or share the reports. To export a report or a folder of reports, select **Export** from the context menu. You can export the following:

- The highest level of **User Defined Reports**
- A folder and subfolders
- Individual reports

If you have created folders to categorize reports, then these folders are ideal to export.

In the same way that you can export folders of reports or individual reports, you can import reports and folders of reports from other users. Any report that you import is added to your personal UserReports.xml file and, as such, it can be edited and deleted as you choose.

Sharing reports through user-defined extensions

If you create a selection of reports that you want to share among team members as read-only reports, you can include these in a separate **Shared Reports** node. These reports are not editable, much like the shipped reports, although they can be copied and added to the **User Defined** reports section and edited at this point. To share reports, you first need to export a set of reports. Once you have the new XML file or reports, place it on a shared server that is available for all the users who need access. Open the **Preferences** dialog from the **Tools** menu, expand the **Database** node in the tree on the left-hand side, and select **User Defined Extensions**. Here, you can add the reports by browsing to the location of the report. The location should include the XML file name. Set **Type** to **REPORT**.

Once you have completed this step, you need to restart SQL Developer for the new extension type to be included. Once reopened, the new **Shared Reports** node will be displayed in the top-level list of folders.

Save shared reports on a web server

You can save the report's XML file on a web server. If the file is stored on a web server, use the full URL for the location of the file in the **User Defined Extensions** settings.

DB Doc generation

One of our more popular features is **DB Doc**. We can generate an HTML documentation selected schema with a right-click.

You can generate a documentation about your schema in the HTML format for your own review or to share with others. Follow these steps to generate and view schema documentation:

1. Connect to the **HR** schema.
2. Right-click on the **HR_ORCL** connection and select **Generate DB Doc**.
3. Select or create a suitable location for the generated files.

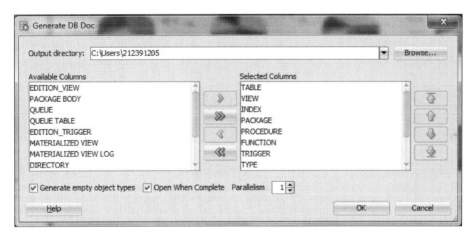

4. An `index.html` file should open automatically in your default browser. If it doesn't, navigate in a browser to the `\working\index.html` file and open it.

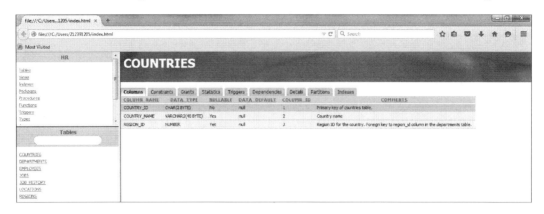

To see the details for any database object in the HTML documentation, select the object type in the schema panel in the top left corner. A list of all the objects of that type will then appear in a panel below the schema panel.

Summary

SQL Developer provides the ability to create and save SQL queries as reports. You can create your own reports using various report styles, including graphs or master-detail reports with sibling detail reports. In addition to being able to create your own reports, SQL Developer supplies a set of shipped reports that access the data dictionary and provide you with an easy start to assessing the status of your application. In this chapter, you saw that by using these SQL reports, you can determine the general health and status of all of the database aspects of the systems you are working with, including the general health of the database, the database objects, and instance data in the application. Using SQL Developer, you can build your own reports and export them to be shared with colleagues by sharing the exported XML file or through the user-defined extension mechanism.

In the next chapter, we'll look at how SQL Developer supports working with PL/SQL Tuning Tools. You'll see how the tool can support you while creating and editing PL/SQL, and how to compile and debug PL/SQL packages, procedures, and functions.

4
Working with PL/SQL

Unique to the Oracle database, PL/SQL code forms the core of many Oracle database applications. Whether a database-centric application or one using open source technologies, if the Oracle database underpins the application, PL/SQL code is almost certainly present and is stored in the database or sent in blocks of code to the database for execution. PL/SQL is a language extension to SQL, offering a procedural language structure in the Oracle Database, which is required for more complex application development. SQL Developer supports PL/SQL development by allowing you to work with text files or develop and test code directly against the database.

In this section, we will review this support and show you how to create, compile, and debug PL/SQL and look at a number of useful features available to facilitate writing PL/SQL. This chapter is not about teaching PL/SQL or best practice programming techniques. Instead, the examples used here serve to illustrate how the tool might be used and are based on the many coding examples available in the Oracle documentation.

Creating, compiling, and debugging PL/SQL

You can use either the SQL Worksheet, or the PL/SQL Editor, to create and edit your PL/SQL code. You can think of the SQL Worksheet as a free format text editor where you can create anonymous PL/SQL blocks or more formal structured program units, such as procedures. Using the PL/SQL Editor, you can edit program units already in the database. In either case, SQL Developer provides you with a set of tools to help you create, edit, refactor, and debug your code. Coding assistants, such as code insight, code templates, or code snippets, are available in both the SQL Worksheet and the PL/SQL Code editors.

However, feedback on errors is only available in the PL/SQL Code editor. We'll start the section by reviewing some of the code editing options available by initially working in the SQL Worksheet with anonymous PL/SQL blocks.

Writing PL/SQL in the SQL Worksheet

The SQL Worksheet is an excellent scratch pad for working with SQL, SQL*Plus, and PL/SQL, and combinations of these. When starting to develop a new program unit, having access to pieces of previously written code is useful. Time-saving code completion means less typing or the need to remember the correct spelling of object names or columns in tables.

Using code insight

SQL Developer provides a facility called code insight that displays in a popup list of possible choices for the next value or statement in the code. Consider the following code:

```
DECLARE
    BONUS NUMBER;
    SAL NUMBER;
    COMM NUMBER;
    EMP_NAME VARCHAR2 (20);
BEGIN
    SELECT LAST_NAME, SALARY, COMMISSION_PCT
    INTO EMP_NAME, SAL, COMM
    FROM EMPLOYEES
    WHERE EMPLOYEE_ID = 157;
    BONUS := (SAL * 0.10) + (COMM * 0.15);
    DBMS_OUTPUT.PUT_LINE('EMPLOYEE '|| EMP_NAME || ' EARNS A NEW BONUS OF '
|| BONUS );
END;
```

If you use the SQL Worksheet and start entering that code, a short list of values is displayed soon after you type BONUS, as shown in the following screenshot:

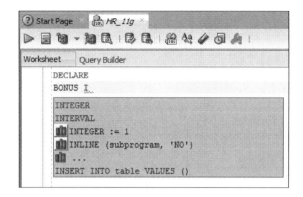

You can tab down, select **NUMBER**, and you're done. You can also type N and the list changes, in general revealing more possible options, thus revealing that the initial selection contained a shortened list of the most commonly used choices (in this case, displaying only **NUMBER**).

You can also choose to type any other letter and change the list of choices altogether. The list of choices here includes schema names, tables, columns, variable declarations, and procedure or function calls.

Each selection from the list reduces and changes the next list displayed. For example, take a package with procedures included. If you start typing the package name, the code insight feature provides a list of all packages with those initial letters. Once you have the package entered, typing the "." invokes the list of public procedures and functions available within the package. In the example that follows, the package and procedure are already in place and the code insight now reveals the parameters and data types required for input:

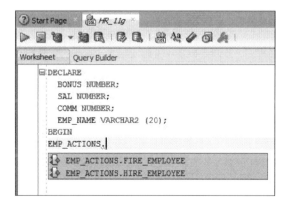

For more detail on controlling or switching off code insight, you can navigate to **Tools | Preferences | Code Editor | Completion Insight**.

Using code snippets and code templates

Code snippets are useful as they provide the framework for larger or smaller chunks of code. By navigating to **View | Snippets**, we can open the **Snippets** pane. There are PL/SQL snippets under the category **PL/SQL Programming Techniques**, in the **Snippets** window (shown in the following screenshot), which provide a useful selection of PL/SQL constructs.

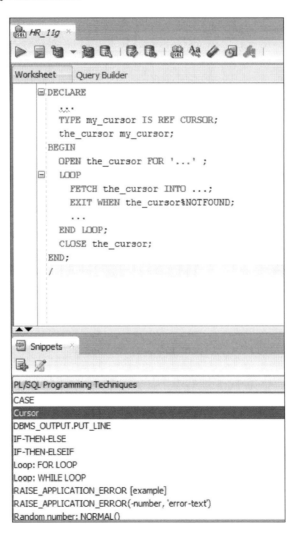

In the preceding example, both the **Snippets** window and the resulting code skeleton, created here by dragging the **Cursor** snippet onto the SQL Worksheet, are shown. You can extend the selection of snippets provided by adding your own.

Code templates are very similar in concept, except that SQL Developer only provides a few default code templates. Instead, you have a blank canvas in which you need to add your own. You invoke code templates by entering the first few letters of the template, which displays the code using code insight. Code templates are useful for frequently used chunks of complete code, such as exception handlers.

For the add, edit, and remove code templates, we can navigate to **Tools | Preferences** and expand the **Database** node in the left pane of the **Preferences** dialog box, as shown in the following screenshot:

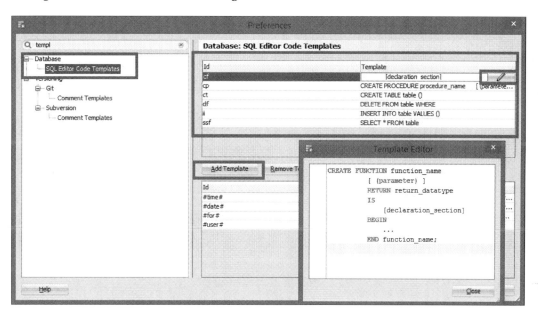

Working with triggers

SQL Developer supports creating, editing, and debugging PL/SQL program units. **Triggers**, **Functions**, **Procedures**, and **Packages** are listed in the **Connections** navigator, and you can view the details of these by selecting and clicking on each to open the display editors. In this section, we'll look at each of these constructs in turn and at the dialogs and utilities associated with them. Oracle Database triggers fire when you manipulate or update data, update database objects (such as dropping a table), or on certain database events (such as logging on). SQL Developer provides a number of utilities and dialogs to simplify creating and working with triggers.

Using the Create Trigger dialog

You can use the SQL Developer worksheet to write the PL/SQL code for the complete database trigger, without having the formal or, if you know the trigger structure very well, perhaps confining restrictions of a dialog. However, if you are a bit unfamiliar with creating triggers, then the **Create Trigger** dialog can be really useful by providing the structure for the DML event clause and any condition details.

Consider the following example:

```
CREATE OR REPLACE
TRIGGER TRACK_SALARY_HISTORY
BEFORE INSERT OR UPDATE OF SALARY ON EMPLOYEES
FOR EACH ROW
WHEN (NEW.EMPLOYEE_ID >0)
DECLARE SAL_DIFF NUMBER;
BEGIN
   SAL_DIFF := :NEW.SALARY - :OLD.SALARY;
   INSERT INTO SALARY_HISTORY (EMP_ID, NEW_SAL, OLD_SAL, INCREASE,
UPDATED_ON)
   VALUES (:NEW.EMPLOYEE_ID,:NEW.SALARY, :OLD.SALARY, SAL_DIFF, SYSDATE);
END;
```

By providing checklists, radio groups, and drop-down lists, the dialog shown in the following screenshot helps you create most of the structure of the trigger:

Once you have completed the dialog, all that is left for you to add are any variable declarations and the body of the PL/SQL block.

The **Create Trigger** dialog also has the advantage of setting a context, so that certain sections of the dialog are only editable for set conditions. For example, if you are creating a trigger that fires before or after **INSERT** or **DELETE**, then it is not relevant to select specific columns since these actions affect the entire record. However, you may want a trigger to fire on **UPDATE** of a specific column. In this case, when you select the **Update** option, the **Selected** and **Available Columns** fields are enabled. It is also not relevant to add a When clause to a **Statement Level** trigger, so this item is only enabled for **Row Level** triggers.

Once you have completed the details in the **Trigger** tab of the dialog, you can select the **DDL** tab to review the code that will be executed, and then click on **OK** to create the trigger. You need to add the PL/SQL trigger body and any additional declarations required, and then compile the code. For this example, before you can compile the code, you need the **SALARY_HISTORY** table. To compile the code, select the **Compile** button:

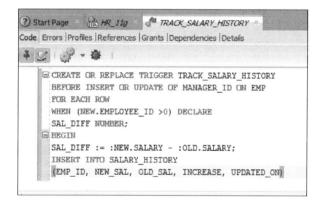

Once a trigger has been compiled, you can test the code by performing the various operations that cause it to fire. In this case, it should fire on inserting a new record, but not on delete. It should fire when updating the salary, but not for updating any other column values. In each case, the auditing table, **SALARY_HISTORY** is updated.

Creating INSTEAD OF triggers

The **Create Trigger** dialog supports creating advanced triggers, which are fired not only on table insert, update, and delete events, but also on these events for views. If a view is updateable, it means you can update the underlying table, or tables, by executing `insert`, `update`, or `delete` statements against the view. In general, complex views are not updateable, meaning that you can't use DML statements directly against the view to update the underlying table or tables. In this case, you can use **INSTEAD OF** triggers. When using the **Create Trigger** dialog, switching the trigger type from **TABLE** to **VIEW** causes the dialog to change to support the **INSTEAD OF** trigger.

In the previous screenshot, the trigger type of **VIEW** was selected, producing the skeleton shown. Once created, **INSTEAD OF** triggers are listed with other triggers in the **Triggers** node and can also be found in the triggers display for the views they are associated with.

Controlling triggers

SQL Developer provides a number of context-sensitive menus which provide a quick route to enabling, disabling, and compiling triggers. Select any trigger in the navigator and invoke the context menu, as shown in the following screenshot:

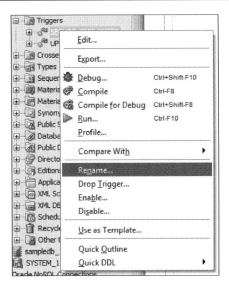

You can also apply global updates to triggers by invoking the context menu selection for tables. This displays a trigger menu that includes the **Enable All** and **Disable All** options.

Adding functions or procedures

You can create functions or procedures using the **Create New Function** or **Create New Procedure** dialogs, or by using the SQL Worksheet. The dialogs for creating functions and procedures are very basic, providing only the structure for naming and adding parameters. For functions, a default **RETURN** parameter is also defined:

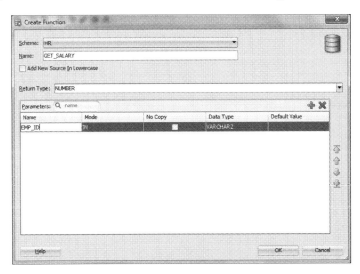

The main content, the body, still needs to be written, but the dialog creates the framework, making it easier to get started. If you have no input parameters and only the return value, you can do this as easily in the SQL Worksheet by just typing the text. The advantage of using the dialog is that the skeleton code is opened in the PL/SQL code editor and you can get the immediate added benefit of the compiler messages. In the examples that follow, we use functions to illustrate the point, but the detail is pertinent to procedures too. For the most part, we'll refer to subprograms to include both functions and procedures.

Consider the following piece of code:

```
CREATE OR REPLACE
FUNCTION GET_SALARY (EMP_ID NUMBER) RETURN NUMBER IS
  CURR_SAL NUMBER;
BEGIN
  SELECT SALARY INTO CURR_SAL FROM EMPLOYEES
      WHERE EMPLOYEE_ID = EMP_ID;
  RETURN CURR_SAL;
END GET_SALARY;
```

Whether you used the SQL Worksheet or the **Create Function** dialog, once you have created the skeleton, open it in the PL/SQL code editor. If you have used the SQL Worksheet, once you execute the code to create the function, refresh the **Functions** node in the navigator, and click on the name of the new function. By way of example, enter the following piece of code in the SQL Worksheet, and press *F5* to run the code:

```
CREATE OR REPLACE
FUNCTION GET_SALARY(EMP_ID NUMBER)
  RETURN NUMBER
  AS
  BEGIN
    RETURN NULL;
END GET_SALARY;
```

To invoke the code editor (shown in the following screenshot), click on the function name in the navigator and select **Code**.

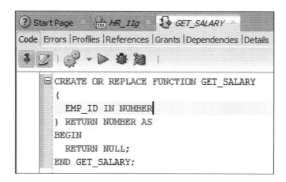

Working with errors

The **Connections** navigator displays all packages, procedures, and functions the user owns, including those that are currently compiled with errors. A red cross overlaying the object icon indicates that the object is compiled with errors. In the following screenshot, the procedure **EMP_ACTIONS** package body has errors, while the **ADD_JOB_HISTORY** function has none. Errors may be syntactical, or might have errors if dependencies have been removed (for example, if a table that the function relies on has been dropped).

The other area to look for compile-time errors is in the editor itself. Once you have compiled a program, the errors are marked:

- Within the code, using a line under the code.
- In the right-hand margin. You can see each message by rolling the mouse over the point in the margin.

In the following screenshot, we have shown all the elements:

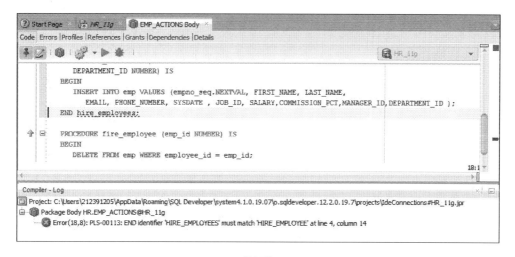

There is a database hard limit of 20 messages displayed in the log window, including both warnings and errors. If you have 20 warnings before the first error is encountered, you will not see the error messages. Oracle Database 11g Release 2 has changed this to 20 errors and unlimited warnings.

Handling multiple error messages

You can control the type of PL/SQL warning messages that are displayed using **Preferences**. Navigate to **Database | PL/SQL Compiler**. The settings control whether the types of warnings are displayed or suppressed, and whether they are treated as errors.

Creating packages

Creating packages requires a specification and body to be created. In this case, the new dialog for the package specification only serves to provide the skeleton, requiring only a name as an input value. Once you click on **OK**, the package specification opens in the PL/SQL **Code** editor and you need to enter all of the required declarations. The following screenshot shows the very basic skeleton created by the **Create PL/SQL Package** dialog:

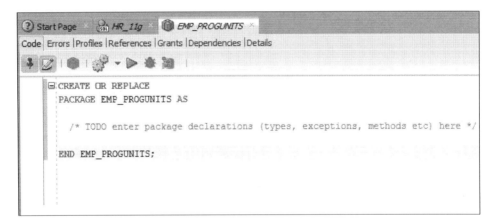

To complete the specification, you need to manually enter the code, such as declaring the public variables, procedures, and functions as needed. We added the following highlighted code to the example:

```
CREATE OR REPLACE
PACKAGE EMP_PROGUNITS AS
 TYPE EMPRECTYP IS
    RECORD (EMP_ID INT, SALARY REAL);
```

```
    CURSOR DESC_SALARY
        RETURN EMPRECTYP;
  PROCEDURE HIRE_EMPLOYEE
      (LAST_NAME VARCHAR2, JOB_ID VARCHAR2,
      MANAGER_ID NUMBER, SALARY NUMBER,
      DEPARTMENT_ID NUMBER);
  PROCEDURE FIRE_EMPLOYEE (EMP_ID NUMBER);
  PROCEDURE ADD_DEPT
      (DEPARTMENT_NAME IN DEPARTMENTS.DEPARTMENT_NAME%TYPE,
      LOCATION_ID IN DEPARTMENTS.LOCATION_ID%TYPE);
END EMP_PROGUNITS;
```

Creating the body

Once you have provided all of the package declarations, using the **Code** editor,
you can use the new package body dialog to create the skeleton. Of all the PL/SQL
Create dialogs, this is the most useful. It provides skeletons in the package body for
each of the procedures or functions declared in the package specification.

To automatically create the body, select the package specification, invoke the context
menu, and select **Create Body...** to invoke the new package body dialog:

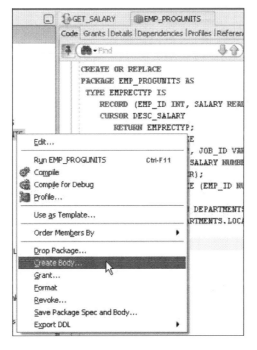

Creating a package body

Save time setting up the package body by defining all of the procedure and function declarations in the package specification, and then using the **Create Body** context menu to automatically create a skeleton of procedures and functions.

Refactoring code

The utilities discussed in this section can once again be used in either the SQL Worksheet or the **Code** editor. While all are not necessarily confined to PL/SQL, such as the **Find DB Object** search utility, it is useful to discuss them here.

Refactoring code is the process of redesigning the code to restructure it or improve the performance, without impacting the resulting behavior. SQL Developer supports a number of refactoring options, which include:

- Surrounding the code with the following PL/SQL constructs
    - The FOR loop
    - The WHILE loop
    - The PL/SQL block

- Extracting a procedure
- Renaming a local variable

Some of these can assist you while writing your code, such as **Surround with...**, and so are as much about being productive as they are about refactoring. One feature that is useful when refactoring is **Extract Procedure...**.

When you are creating PL/SQL code, it is often recommended that you create chunks of code that you can call from another program unit. This introduces reusability and readability to your code. In particular, it is recommended that you keep the lines of code in your triggers to a minimum, calling procedures from the trigger, instead of writing the full text in the trigger itself. Often, at the time of writing, you don't see the need for this chunking, nor does it seem to be necessary. However, as the code grows and becomes possibly less manageable, it is advisable to return to the code and rework or refactor it.

Consider the trigger, which is part of the HR schema, as shown in the following code:

```
CREATE OR REPLACE TRIGGER SECURE_EMPLOYEES
   BEFORE INSERT OR UPDATE OR DELETE ON EMPLOYEES
BEGIN
```

```
IF TO_CHAR (SYSDATE,'HH24:MI') NOT BETWEEN '08:00' AND '18:00'

OR TO_CHAR (SYSDATE, 'DY') IN ('SAT', 'SUN') THEN

   RAISE_APPLICATION_ERROR (-20205, 'YOU MAY ONLY MAKE CHANGES DURING
NORMAL OFFICE HOURS');

   END IF;

END SECURE_EMPLOYEES;
```

This is not a large piece of code in the body of the trigger. We'll use it to illustrate the refactoring capabilities in SQL Developer. Select and highlight the code that can stand alone as a procedure, invoke the context menu, and navigate to **Refactoring | Extract Procedure…**:

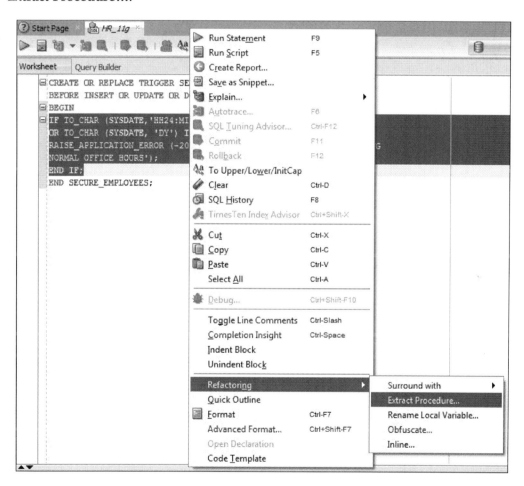

If you have selected an incomplete piece of code, an error message will display stating that you have not selected a complete set of PL/SQL statements. If the code is acceptable, you are shown a dialog where you can provide the name of your new procedure:

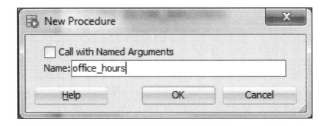

Once you have provided a name for the new procedure, a new editable screen is displayed (shown in the following screenshot), allowing you to modify the procedure before you accept the code. You can of course just accept the code straightaway and make any additional modifications in the code editor. However, the intermediate code window allows you to review the code before accepting the changes. This is particularly useful if you've selected too much or too little code to refactor. Until you have accepted the dialog, the underlying trigger or procedure is not affected.

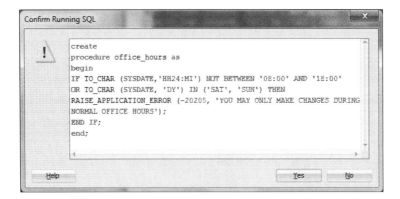

Once you have accepted the new procedure, the refactored trigger now includes the call to the new procedure, replacing the chunk of code, and the new procedure joins the others in the list of available procedures in the **Connections** navigator:

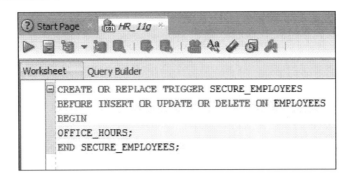

Searching for code

SQL Developer provides a number of utilities to search for strings of text. To search for strings within a piece of code, use the menu choice **Find** or **Replace**. There are also **Incremental Find Forward** and **Incremental Find Backward** to search for strings. Often, developers want to search for tables within a schema or across schemas or for PL/SQL declarations. The **Find DB Object** mechanism provides this facility.

Finding a DB Object

You can use the **Find DB Object** feature, on the **View** menu, to look for object types such as tables, views, and procedures in all databases supported by SQL Developer. The **Find DB Object** and **Extended Search** have been incorporated into a single search dialog. Therefore, you are able to search for objects and to drill down and search for variable declarations and references. To search for variable declarations, you need to be connected to Oracle Database 11g or above, as this search mechanism takes advantage of the PL/Scope facility that was introduced in Oracle Database 11g.

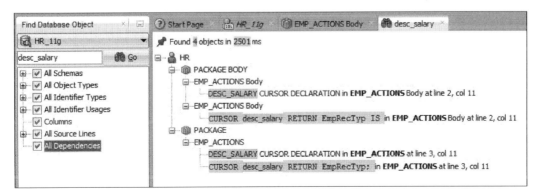

If you have access to Oracle Database 11g, then you can click on the **More...** button on the **Find Database Object** dialog (shown in the previous screenshot). This extends the dialog to include the **Type** and **Usage** options, which allow you to drill into the PL/SQL code units. Once you complete the search, select the required return links and the program unit is invoked in the **Code** editor in the background, with the cursor highlighting the point of reference.

Debugging PL/SQL code

Once your PL/SQL code has successfully compiled, it is important to review it to make sure it does what is required to do and that it performs well. You can consider a number of approaches when tuning and testing code. These approaches include:

- **Debugging**: Run the code and add break points to stop and inspect areas of concern.

- **SQL performance**: Use Explain Plan results to review the performance.

- **PL/SQL performance**: Use the PL/SQL Hierarchical Profiler to identify bottlenecks.

- **Unit testing**: Review edge cases and general function testing. Does the code do what you intended it to do?

In this section, we'll review the debugger. SQL and PL/SQL code may execute cleanly, and even produce an output. PL/SQL code may compile and produce results, but this is part of the task. Does it do what you are expecting it to do? Are the results accurate? Does it behave as expected for high and low values, odd dates, or names? Does it behave the same way when it's called from within a program as it does when tested in isolation? Does it perform as well for massive sets of data as it does for a small test case? All of these are aspects to consider when testing code, and many can been tracked by debugging the code.

Using the debugging mechanism in SQL Developer

Once again, you need a piece of compiled, working code. For this exercise, we will use the following piece of code:

```
CREATE OR REPLACE PROCEDURE EMP_DEPTS
   (P_MAXROWS VARCHAR2)
AS
CURSOR EMPDEPT_CURSOR IS
SELECT D.DEPARTMENT_NAME, E.LAST_NAME, J.JOB_TITLE
FROM DEPARTMENTS D, EMPLOYEES E, JOBS J
```

```
WHERE D.DEPARTMENT_ID = E.DEPARTMENT_ID
  AND E.JOB_ID = J.JOB_ID;
EMP_RECORD EMPDEPT_CURSOR % ROWTYPE;
TYPE EMP_TAB_TYPE IS TABLE OF EMPDEPT_CURSOR % ROWTYPE INDEX BY BINARY_
INTEGER;
EMP_TAB EMP_TAB_TYPE;
I NUMBER := 1;
BEGIN
  OPEN EMPDEPT_CURSOR;
  FETCH EMPDEPT_CURSOR
  INTO EMP_RECORD;
  EMP_TAB(I) := EMP_RECORD;
  WHILE((EMPDEPT_CURSOR % FOUND) AND(I <= P_MAXROWS))
   LOOP I := I + 1;
   FETCH EMPDEPT_CURSOR
    INTO EMP_RECORD;
    EMP_TAB(I) := EMP_RECORD;
   END LOOP;
 CLOSE EMPDEPT_CURSOR; FOR J IN REVERSE 1 .. I
   LOOP DBMS_OUTPUT.PUT_LINE('THE EMPLOYEE '|| EMP_TAB(J).LAST_NAME || '
WORKS IN DEPARTMENT '|| EMP_TAB(J).DEPARTMENT_NAME);
   END LOOP;
END;
```

Before you can debug code, you need to have the following privileges:

- EXECUTE and DEBUG: You need to be able to execute the required procedure
- DEBUG CONNECT SESSION: This is used in order to be able to debug procedures you execute in the session

Note, when granting the system privilege DEBUG ANY PROCEDURE, you are granting access to debug any procedure that you have execute privilege for and has been compiled for debug.

Using the Oracle debugging packages

Oracle provides two packages for debugging PL/SQL code. The first, DBMS_DEBUG, was introduced in Oracle 8i and is not used by newer IDEs. The second, DBMS_DEBUG_JWP, was introduced in Oracle 9i Release 2, and is used in SQL Developer when debugging subprograms.

Debugging

When preparing to debug any code, you need to set at least one breakpoint, and then you should select **Compile for Debug**. In the following screenshot, the breakpoint is set at the opening of the cursor, and the **Compile for Debug** option is shown in the drop-down list in the following screenshot:

 Instead of using the drop-down list to select the **Compile** or **Compile for Debug** options, just click on the **Compile** button. This compiles the PL/SQL code using the optimization level set in the **Preferences**. Navigate to **Database | PL/SQL Compiler**. By setting the **Optimization Level** preference to 0 or 1, the PL/SQL is compiled with debugging information.

Any PL/SQL code that has been compiled for debugging will show the little green bug overlaying the regular icon in the **Connections** navigator. The next screenshot shows that the **EMP_DEPTS** procedure and the **GET_SALARY** function have both been compiled for debug:

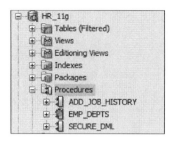

Compile for debug

Once you have completed a debugging session, be sure to compile again afterwards to remove any debug compiler directives. While negligible, omitting this step can have a performance impact on the PL/SQL program.

You are now ready to debug. To debug, click on the **Debug** button in the toolbar. SQL Developer then sets the sessions to a debug session and issues the command **DBMS_DEBUG_JDWP.CONNECT_TCP** (hostname, port), and sets up the debug windows, as shown in the following screenshot:

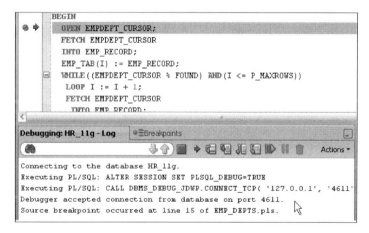

This connects you to a debugger session in the database. In some instances, the port selected is not open, due to firewall or other restrictions. In this case, you can have the SQL Developer prompt for the port. To set this option, open the **Preferences** dialog, and select the **Debugger** node. You can also specify the port range available for SQL Developer to use. These options mean that you can have more control over the ports used.

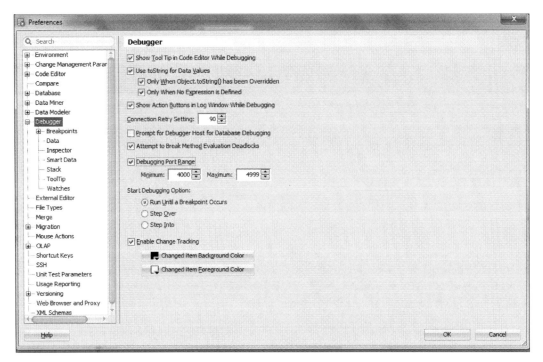

Working with Explain Plan

Oracle puts together a sequence of operations, called an execution plan, required to run SQL statements. Working specifically with DML statements SELECT, INSERT, UPDATE, and DELETE, the EXPLAIN PLAN statement displays the execution plans prepared by the optimizer and inserts rows into a global temporary table called the PLAN_TABLE. If you use SQL*Plus, you need to write queries to display the execution plans in the PLAN_TABLE . However, if you use SQL Developer, you need to only use the **Explain Plan** button to output the execution plan report below your query.

If you are new to these execution plans, then write a few basic queries and see the impact the query has on the output. In the first screenshot, we have used a simple SELECT statement, SELECT * FROM EMPLOYEES;. Click on the **Explain Plan** button, or press *F10*, to show the results. Notice that this is a full table scan, which makes sense as you have selected all columns and all rows from the table:

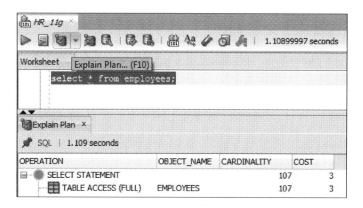

A full table scan has a high impact on resources, and is not advisable for large tables. More often than not, we want to look at a restricted set of records, and so we need to learn to write queries that restrict the records returned. A simple WHERE clause restricts records, but even that can be written more efficiently depending on the search conditions provided. If we restrict the query as shown in the next query, the **Explain Plan** output differs considerably:

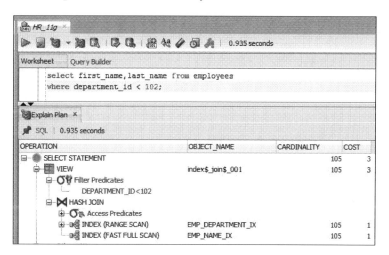

In this case, you see the indexes are now being used and that the index on the DEPARTMENT_ID column is used in a range scan.

Controlling the Explain Plan output

SQL Developer provides options for controlling what is displayed in the **Explain Plan** output. In the previous screenshot, the predicate detail is shown in its own column, but on switching the preference and selecting the **Predicates** option, the details are included in the tree as shown in the following screenshot:

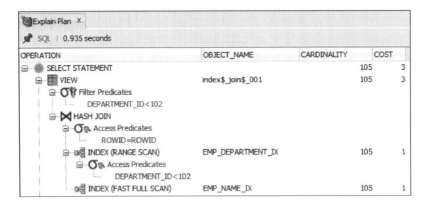

To control the detail in the **Explain Plan** report, use the **Tools | Preferences** menu to invoke the **Preferences** dialog, and then navigate to **Database | Autotrace/Explain Plan** and select or deselect the settings as required:

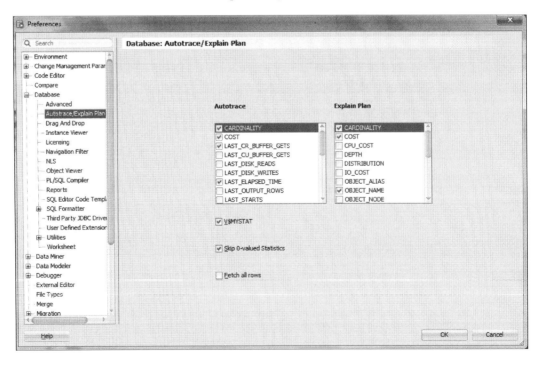

Execution plan details

Depending on which preferences you have selected, the **Explain Plan** report in SQL Developer displays the following details:

- **Operation**: This part of the execution plan tree is always displayed and lists the method of access being used. This includes table access, or sort operations, and includes the join methods if used in the statement.

- **Object Name**: This includes the tables referenced in the statement.

- **Options**: This is the access method used, whether it's a full or range scan, for example.

- **Cost**: This is used to optimize the query and is the relative cost of the operation based on a number of factors, such as initialization parameters, bind variable types if used, or statistics, if calculated for the tables.

- **Predicates**: This lists the predicates used in the query and by the statement.

Using SQL reports

In the previous section, we looked at SQL statements and at how using the **Explain Plan** output can assist you when you are learning to write queries that perform better. It is good to try to write sound queries from the outset, but more often than not, what happens is that users come back to the developers complaining about performance. In this case, there is no sense in starting to wade through all of the code in the application, instead you need to determine which queries have the greatest impact on the system, such as the top running SQL statements. Once you have determined where the offending code is, you can review the execution plans for each of these and then work at reducing the impact these have on the system by improving the statements.

SQL Developer provides a number of packaged reports that you can use when tuning your queries. You can start by navigating to **Data Dictionary Reports | Table | Statistics**. These are simple reports, which report when the table was last analyzed and at the number of rows per table.

In the following example, the new **CUSTOMERS_PART** table has been analyzed and the row count of each of the tables in the schema is displayed. Knowing which are the smaller tables in a system is useful when writing queries that join multiple tables.

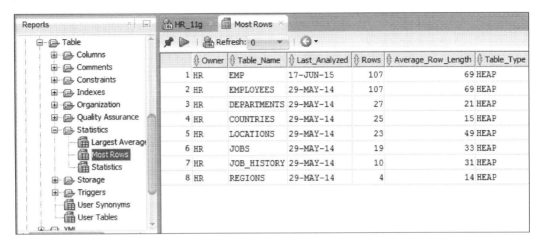

Running the Top SQL reports

In the packaged reports are six reports that look at the top SQL statements executed in the system. These include all of the SQL statements that are being executed and can be quite daunting when you first run the report. You can find these reports by navigating to **Data Dictionary Reports** | **Database Administration** | **Top SQL**.

If you select **Top SQL by CPU**, the output might look a little like the one we have illustrated in the following screenshot:

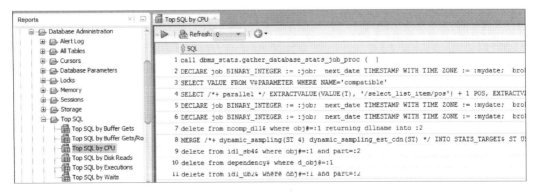

SQL Developer also provides a selection of **ASH** (Active Session History) and **AWR** (Automatic Workload Repository) reports. Statistical details useful for diagnosing performance issues are stored in the AWR and the **Automatic Database Diagnostic Monitor (ADDM)** analyzes this data. To review the SQL Developer reports, navigate to **Data Dictionary Reports | ASH and AWR**:

 ASH, AWR, and ADDM are part of the Oracle Diagnostic Pack, an Oracle Database 11g Cost Option, and as such are an additional cost.

Summary

SQL Developer supports creating, editing, and compiling PL/SQL code. The SQL and PL/SQL parsing capabilities provided by the tool mean that additional utilities, such as code insight and completion, can be an invaluable resource to developers working with many objects to hand. Utilities as simple as a small dialog, save time by providing frameworks of code, while code templates and code snippets mean that frequently used code is not far out of reach. Using the utilities provided, and adding your own code to them, can be an invaluable coding resource.

In the next chapter, we'll show you the different utilities that SQL Developer provides to help a DBA in his daily work and tune problem areas in the databases.

5
SQL Developer for DBAs

Initially, SQL Developer was considered to be a developer tool that can make the database client connections work with the privileged database objects. Over the years, the Oracle SQL developer tool has been continuously evolving and maturing as a full-fledged product that has largely changed the usage of SQL developer from a user perspective.

One of the major features is the SQL Developer's DBA panel that allows a database administrator to carry out DBA activities with much more ease and supports the 12c database with a multi-tenant architecture and its cloud features fully.

Database instance viewer

The database instance viewer window is a very useful feature for DBAs who can look at the target database with a 360 degree view. To open the instance viewer, we can use the navigation **View | DBA**.

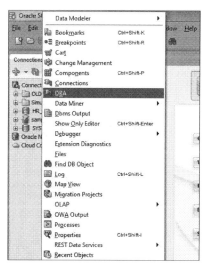

We should add the DBA connection (preferably the system connection that we have already defined in the connections navigation pane).

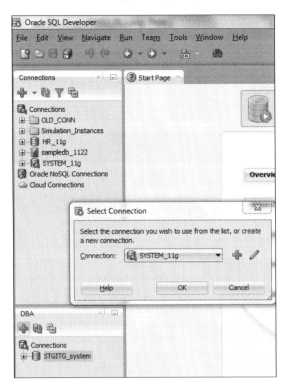

Once the DBA connection is made, open the database status node, click on the database status needed, as shown in the following screenshot:

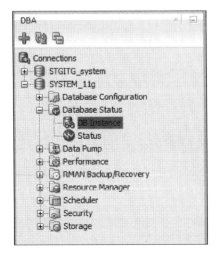

The information shown in the instance status window might take a while to come up, as shown in the below screenshot. This window is otherwise called as **Instance Viewer** and we have detailed information about all our database sessions, processes, wait events, CPU, memory, and storage details.

A double-click on each of these graphs will take us to more detailed information. For example, a double-click on the sessions graph will take us to more drill-down information on the database sessions.

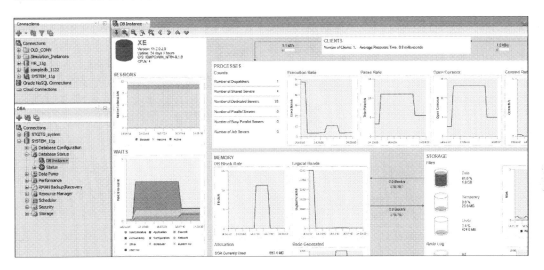

Instance viewer is helpful in quickly looking into the activities of a database instance in a 360 degree view.

Finding database objects

We can find all types of database objects (tables, columns, declarations within functions, or procedures) associated with an Oracle database connection; after finding these objects, we can edit them quickly with editing panes. To open the **Find Database Object** pane, right-click a connection name in the **Connections** navigator and select **Find DB Object**. You can also click on **VIEW** and then on **FIND DB Object**.

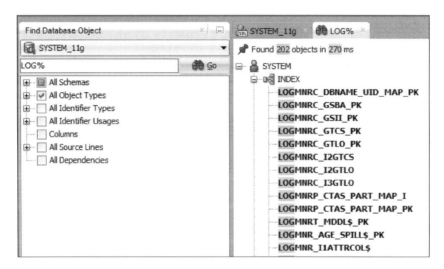

Database configuration – initialization parameters

Our database configuration depends on the parameters defined in this initi.ora file. To quickly see what the parameters are and to determine the values set for these parameters, we can click on the **Database Configuration** node and then on the **Initialization Parameters** option, which readily starts showing us all the defined parameters for our database, as shown in the following screenshot:

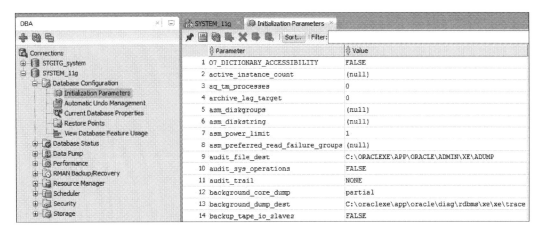

A right-click on the **Initialization Parameters** gives us three more options for editing our recoverability settings for Instance recovery (desired recovery time), Media recovery (log archive file format), and Flash recovery (flash recovery area, size, retention, and so on).

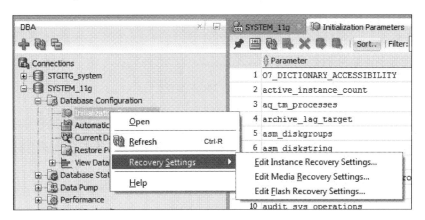

Automatic undo management

Oracle provides a fully automated automatic undo management for managing the undoing of information and space. With **Automatic Undo Management**, the database manages undo segments in an undo tablespace. In Release 11g and above, the **Automatic Undo Management** is the default mode.

Though the importance of UNDO data and undo tablespace is out of the scope of this chapter, the following screenshot shows the complete information of our UNDO settings for the database:

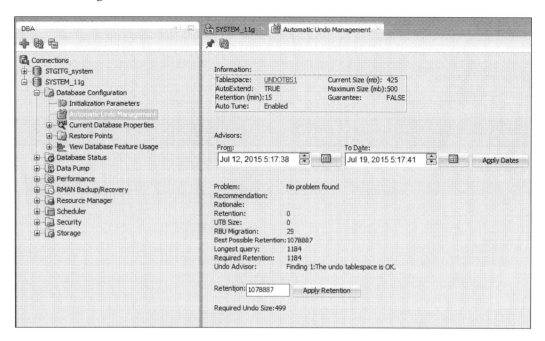

Current database properties

Database properties help us to view and control the behavior of databases, for example, NLS configuration. There are basically two types of database properties, namely monitorable (Read-Only) database properties and configurable database properties. Clicking on the **Current Database Properties** shows the complete list of database properties set for our target database, as shown in the following screenshot.

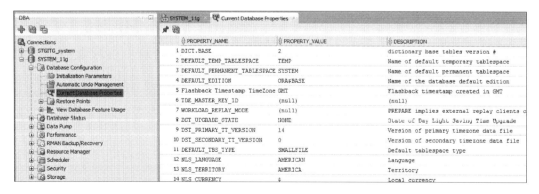

Restore points

Oracle Flashback database and restore points enable us to rewind the database back in time to correct any problems caused by logical data corruption or user errors, and it doesn't require any restoration of backup. There are two types of restoration points, which are as follows:

1. **Normal Restore Point:** Assigns a restore point name to an SCN or specific point in time. The control file stores the name of the restore point and the SCN.

2. **Guaranteed Restore Point**: Is a normal restore point, but additionally serves as an alias for an SCN in recovery operation. The only difference is that the guaranteed restore points never age out of the control file and must be explicitly dropped.

   To create a restore point or view existing restore points, click on **Restore Points**.

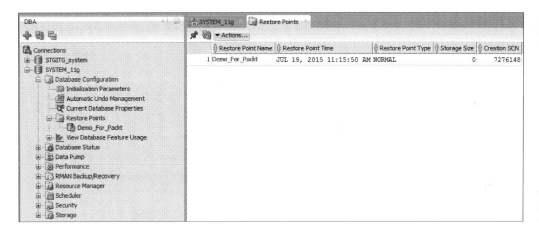

3. **View Database Feature Usage:** Selecting this option shows us the list of all available database features and the detected count of usages and versions of all those features.

Data Pump

Data Pump is an important logical backup and restore mechanism used by DBAs. The Data Pump feature helps us to export database, table spaces, schemas, and tables logically from one database and import it to another database. The DBA navigation pane gives us the export and import data pump wizards to carry out Data Pump jobs, as shown in the next screenshot.

Export Jobs

This option shows us all the Data Pump export jobs. Right-clicking and selecting **Data Pump Export Wizard** will help us creating an export job easily.

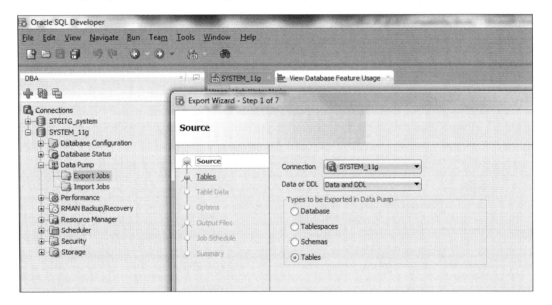

Import Jobs

Similar to Export Jobs, a right-click and a select on **Data Pump Import Wizard** helps us to create import jobs quickly and easily. This way, we can also monitor the ongoing import jobs (if any).

Performance

This section gives us the options to create objects and view reports related to the use of database statistics. **Automatic Workload Repository (AWR)** snapshots are created at regular intervals, which capture the statistics at all levels with delta cumulatively. These snapshots provide us with the historic data, which can help us identify and resolve performance issues.

Snapshots (filtered)

Snapshots are the historic data for the defined time period (the default is every hour and is retained for 8 days) that can be used by **Automatic Database Diagnostic Monitor (ADDM)** for comparison and helping us to identify the performance issues. ADDM does the comparison of these snapshots and also comes up with some advisories and the rationale behind those advisories.

For creating a snapshot, the database should be licensed with the **Diagnostic Pack** or the user will find the following warning while trying to create a manual snapshot:

```
Failed to process SQL command
ORA-13716: Diagnostic Package License is needed for using this feature.
```

Baselines

Baselines are a set of snapshots taken between specific intervals which will be used for comparison with any other snapshots when a performance issue occurs. For example, we can have a base line created for a period between 10 AM to 11 AM during business hours and keep it as a baseline for optimal performance. The baseline can be used to compare with another snapshot taken during the same interval but on a day when the performance is really bad. This could help us in quickly isolating the performance issues.

Baseline templates

Baseline templates help us in creating baselines for a contiguous time period in the future. Baseline templates are basically of two types, namely **Single** and **Repeating**.

Automatic Database Diagnostic Monitor (ADDM)

ADDM uses the AWR snapshots for the comparison of database statistics between two intervals and comes up with a detailed advisory. ADDM also helps us to find the root cause for the observed performance issues with the rationale behind the issue. It provides recommendations for correcting the problem areas and identifies the non-problem areas of the database system.

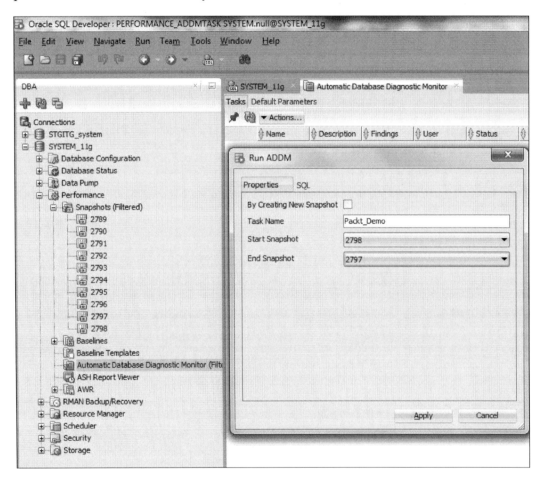

ASH Report Viewer

ASH report helps us to diagnose and perform detailed analysis on the sampled activity of database sessions. Every second, Active Session History polls the database to identify the active sessions and dumps relevant information about each of them.

Click on the **ASH Report Viewer**, and on the window, click on the **Generate Report** button to generate a new ASH report for a specified time interval.

The following screenshot shows how to generate the ASH report and view it:

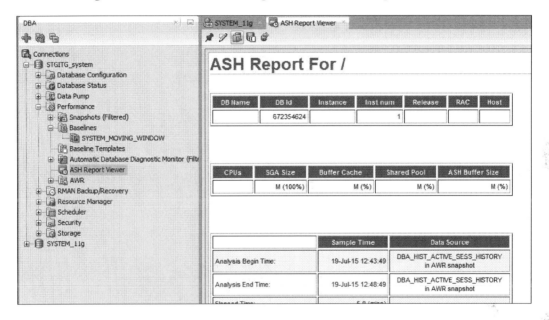

AWR

AWR reports are the first thing DBAs would generate when a performance issue is reported during an interval. An AWR report shows us the data captured between two snapshots. The AWR report has the workload profile of the database system. The AWR option in SQL Developer gives us three more options, which are as follows:

- **AWR Report Viewer**: AWR report can be generated between two snapshots or baselines

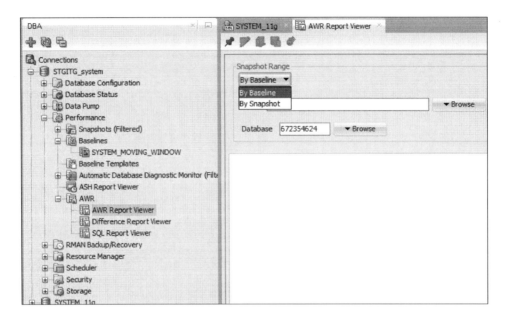

- **Difference Report Viewer**: AWR difference report can be generated between two snapshots or baseline periods.

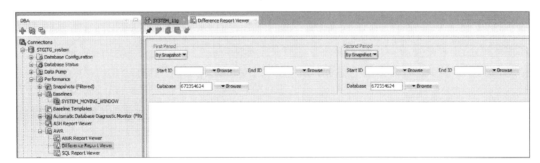

- **SQL Report Viewer**: Generates a Workload Repository SQL Report for a baseline or a snapshot range for a specific SQL statement

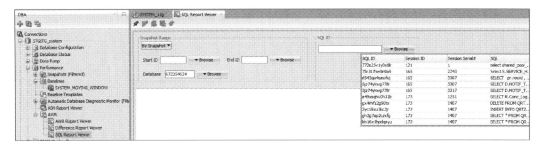

RMAN Backup/Recovery

Selecting this option configures database backup and recovery options. The **Oracle Database Recovery Manager (RMAN)** feature is used for these options; DBAs familiar with RMAN concepts and techniques can use these options with ease.

In any dialog box or wizard for RMAN operations, you can click the SQL or **Summary** tab to see the statements that will be used to implement the specified options.

Create Backup Wizard (in the context menu) displays a wizard where you specify **Backup Properties** (type of backup and whether to use RMAN encryption) and **Script Properties** (save to file and where to save the script file or **Run Scheduler Job** and specify a credential or create a new one).

For **Create New Credential**, specify the credential name, username, and user password on the server system.

Backup jobs

This displays the backup jobs that have been previously run and lets you create and run new backups. (Note that backup jobs are distinct from action jobs.)

Backup sets

This displays the backup sets that have been created by previous backup jobs and that can be used for recovery.

Image copies

This displays the image copies that have been created by previous backup jobs and that can be used for recovery.

RMAN settings

This displays settings for backup and recovery. (These settings are stored in the server and are used and managed by RMAN.)

Scheduled RMAN actions

For Oracle database 11.1 and later connections, this displays DBMS_SCHEDULER jobs that have been used to execute RMAN scripts and lets you view log files.

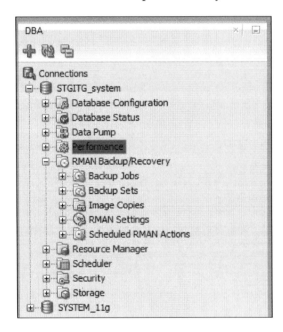

Resource manager

The Oracle database resource manager (the **Resource Manager**) enables us to optimize resource allocation among the many concurrent database sessions. When database resource allocation is done by the operating system, we may encounter the following problems with workload management:

- Excessive overhead results from the operating system context by switching between Oracle database server processes

- The operating system de-schedules database servers while they hold latches, which is inefficient

- The operating system distributes resources equally among all active processes and cannot prioritize one task over another

- Inability to manage database specific resources, such as parallel execution servers and active sessions

Consumer group mappings

A consumer group mapping defines the mapping rules for the **Resource Manager** to limit I/O and CPU resources automatically assigned to each session on start-up based upon session attributes. The **Consumer Group Mappings** option displays for each attribute its priority, value, and associated consumer group:

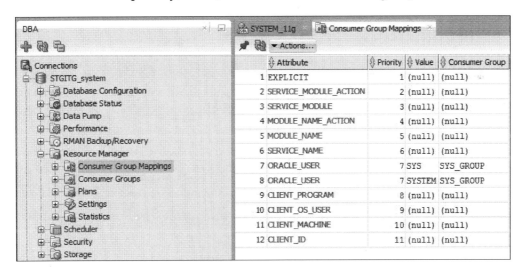

Consumer groups

A resource consumer group is a group of sessions that are grouped together based on resource requirements. The **Resource Manager** allocates resources to resource consumer groups, not to individual sessions. The **Consumer Groups** option displays for each consumer group its description and whether it is mandatory.

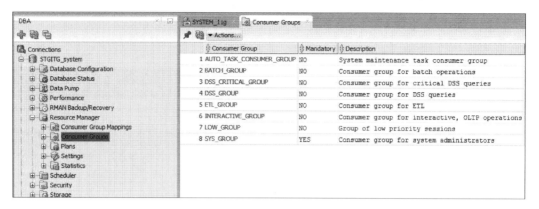

Plans

A resource plan has all the directives that specify how resources are allocated to CPU, IO, and MEM resource to consumer groups.

We can define how the database allocates resources by activating a specific resource plan. The **Plans** option displays for each plan its description and if its status is **Active**.

Settings

As shown in the following screenshot, there is only one active resource plan for my target database.

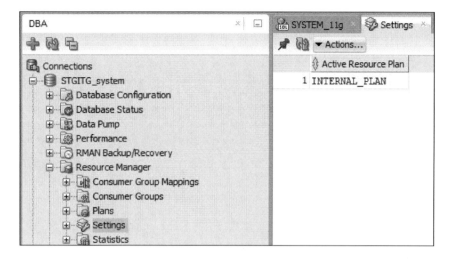

Statistics

This option lists all the resource related statistics as listed here:

- CPU Consumed
- I/O Requests Issued per Second
- Megabytes of I/O Issues Per Second
- Waits for CPU
- Queued Sessions
- Runaway Queries
- Idle

Scheduler

Scheduler gives you the option to schedule jobs using SQL developer. It's at the very end of a very long tree list. If you connect to your database and expand a **SCHEMA**, you'll see **SCHEDULER** at the very bottom.

There's a wizard interface that will walk you through the entire process of creating a new job, or you can use the traditional forms to create and alter existing jobs and schedules.

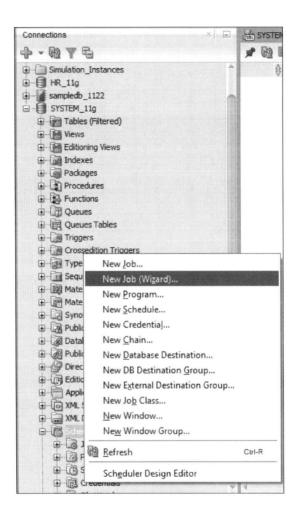

 All the objects under **Scheduler** in the DBA navigator are for objects that are owned by the SYS user and that can be created and modified only by users with DBA privileges. Other objects are listed under **Scheduler** for users in the **Connections** navigator.

Global Attributes

The **Global Attributes** display shows us all the attributes and enables us to edit the attributes such as the default time zone, the email sender and server, event expiry time, log history retention, and maximum job slave processes.

Job Classes

The **Job Classes** display helps us to view and edit information about job classes. The information for each job class includes the job class name, logging level, log history, resource consumer group, service, and comments.

External Destinations

The **External Destinations** display lets you view information about external destinations for jobs.

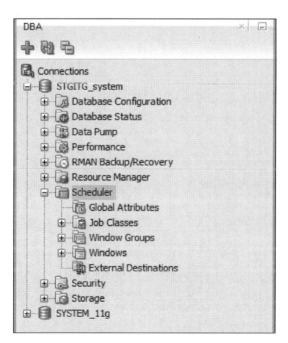

Security

The **Security** option in the **DBA** pane is related to database security management, for creating and managing profiles, roles, and users. Also, we can create new objects of any type, edit, and drop existing objects.

Audit Settings

The **Audit Settings** displays audit trail settings for our database, whether SYS or any other user operations are audited, and the location for the audit file. Failed logins, privileges trail, objects trail, audited privileges, audited objects, and audited statements are some of the information provided using this option.

Profiles

A profile is a set of limits on database resources. If you assign the profile to a user, then that user cannot exceed these limits. The **Profiles** option displays any limits on activities and the resource usage for each profile.

Roles

A role is a set of privileges that can be granted to users or to other roles; you can use roles to administer database privileges. The **Roles** option displays the roles and their authentication settings.

Users

A database user is an account through which you can connect to the database. The **Users** option displays status and usage information about each database use.

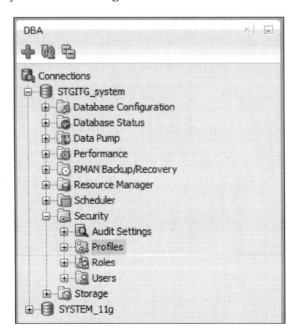

Storage

This option in **DBA** pane shows the complete database storage management details for the **Archive Logs**, **Control Files**, **Datafiles**, **Redo Log Groups**, **Rollback segments**, **Tablespaces & Temporary tablespace** groups. DBAs can quickly access these storage details with a single click and perform certain allowed actions on each of these components by clicking on the **Actions** button.

Archive Logs

This option, with a single click, shows all the archive logs generated for that database, its location, the `sequence#`, and the `thread#`. This option can be helpful for finding a particular archive file without even logging into the server and its details.

Control Files

This option shows up all the multiplexed control files used by the database and also the option to back up the control file to trace.

Datafiles

The data files can be located either in an operating system file system or Oracle ASM disk group. The **Datafiles** option displays for each data file its file name, tablespace, status, and other information. Additionally, a new datafile creation is also easy through the **Actions** button.

Redo Log Groups

A redo log group contains one or more members: each online redo log member belongs to a redo log group. The contents of all members of a redo log group are identical. The **Redo Log Groups** option displays for each redo log group its status, the number of members, and other information.

Rollback Segments

A rollback segment records the before-images of changes to the database. The **Rollback Segments** option displays for each rollback segment its name, status, tablespace, and other information.

Tablespaces

The database data files are stored in tablespaces. The **Tablespaces** option displays for each tablespace its name megabytes allocated, free, used, and other information.

Temporary Tablespace Groups

A temporary tablespace group is a tablespace group that is assigned as the default temporary tablespace for the database. The **Temporary Tablespace Groups** option displays for each tablespace group its name, the number of tablespaces in the group, the total size of the tablespaces, and whether the group is the default temporary tablespace.

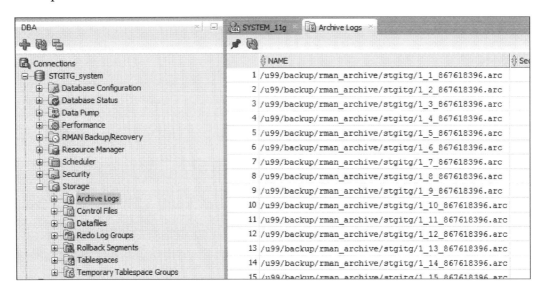

Summary

The **DBA** panel in SQL Developer was born since version 3.0, starting with the **Manage Database** (Context Menu) option in the **Connection** pane, then followed by the actual DBA pane in Version 3.1. Since then, this **DBA** panel has been continuously adding the features that has made this tool helpful for DBAs as well. The support for 12c features is, however, out of scope of this chapter, but definitely the support for Oracle 12c features like redaction, multi-tenant, cloning of pluggable databases, and so on, are great features for this tool and make it truly cloud ready. In the next chapter, we will be discussing more on the SQL developer accessibility information.

6

SQL Developer Accessibility

SQL Developer has a **Connections** node for establishing a database session with the target database. The connections may be either newly created or an imported and existing connection that we already had in the previous version of SQL Developer. To create a new database connection, right-click on the **Connections** node and select **New Database Connection.** You can also connect to schemas for MySQL, TimesTen, and Hive, as well as some select third-party (non-Oracle) databases, such as Microsoft SQL Server, Sybase Adaptive Server, and IBM DB2, to view metadata and data. However, providing details on such third-party database connections are out of scope of this book. The existing connections are always displayed in the connections pane automatically every time the SQL Developer is started. This list of existing connections is fetched from either `tnsnames.ora file` (if it exists); otherwise, the connections information is stored in a `connections.xml` file under `C:\Users\212391205\AppData\Roaming\SQLDeveloper\system4.1.0.19.07\o.jdeveloper.db.connection.12.2.1.0.42.150416.1320.`

Screen reader readability

Screen reader readability is based on the US Federal law of 1973, under which all electronic and information technology products and services meet the standards which can provide an extension, that can be used by people with disabilities.

The following of technologies provide the screen reader readability feature:

- Java J2SE 1.6.0_24 or higher, but one that comes before Java 7 Update 6 (you need to manually install Java Access Bridge 2.0.2 after you install the screen reader).

- Java Access Bridge for Windows version 2.0.2. This can be downloaded; the file you will download is `accessbridge-2_0_2-fcs-bin-b06.zip`. It is available at `http://www.oracle.com/technetwork/java/javase/tech/index-jsp-136191.html`.

- JAWS 12.0.522 (Job Access With Speech)

To set up a screen reader and Java Access Bridge, use the following procedure:

1. Install the screen reader. Oracle recommends JAWS, which can be downloaded from `http://www.freedomscientific.com/Products/Blindness/JAWS`.

2. Install SQL Developer 4.1; we already have one.

3. Download and Install Java Access Bridge version 2.0.1 for Windows' 32-or 64-bit version. It is available at `http://www.oracle.com/technetwork/java/javase/tech/index-jsp-136191.html`.

4. Confirm that the following files have been installed in the Windows `System32` directory or copy them from `C:\accessbridge_home\installerfiles` because they must be in the system path in order to work with SQL Developer:

   ○ `JavaAccessBridge.dll`

   ○ `JAWTAccessBridge.dll`

   ○ `WindowsAccessBridge.dll`

5. Confirm that the following files have been installed in the `C:\Program Files\Java\jdk1.8.0_45\jre\lib\ext` directory, or copy them from `C:\accessbridge_home\installerfiles`:

   ○ `access-bridge.jar`

   ○ `jaccess-1_4.jar`

6. Confirm that the `accessibility.properties` file has been installed in the `C:\Program Files\Java\jdk1.8.0_45\jre\lib` directory, or copy it from `C:\accessbridge_home\installerfiles`.

7. Start screen reader.

8. Start SQL Developer by running the `sqldeveloper.exe` file located in the `C:\sqldeveloper-4.1.0.19.07-no-jre\sqldeveloper` folder.

Keyboard access

Almost all the menus are accessible with appropriate keyboard shortcuts. Some of the key features of SQL Developer that can be accessed via keyboard are listed as follows:

- Users can navigate to and invoke all menu items:

- All toolbar functions are accessible through menu items:

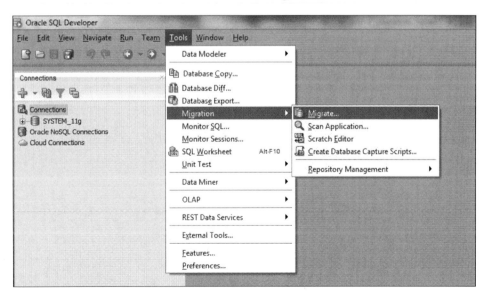

- All menus and menu items have unique and functioning mnemonic keys. All the yellow shaded keys in following screenshot give the examples of the existing mnemonic keys:

- All context menus within the navigators and source editor can be invoked:

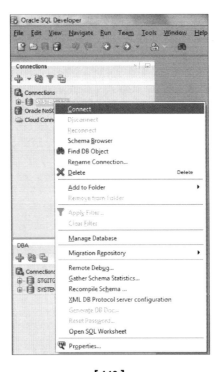

- Frequently used menu items have unique accelerator keys:

The following functionalities are available in SQL Developer windows. You can do the following:

- Navigate between all open windows, to all nodes within a window or pane, and between tabs in a window

- Set focus in a window or pane

- Invoke all controls within a window or pane, and perform basic operations

- Navigate and update properties in the Property Inspector

- Use Completion Insight and Code Templates in the source editor

- Invoke context-sensitive help topics, navigate to and open all help topics, and navigate between the navigation and viewer tabs

- Open, close, dock, undock, minimize, restore, and maximize the applicable SQL Developer window

Font and color choices

Visually impaired people using SQL Developer have the choice to select the font size and font type for a better viewing experience. The next screenshot shows the font and color features that are included.

Users can specify both the font and the size in which the font displays for code editors by navigating to **Tools** | **Preferences** | **Code Editor** | **Fonts**:

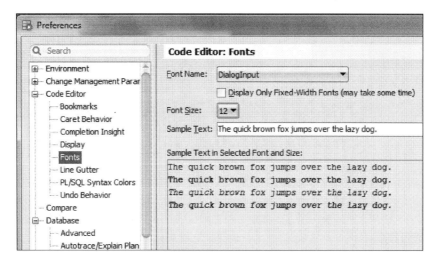

Black text on a white or gray background tone used in SQL Developer gives a good contrast and better viewing to the users.

No audio-only feedback

In case of an exceptional erroneous situation the in SQL Developer, users get audible feedback accompanied by a prompt on the screen. For example, a prompt accompanies the bell sound that occurs when an error or illegal action has taken place.

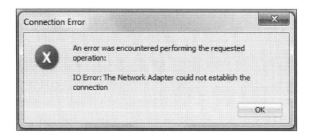

Screen magnifier usability

During some presentations, there may be a need to use screen magnifiers. These are used to magnify a section of the SQL Developer window pane and its contents to alleviate reading difficulties:

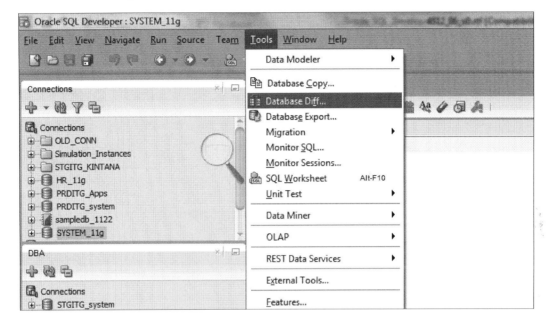

Change the editor or tabbed view of a file

By default, any database connection under **Connections Navigator** opens the default editor for that file. To toggle between different editors, such as Worksheet or Query Builder, you can make use of the *Alt + Page Up* and *Alt + Page Down* accelerators to invoke the **Navigate | Go to Window | Right Editor** and **Navigate | Go to Window | Left Editor** menu commands, respectively. This is shown in the following screenshot:

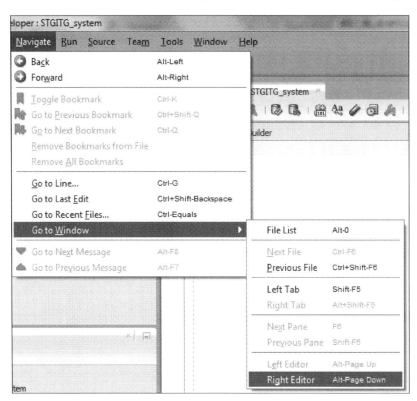

Read text in a multi-line edit field

To have the text in a multi-line edit field read by a screen reader, you can select the text by holding down the *Shift* key while moving the cursor either up or down with the arrow keys, depending on the initial cursor position.

Read the line number in the source editor

While using screen reader, it will read out the line number in the source editor when *Ctrl + G* is pressed. For visually impaired people, this feature helps them to know the line number of the code that they are editing.

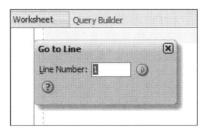

Customize the accelerators keys

The accelerator keys for Oracle SQL Developer can be edited by going to **Tools | Preferences | Shortcut Keys**. You can also load the preset keymaps that you are accustomed to using.

Also, you can pass a conflicting accelerator key to JAWS 12.0.522 (Job Access with Speech) by preceding the accelerator key combination with *Insert + F3*.

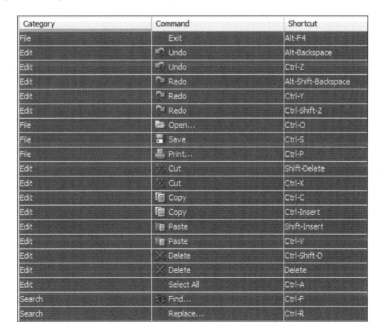

Category	Command	Shortcut
File	Exit	Alt-F4
Edit	Undo	Alt-Backspace
Edit	Undo	Ctrl-Z
Edit	Redo	Alt-Shift-Backspace
Edit	Redo	Ctrl-Y
Edit	Redo	Ctrl-Shift-Z
File	Open...	Ctrl-O
File	Save	Ctrl-S
File	Print...	Ctrl-P
Edit	Cut	Shift-Delete
Edit	Cut	Ctrl-X
Edit	Copy	Ctrl-C
Edit	Copy	Ctrl-Insert
Edit	Paste	Shift-Insert
Edit	Paste	Ctrl-V
Edit	Delete	Ctrl-Shift-D
Edit	Delete	Delete
Edit	Select All	Ctrl-A
Search	Find...	Ctrl-F
Search	Replace...	Ctrl-R

The look and feel of SQL Developer

The look and feel of the SQL developer is the visual characteristics of the tool, which again can be customized as per our needs. To do this, go to **Tools** | **Preferences** | **Environment**:

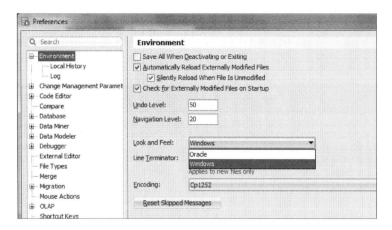

The preceding screenshot shows the **Environment** node under **Tools** | **Preferences** and the options that you can enable for external files and its dynamic actions on SQL Developer startup. Look and feel has Oracle and Windows options; any change made will prompt for a SQL Developer restart for the changes to reflect.

Once the SQL developer is restarted, the environment's look and feel completely changes like a windows screen, as shown in the following screenshot:

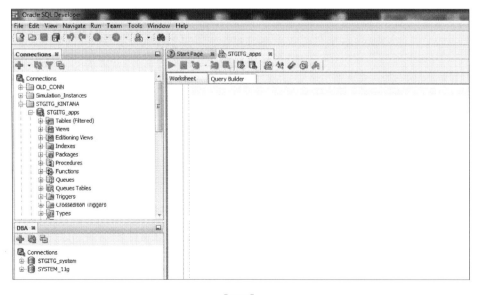

The **Environment** node also has two other options, **Local History** and **Log**.

Local History controls the number of days to keep the file history and number of revisions per file:

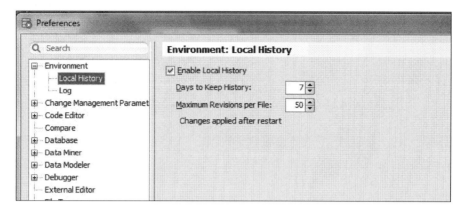

The **Log** option enables us to set the required colors for the logs such as hyperlink, program output, error, and input colors:

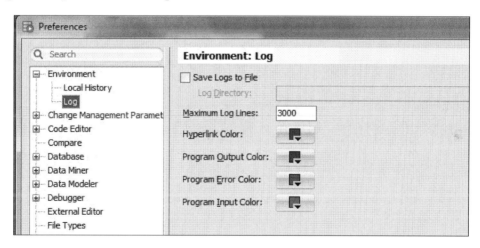

Customize syntax highlighting

Sometimes PL/SQL blocks run to 1,000 or more lines. In this case, it would be nice to have the keywords and syntax highlighted. To change or edit the font style and enable the syntax highlighting for the PL/SQL blocks within the source editor, go to **Tools | Preferences | Code Editor | PL/SQL Syntax Colors**. The following screenshot shows the window where such settings can be done:

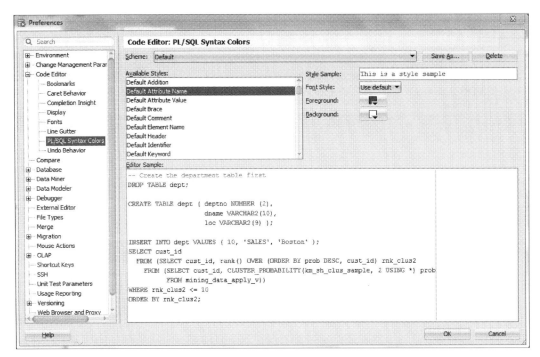

 Enabling the syntax highlighting is a good feature for PL/SQL developers who are required to edit or make changes to large PL/SQL blocks. Any syntax error or a bracket mismatch can be easily identified.

Display line numbers in Code Editor

The display of line numbers in the source code editors is another very useful feature for developers while working on large PL/SQL blocks. Debugging the code becomes easier as the errors on a particular line can be quickly addressed. To display or hide line numbers in the source editor, go to **Tools | Preferences | Code Editor | Line Gutter**:

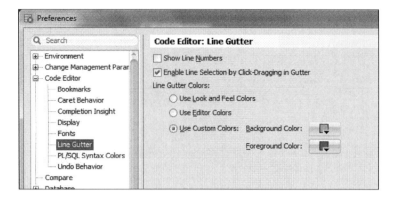

Timing for completion insight

Most of the time, it is very difficult to remember the PL/SQL syntax and object names during coding. SQL Developer provides developers with the great feature of providing completion insights as they progress with their coding.

The completion insights and their settings can be controlled by going to **Tools | Preferences | Code Editor | Completion Insight**, as shown in the following screenshot:

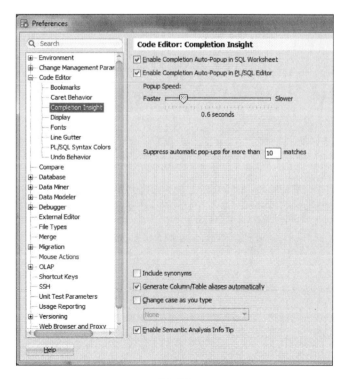

Specify the columns in the Debugger

You can choose the columns and types of information that display in the Debugger by navigating to **Tools | Preferences | Debugger**.

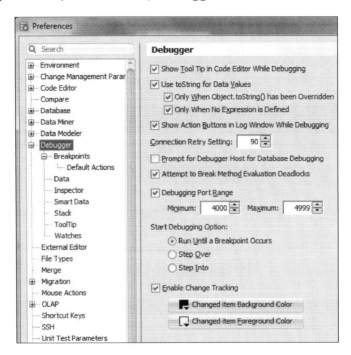

Summary

This chapter introduces information on the accessibility features of Oracle SQL Developer 4.1. It includes using a Screen Reader and Java Access Bridge with Oracle SQL Developer for visually impaired users, Oracle SQL Developer features that support accessibility, recommendations for customizing Oracle SQL Developer and the highly visual features of Oracle SQL Developer that make the tool very user-friendly. In the next chapter, we will be discussing *Importing, Exporting, and Working with Data*.

7
Importing, Exporting, and Working with Data

Working with one or more databases during development cycles will invariably mean that developers need to replicate schemas between different databases, such as test and production, or they need to test data based on a subset of instance data. To do this, developers need to produce easily replicable scripts that copy and move data from one database instance to another, or from one schema to another.

"Data" means many things to people. Here, data is both the instance data (rows in a table) and metadata (object definitions, such as tables, stored in the **Data Dictionary**). In this chapter we look at the variety of options offered in SQL Developer, specifically, exporting instance data and metadata, and importing instance data. You will see the different options available when copying instance and metadata from one schema to another and when comparing metadata between two schemas. We'll look at how to create and then use the scripts produced. The choices you make depend on the activity and the desired results.

Exporting data

In this section, we'll look at the various options and utilities provided by SQL Developer to export either instance data or metadata. The utilities range from copy and paste to wizard-driven export and import, and we'll progress from quick and easy towards more depth.

Exporting instance data

Throughout SQL Developer, data of different types is displayed in data grids, whether you are querying the definitions of a table by clicking on the table in the **Connections** navigator, running a report, running a query from the SQL Worksheet, or selecting the **Data** tab for a table. All of these data grids have a set of standard context menus, which include exporting the data in the grid to various file formats. In the following example, the **Export Data** context menu has been invoked for the **EMPLOYEES** table's **Columns** display editor:

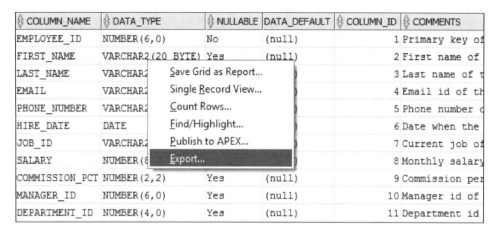

Another powerful method of exporting the data is to specify a query in the SQL Worksheet. Run the query using the **Run Statement** (*F9*) command. This returns the data in a grid and you'll have access to the same context menu as before.

The choice of file formats (wizard) for exporting the data is obtained by clicking on the **Export** context menu as shown in the preceding image. Here are some of the file formats mentioned:

- CSV—comma separated values
- Delimited
- excel 2003+ (xlsx)
- excel 95-2003 (xls)
- excel.xml
- fixed—space delimited file
- html—HTML tagged text
- insert—SQL DML commands
- JSON

- loader—SQL Loader file format
- pdf
- text—unstructured text
- ttbulkcp—TimesTen Bulk Copy
- xml—XML tagged text

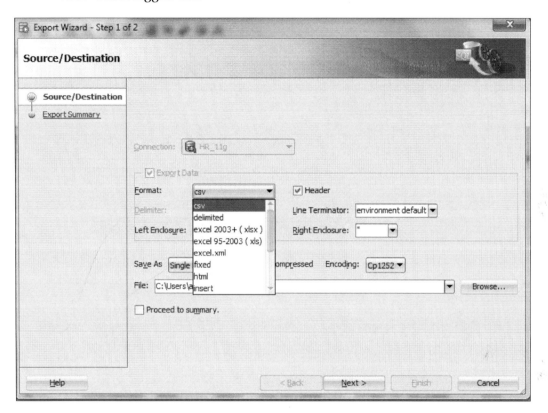

Exporting table data

To export the data for a specific table, select the table in the **Connections** navigator, and right-click to invoke the **Export Data** context menu. This displays the same **Export Data** menu shown on any data grid. The advantage of using the context menu in the navigator is that it pre-populates the **Table** name in the dialog.

For each of these output formats, as shown in the preceding screenshot, you can elect to write the text to a file, specifying the location or copy it to the clipboard and paste it to a location of your choice.

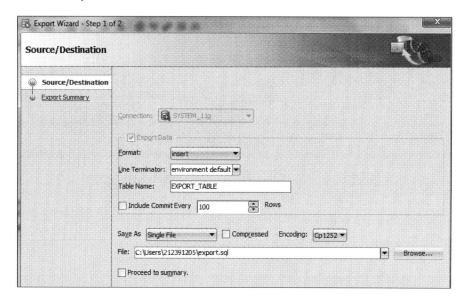

You can browse to find and set the file location, or you can set the default export location in the **Preferences** dialog. Select **Database** from the tree, and set the default location, as shown in the following screenshot:

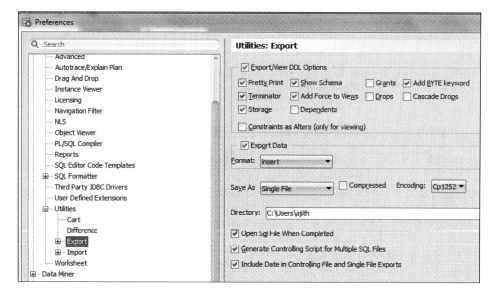

You can set a preference to handle file encoding on export. Go to **Tools | Preferences**, select the **Environment** node in the tree, and set **File Encoding**. The export output is given using the specified encoding. There is an additional **File Encoding** drop-down list on the **Export File Chooser** dialog. If selected, this overrides the preference set.

Setting up the export file

Whether you are invoking **Export Data** for a particular table in the **Connections** navigator or from the table's data grid, the default output includes all of the columns and data. This is also true if you have run one of the shipped SQL Developer reports. If you want to export any subset of data from any of these or the other data grids available, you can change the number of rows of data exported, or even the columns in the grid, using the **Export Data** dialog to restrict the export detail. The first choice is selecting the columns that you want to export:

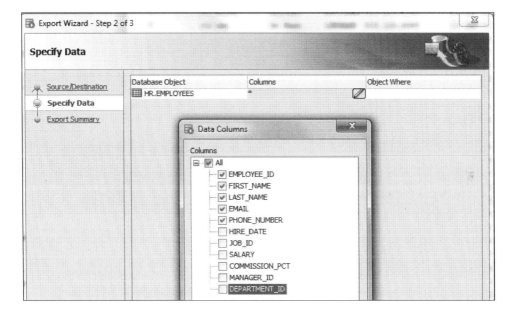

Once you have the columns selected, you can also restrict the data returned. Add the **WHERE CLAUSE** restriction criteria and click on **Go** to restrict the data returned.

 If you modify the number of rows returned by including the **WHERE CLAUSE**, the query is only re-run by clicking on **Go**, and not on **Apply**, which merely writes the data to the file.

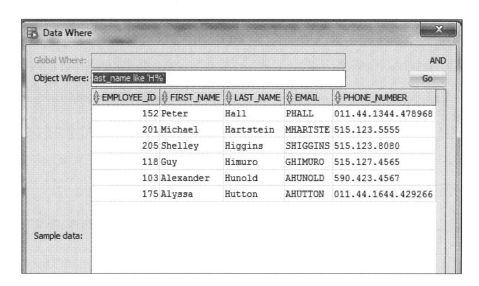

Instead of using the dialog, if you set up the query in the SQL Worksheet, you'll need to write the query to ensure it contains exactly the data that you want to export. Indeed, some file formats, such as XLS, have a maximum records file size. Therefore, you're advised to limit the data you want to export. Once the data is prepared and ready, you can simply invoke the context menu to export the data. Select the file format and location, and run the export.

 Preparing the contents of a data grid for export

You can sort, filter, and rearrange the column order on data grids. If you make any changes to the data grids before exporting the data, the updated detail is reflected in the exported file.

Exporting SQL DML

Creating an SQL script file of insert commands is very useful when creating sets of test data. You can then modify and update the data at will and then rerun the script to restore the data to the initial state. To create the SQL DML commands, go to **Export Data | Insert** from the context menu.

If you export this format to the clipboard, after that open an SQL Worksheet and paste (*Ctrl+V*); you are then in an ideal position to run the script. Ensure that you provided the correct table name in the **Export Data** dialog. If, for example, you write an SQL query and then invoke the **Export Data** dialog, the **Table** field is "table_ export", so you'd need to update that field as needed.

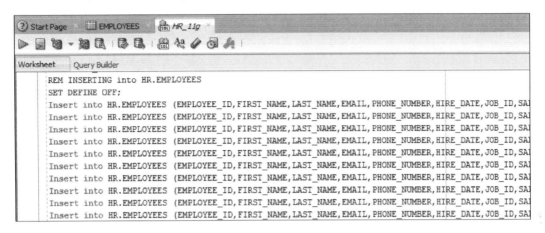

Exporting to HTML

You can export the data to the HTML format. To create the HTML, go to **Export Data | HTML** from the context menu. Once created, you can store the file on a central server and display it in a browser. This is very useful when you need to share data with other users, without providing any update permissions. The exported HTML file includes a basic search box, allowing users to further restrict the records displayed. In the following screenshot, the file shown is open in a browser:

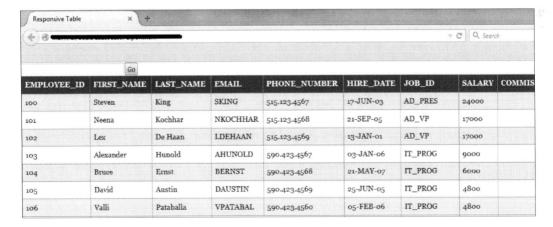

Supporting export for SQL*Loader

SQL Developer supports exporting data to an SQL*Loader file. Go to **Export Data | Loader** from the context menu to create the SQL*Loader file. Once created, you can use SQL*Loader to load the data into the Oracle database. The file format is set by SQL Developer, so you don't have the option to set parameters to control the Loader file format.

To create a working example, enter the following query into the SQL Worksheet and use the steps listed next:

```
select E.FIRST_NAME,
   E.EMAIL ,
   E.HIRE_DATE ,
   E.LAST_NAME,
   D.DEPARTMENT_NAME
from EMPLOYEES E,
   DEPARTMENTS D
where E.DEPARTMENT_ID = D.DEPARTMENT_ID;
```

1. Click on the **Run Statement** button (or press the *F9* key).
2. Right-click on the data grid and navigate to **Export Data | Loader** from the context menu.
3. Set the **Table** and **File** values as required.
4. Click on **Apply**.

The default control file created in SQL Developer, based on the example that we have just seen, is structured as follows:

```
LOAD DATA
INFILE *
TRUNCATE
INTO TABLE "EMPLOYEES"
FIELDS TERMINATED BY '|'
TRAILING NULLCOLS (
FIRST_NAME,
EMAIL,
HIRE_DATE timestamp "DD-MON-RR",
LAST_NAME,
DEPARTMENT_NAME)
begindata
Whalen|Jennifer|JWHALEN|17-SEP-87|Administration
Hartstein|Michael|MHARTSTE|17-FEB-96|Marketing
Fay|Pat|PFAY|17-AUG-97|Marketing
```

Exporting to Microsoft Excel

SQL Developer supports the export of data to the Microsoft Excel (XLS) format. This is one of the more popular export formats. The data, once in a Microsoft Excel spreadsheet, is easily used for graphs and statistical review. To create the Microsoft Excel file, go to **Export Data | xls** from the context menu. In this instance, the **Table** field in the **Export Data** dialog is not available. You only need to provide a filename and make the columns and **Where clause** choices. The new file, when opened in Microsoft Excel, also includes the column headings.

It's important to be aware of the fact that there are limitations when working with large sets of data. There is a 65,536 row limit in Microsoft Excel, so SQL Developer writes the records to new worksheets when 65,000 is reached. In addition, working with an XLS file, SQL Developer loads all of the records into memory before writing. If the XLS file is significantly large, you can run out of memory. If this is an issue, then edit the `sqldeveloper.conf` file in the `<YourDirectory>\sqldeveloper\sqldeveloper\bin` directory and increase the heap size by increasing the default value set to `AddVMOption -Xmx1024M`.

Exporting to XML

The SQL Developer **Data Export** also supports exporting to XML. To create an XML file, based on the data in the grid, go to **Export Data | xml** using the context menu. A single row of data (in this case from the **EMPLOYEES** table) exported to XML follows a structured format as follows:

```
<ROW>
  <COLUMN NAME="EMPLOYEE_ID"><![CDATA[100]]></COLUMN>
  <COLUMN NAME="FIRST_NAME"><![CDATA[Steven]]></COLUMN>
  <COLUMN NAME="LAST_NAME"><![CDATA[King]]></COLUMN>
  <COLUMN NAME="EMAIL"><![CDATA[SKING]]></COLUMN>
  <COLUMN NAME="PHONE_NUMBER"><![CDATA[515.123.4567]]></COLUMN>
  <COLUMN NAME="HIRE_DATE"><![CDATA[17-JUN-87]]></COLUMN>
  <COLUMN NAME="JOB_ID"><![CDATA[AD_PRES]]></COLUMN>
  <COLUMN NAME="SALARY"><![CDATA[24000]]></COLUMN>
  <COLUMN NAME="COMMISSION_PCT"><![CDATA[]]></COLUMN>
  <COLUMN NAME="MANAGER_ID"><![CDATA[]]></COLUMN>
  <COLUMN NAME="DEPARTMENT_ID"><![CDATA[90]]></COLUMN>
</ROW>
```

Exporting data to XML is very beneficial in broader application development, since the structure of the XML file enables you to use this data in other applications. It may be more common to export the metadata for reuse than the instance data in this case.

Exporting DDL (Metadata)

One of the most basic tasks you can perform with SQL Developer, once you have created a connection, is to select a table in the **Connections** navigator. In earlier chapters, we discussed the various display editors that are invoked by this action. At this point, we're only interested in the SQL display editor. The SQL display editor, for any object selected in the **Connections** navigator, displays the SQL code required to recreate the object in question, which is the **Data Definition Language** (**DDL**). The SQL is derived from executing procedure calls to the `DBMS_METADATA` package. Once opened, you can simply select, copy, and paste the SQL text into the SQL Worksheet to run it or save it to a file and run it later.

Exporting table DDL

If you're working with the default settings provided by SQL Developer, selecting the SQL display editor for a table reveals an involved `CREATE TABLE` statement, as shown in the following screenshot:

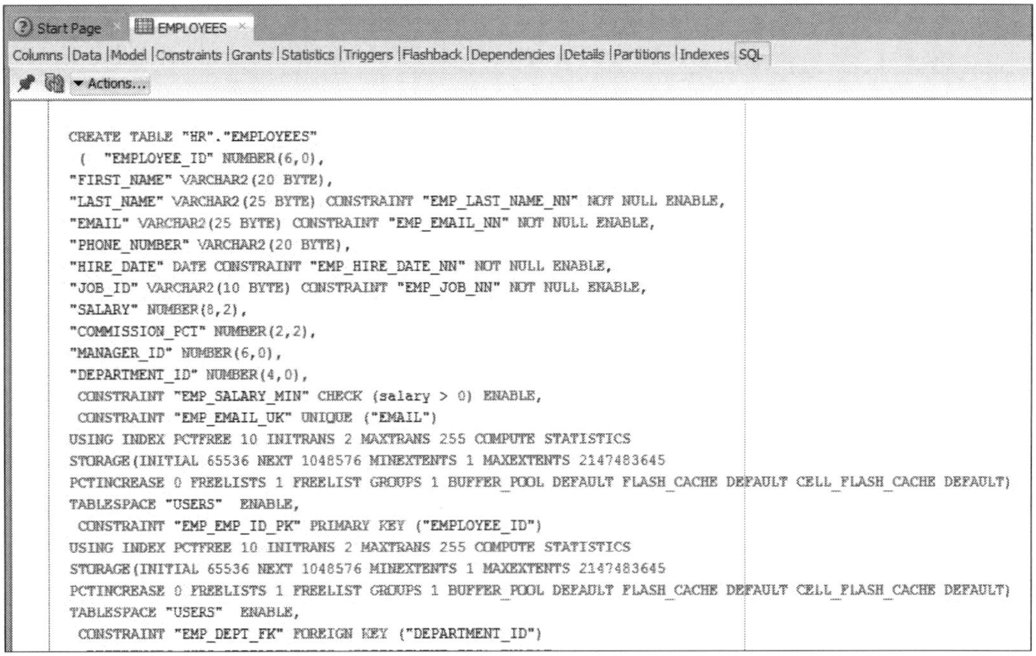
Start Page
EMPLOYEES
Columns | Data | Model | Constraints | Grants | Statistics | Triggers | Flashback | Dependencies | Details | Partitions | Indexes | SQL
Actions...
CREATE TABLE "HR"."EMPLOYEES"
("EMPLOYEE_ID" NUMBER(6,0),
"FIRST_NAME" VARCHAR2(20 BYTE),
"LAST_NAME" VARCHAR2(25 BYTE) CONSTRAINT "EMP_LAST_NAME_NN" NOT NULL ENABLE,
"EMAIL" VARCHAR2(25 BYTE) CONSTRAINT "EMP_EMAIL_NN" NOT NULL ENABLE,
"PHONE_NUMBER" VARCHAR2(20 BYTE),
"HIRE_DATE" DATE CONSTRAINT "EMP_HIRE_DATE_NN" NOT NULL ENABLE,
"JOB_ID" VARCHAR2(10 BYTE) CONSTRAINT "EMP_JOB_NN" NOT NULL ENABLE,
"SALARY" NUMBER(8,2),
"COMMISSION_PCT" NUMBER(2,2),
"MANAGER_ID" NUMBER(6,0),
"DEPARTMENT_ID" NUMBER(4,0),
CONSTRAINT "EMP_SALARY_MIN" CHECK (salary > 0) ENABLE,
CONSTRAINT "EMP_EMAIL_UK" UNIQUE ("EMAIL")
USING INDEX PCTFREE 10 INITRANS 2 MAXTRANS 255 COMPUTE STATISTICS
STORAGE(INITIAL 65536 NEXT 1048576 MINEXTENTS 1 MAXEXTENTS 2147483645
PCTINCREASE 0 FREELISTS 1 FREELIST GROUPS 1 BUFFER_POOL DEFAULT FLASH_CACHE DEFAULT CELL_FLASH_CACHE DEFAULT)
TABLESPACE "USERS" ENABLE,
CONSTRAINT "EMP_EMP_ID_PK" PRIMARY KEY ("EMPLOYEE_ID")
USING INDEX PCTFREE 10 INITRANS 2 MAXTRANS 255 COMPUTE STATISTICS
STORAGE(INITIAL 65536 NEXT 1048576 MINEXTENTS 1 MAXEXTENTS 2147483645
PCTINCREASE 0 FREELISTS 1 FREELIST GROUPS 1 BUFFER_POOL DEFAULT FLASH_CACHE DEFAULT CELL_FLASH_CACHE DEFAULT)
TABLESPACE "USERS" ENABLE,
CONSTRAINT "EMP_DEPT_FK" FOREIGN KEY ("DEPARTMENT_ID")

Selecting multiple tables for DDL export

Selecting the SQL display editor is an easy way to get the DDL for a single table. Selecting **Export DDL** from the context menu in the **Connections** navigator provides the additional capability of generating the DDL for one or more tables at a time. For the DDL export, select the table(s) and write the DDL to file, clipboard, or directly to the SQL Worksheet:

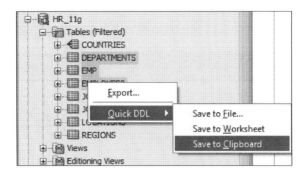

The structure of the DDL in the **Export DDL** menu is driven by the same preferences that shape the SQL in the SQL display editor: **Database | ObjectViewer**.

Using the Database Export wizard to export DDL and data

You can use the preceding utilities to set up and save the DDL or DML scripts. Generally, you'd use them for ad hoc statements to quickly create a table and populate it with data. There are occasions when you'll want a script that you can use repeatedly for many tables or objects. You can use the **Database Export** wizard to create a file that you might use to do the following:

- Run on a regular basis
- Share across teams
- Ship as an initial setup script

Starting the export wizard

The **Database Export** follows a series of steps and choices, allowing you to choose the object types, the specific objects, and to select or restrict the data exported. Go to **Tools | Database Export...** to invoke the wizard.

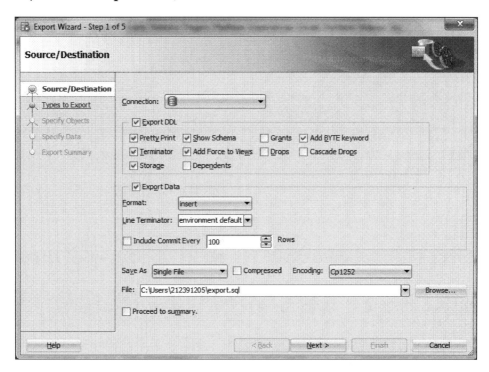

The outcome of the **Database Export** is a file containing DDL and possibly DML statements. The DDL statements are almost all CREATE object statements, although you can also include GRANT statements, and the DML comprises INSERT statements. You can control the structure of the statements in the first stage by setting different options. Set the file location and the schema driving the export on this first page.

> **Controlling the default export location**
>
> Set the default export location in the **Preferences** dialog. Select **Database** from the tree and then set the default location.

The DDL is again derived from executing procedure calls to the DBMS_METADATA package. Most of the options set on this first page are parameters sent to this package, except some, such as the **Include Drop Statement**. In the preceding screenshot, the lowest three statements are not set by default.

By selecting **Include Drop Statements**, you can create a script that is useful in a test environment. By including the DROP commands, you can rerun the script repeatedly, by first dropping the tables, then creating them, and then inserting the data. Oracle supplies many similar scripts. demobld.sql, which creates the EMP and DEPT tables, is one such example.

Although many of the scripts run are for a single schema, you can also create scripts for a number of schemas by including the **Include Grants** option. The wizard reads and replicates the current object privileges in the schemas. If you are selecting objects from multiple schemas, you need to include **Show Schema** to ensure the appropriate schema prefixes each object created.

Selecting objects for generation

Once you have set the options driving the DDL, you need to select the objects for generation. By default, all of the objects are selected, including **Data**. This means you can select **Proceed to Summary** and then **Finish**, and the DDL and DML for the full schema and data will be created. To restrict the choice of objects, deselect the **Toggle All** checkbox, which then gives you the option of selecting individual items by allowing you to just select only those object types you want to appear in the file. On the next page of the wizard, you select the specific, named items.

> **Including dependent objects**
>
> If you select **Automatically Include Dependent Objects** with the other DDL options, you only need to select tables on the **Object Types** page. The related constraints and triggers are then included. Left deselected indicates that you need to select named tables, constraints, and triggers.

Select **Data** to ensure that the DML for the selected tables is also created.

Specifying objects

The details in step 3 of the wizard are driven by the choices made on the previous pages. The schema selected controls the objects you have access to, both in the schema itself and across other schemas. You only need to select a starting schema, such as SCOTT, or another schema with very few privileges, to see how few tables are available.

The HR sample schema can query and therefore can produce the DDL for some of the HR tables. In the screenshot that follows, the four areas marked are as follows:

1. A drop-down list of all available schemas. For each schema selected, the associated objects are displayed.

2. A drop-down list that displays the object types selected on the previous page. This helps reduce the list of objects displayed in area #3.

3. Objects belonging to the schema selected and are driven by the object types in the object list #2.

4. Move any required objects here to reduce the list to just those selected. If none are selected, then by default, the DDL for all objects is created.

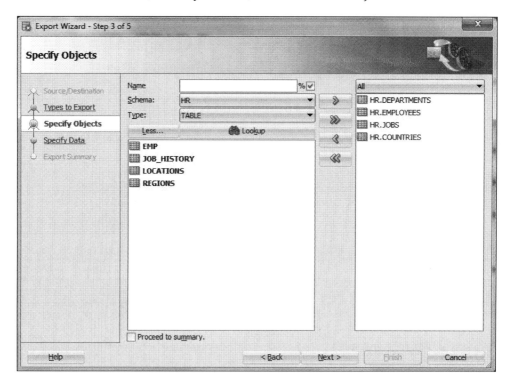

 All objects are selected by default. Select **Proceed to summary**, or click on **Next** to move on. Shuttling a few objects restricts this list to the objects selected.

Running the script

Taking the example we have been working on in the wizard, the output is sent to the SQL Worksheet as a single file that you can run. Notice that the start of the script includes a DROP statement for all objects to be created, in this case, tables and sequences. Once these have been dropped, the path is clear to create new objects, and then insert the data. The connections drop-down list on the right-hand side makes it easier to select an alternate schema to run the script against.

Export full schema

On the initial screen in the **Export** wizard, set the required DDL options and select **Proceed to Summary**. Click on **Next** and **Finish**. All of the objects and data in the schema are exported.

Importing data

Using SQL Developer, you can also import data into tables. The most common approach is running a well-formed (syntactically correct) script file of INSERT statements. The **Import Data** wizard is available from the context menu of existing tables and on the context menu of the **Tables** node, where you can import data and create the table in a one-step operation. The import wizard allows you to import data from a delimited format file or a Microsoft Excel XLS file. In this section, we'll look at three of the supported SQL Developer **Data Export** file formats.

Importing data from SQL script files

When importing data into tables from a file, the structure of the file, whether it is SQL or XLS, determines how the import works. For an SQL script file of insert statements, you only need to run the script from the SQL Worksheet, or open the file in the SQL Worksheet, and then run it against a particular schema to import the data.

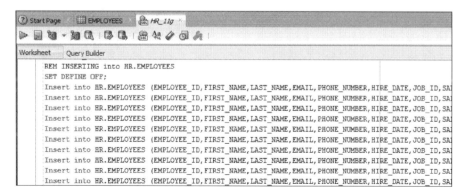

In the example in the preceding screenshot, the file is open in the worksheet. You can run this script against any schema with an EMPLOYEES table, assuming the columns match and any constraints are met. A typical use would be if you had run the DDL to create the table, and then run the DML to populate it.

Importing data from XLS and CSV files

SQL Developer provides you with the ability to import data from CSV and XLS files into a table. To import a spreadsheet of data into an existing table, select the table and select **Import Data** from the context menu, as shown in the following screenshot:

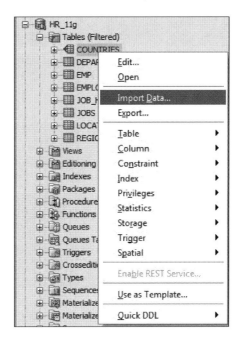

This invokes the **Import Data** wizard (shown in the next screenshot). If the **Import Data** wizard has recognized the file format, it will display the columns and data having opened the dialog. You can also review the SQL Query that produced the spreadsheet, if available.

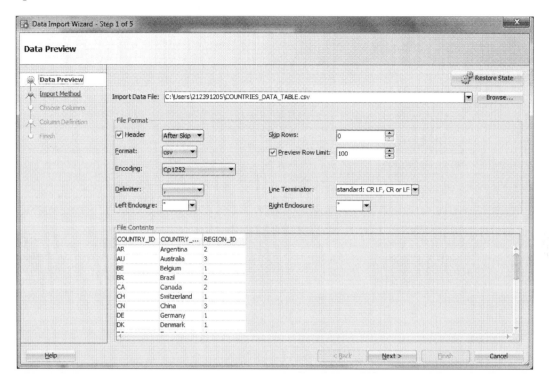

By stepping though the wizard, you can select the columns that you want to import and rearrange the order of those selected. The fourth page of the wizard is where you need to match the columns that you've selected from the file with the columns in the table that you have chosen to import into. The wizard tries to match the columns in the spreadsheet to those in the table, based on the column header. If this is not selected, or the column headers are not an exact match, then you need to select each column in turn, as shown in the following screenshot:

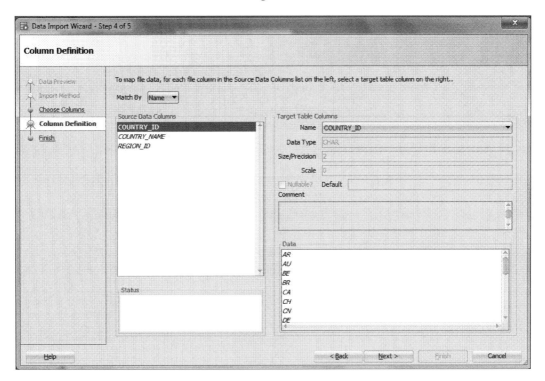

The last page of the wizard runs a verification test to ensure that the data in the spreadsheet or chosen file can be imported into the table of choice. At this stage of the import, only data mapping and matching is verified. If there are duplicate records in the table, or other data issues that cause constraints to fail or triggers to fire, this will only be encountered as you run the import.

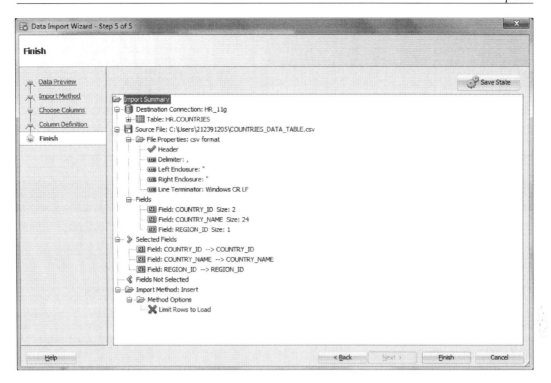

If you do not check this option, then the insert is handled by Java batch inserts. The preference **Database | Advanced | Sql Array Fetch Size** controls the size of the batch, with a bigger batch size providing faster performance. In this case, all of the rows in the batch may be rejected if there is an error. The bad file identifies the error and contains INSERT statements for the rows not inserted.

The **Import Data** wizard also supports the import of a CSV file. The only real difference here is that the first page does not provide you the choice of a Worksheet or SQL Query.

Creating a table on XLS import

If you have a structured Microsoft Excel file, you can use SQL Developer to create a new database table, based on the details in the file. To invoke the **Import Data** wizard for this activity, you need to select the context menu at the table level, as shown in the following screenshot:

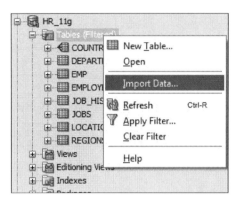

The **Import Data** wizard supports both XLS and CSV formats to create a table. The initial page in the wizard displays the structure of the file and the data. As you step through the wizard, you'll see the same options as you do when you are importing from a spreadsheet to an existing table.

Summary

SQL Developer provides a number of quick and easy-to-use utilities to work with data, whether it's instance data in your tables or metadata that defines your schema. You can create DDL and DML to save and run at a later stage by using a context menu option or by running going step-by-step. In the next chapter, we'll revisit the process of making database connections. Even though you have been using a connection throughout the book to this point, the options in the next chapter take connections a little further and discuss the alternatives and merits of the different connection types available.

8
Database Connections and JDBC Drivers

SQL Developer provides a variety of options when making database connections by supporting connections to both Oracle and non-Oracle databases. For all of these connections, you'll need the required JDBC drivers. Within the Oracle connections, there are a variety of connection types (such as TNS or LDAP connections) and authentication methods (such as OS or Kerberos authentication).

In this chapter, we'll review the basic connection type used in the examples earlier in the book. We'll see how to add these additional Oracle connection types and review the connections for the supported authentication methods. We'll also look at how to add the required drivers and set up the connections for non-Oracle databases.

Working with Oracle connections

We'll start by reviewing the various Oracle connection types available. We'll then look at the authentication methods supported by SQL Developer.

Using alternative Oracle connection types

SQL Developer focuses on ease of use right from the start. With a mantra of *Download, unzip to install and you're ready to start*, this intended ease of use means that you do not need any additional Oracle clients on your machine to connect to an Oracle database. However, in many Oracle environments, having an **Oracle Home** is standard. Therefore, you can access the alias in a `tsnames.ora` file.

To create a new connection, navigate to **File | New... | Database Connection** or right-click on the **Connections** node and select **New Connection**. By now, you should be familiar with the default settings in the **Connections** dialog, as shown in the following screenshot:

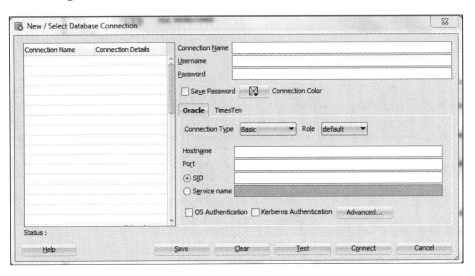

The databases listed in the default **Database Connection** dialog are Oracle and Microsoft Access. Access, which is displayed only for SQL Developer on Microsoft Windows, is available by default as it uses the JDBC-ODBC bridge and requires no additional drivers. For all other database support, you'll need to add the required drivers, which will be discussed later in the chapter.

For the Oracle connections, the different options are in the **Connection Type** drop-down list. As you make each selection, the dialog and required input values change, as shown in the following screenshot:

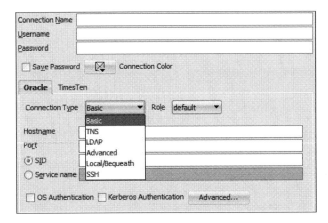

Reviewing the Basic connection

The default connection is the **Basic** connection. It uses a thin JDBC driver that's shipped with SQL Developer and which allows you to connect to the Oracle database without other Oracle clients on your machine. The default **SID** is set for XE, which is the default SID for Oracle Express Edition, the free Oracle 11g database. When using the **Basic** connection type, all that you need to know is the location of your database, the port, and the **SID** or the **Service name**.

When creating an Oracle Agent, there are two types of connection. The differences between these two connections are explained as follows:

- SID: This is the unique name of your database
- SERVICE_NAME: This is the alias used when connecting

> Selecting the **Save Password** checkbox saves the password to an encrypted file. This makes it secure. However, a better level of security is to not save the password at all. That way, there is no file that can be compromised. Disable the **Save Password** option.
>
> To disable the checkbox to save the password, add the following entry to the sqldeveloper.conf file:
>
> ```
> AddVMOption -Dsqldev.savepasswd=false
> ```

Accessing the tnsnames.ora file

The **New Connection** dialog provides two options when you switch to the **TNS** connection type. These are the **Network Alias** drop-down list, which is read from the tnsnames.ora file, or the **Connect Identifier**.

By default, the tnsnames.ora file is defined in the $ORACLE_HOME/network/admin directory. However, you can set the TNS_ADMIN environment variable to specify an alternate location.

The following code is an example of what an entry in the tnsnames.ora file looks like:

```
ajith11grac=
(DESCRIPTION=
(ADDRESS= (PROTOCOL=TCP) (HOST=localhost) (PORT=1521)
 )
(CONNECT_DATA= (SERVER=dedicated)
(SERVICE_NAME=ajith1)
 )
 )
```

In this example, `ajith11grac` can be used as the network alias and the remaining lines can be used as the connect identifier to make the connection.

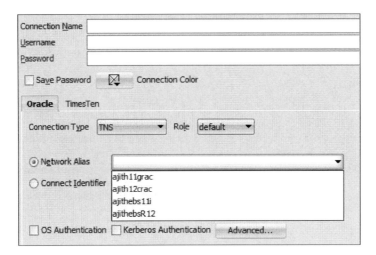

By default, the `tnsnames.ora` file is defined in the `$ORACLE_HOME/network/admin` directory. However, you can set the `TNS_ADMIN` environment variable to specify an alternate location.

You may have multiple `tnsnames.ora` files set up on your machine. SQL Developer only reads one of these, searching for the file in the following order of priority:

1. `$HOME/.tnsnames.ora`
2. `$TNS_ADMIN/tnsnames.ora`
3. `/etc/tnsnames.ora` (for non-Microsoft Windows environments)
4. `$ORACLE_HOME/network/admin/tnsnames.ora`
5. **Registry Key** accessing the correct **TNS Names** file

If SQL Developer does not locate the required `tnsnames.ora` file, you can set the directory location using the **TNS_ADMIN** system environment variable.

In Microsoft Windows, you can create the **TNS_ADMIN** environment variable using the **Control Panel**. Navigate to **System | Advanced | Environment Variables** and add or update the value for the **TNS_ADMIN** variable.

Although not a recommended approach, you can also directly set the registry variable. To set the **Registry Key**, open the registry editor and find the **HKEY_LOCAL_MACHINE\SOFTWARE\ORACLE** entry. Locate or create the **TNS_ADMIN** entry and set it to the required path.

SQL Developer gives a preference to specify the directory location of the `tnsnames.ora` file. This setting overrides all the aforementioned settings. The preference is the **Tnsnames Directory** setting in the **Database** | **Advanced** section of the **Tools** | **Preferences** dialog.

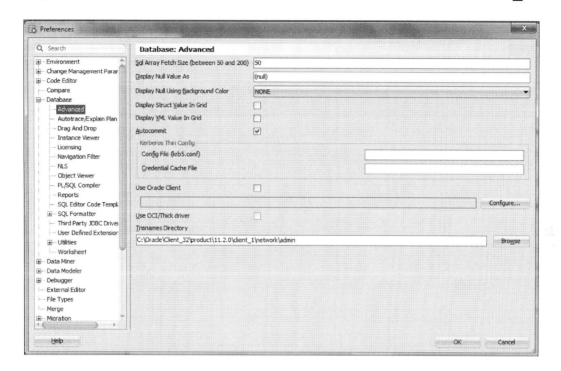

Accessing LDAP server details

SQL Developer provides LDAP authentication to access database service names in the **Oracle Internet Directory (OID)**. **Lightweight Directory Access Protocol (LDAP)** is an application protocol that's used to query and modify directory services. The OID is a directory service that stores and manages net service names in a central location. In order to use or access an LDAP server, you need to have the LDAP parameter set in the `sqlnet.ora` file, as follows:

```
NAMES.DIRECTORY_PATH=(LDAP)
```

The `ldap.ora` file should have an entry that's similar to the one shown in the following sample:

```
DIRECTORY_SERVERS= (localhost:389:636)
DEFAULT_ADMIN_CONTEXT = ""
DIRECTORY_SERVER_TYPE = OID
```

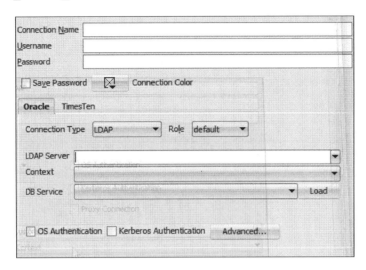

SQL Developer reads the `ldap.ora` file in the same way that it reads the `tnsnames.ora` file and populates the **LDAP Server** drop-down list. Alternatively, you can type in the details for the LDAP server, as shown in the previous screenshot. Once you have entered the LDAP server details, click on the **Load** button to populate the **Context** and **DB Service**.

Creating advanced connections with JDBC URLs

Instead of using the preconfigured connection types that provide the appropriate drop-down lists based on the information that's given, you can use the **Advanced** connection type, which connects directly to the database using Java. Selecting this provides an empty field where you can enter the full **connection** string and specify the driver type in the URL. For example, the **connection** string can be `jdbc:oracle:thin:@localhost:1521:orcl`. In the following example, there is no **Username** and **Password** provided. Therefore, we can't use **Test** or **Connect** in the dialog (you can of course include these in the URL and then test the connection). If you save and close the dialog, when you try to connect, you are prompted for the connection username and password, as shown in the following screenshot, and can then connect:

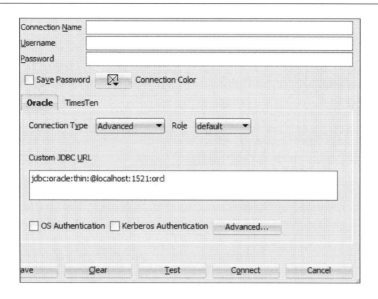

Connecting to Oracle TimesTen

You can connect to an Oracle TimesTen In-Memory Database using SQL Developer. The connection details are available through a separate tab, which only appears alongside the Oracle connections tab if you have TimesTen set up in your environment. The ability to work with the TimesTen In-Memory database is integrated into SQL Developer 1.5 and above. For more details on setting up Oracle TimesTen, refer to the documentation on the Oracle Technology Network, which is available at `http://www.oracle.com/technology/products/timesten/`.

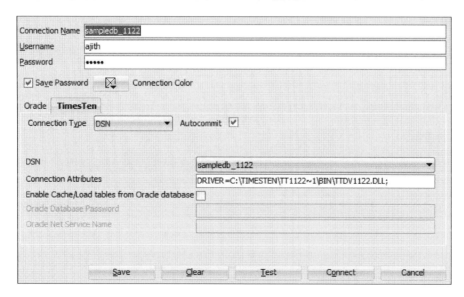

Once you have created a connection, you can connect to and work with the objects as you do for other database connections:

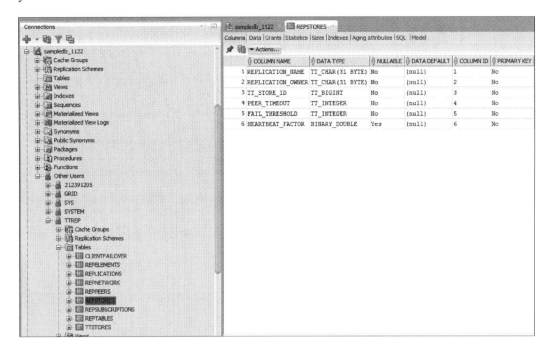

Reviewing JDBC drivers

We have now reviewed connections that seamlessly use either the thin or thick JDBC drivers. Before we look at further connections that use these or when you should force the use of the thick driver, we'll provide a brief explanation of the two driver types and when you need additional client software. We'll also highlight a few points that you need to watch out for.

Oracle JDBC thin driver (Type IV driver)

The JDBC thin driver, also referred to as the **Type IV driver**, is platform independent and as such does not need an Oracle client, **Oracle Call Interface** (OCI), or SQL*Net on the machine. This is the driver that SQL Developer uses by default and which you access when using the **Basic** connection type.

Oracle JDBC thick driver (Type II driver)

Installing Oracle Database or any other Oracle tools sets up an Oracle Home. In examples like this, you are likely to have a `tnsnames.ora` file in your environment, which can be used when connecting to the database using SQL Developer. In this case, you can generally use the "thick" JDBC OCI (Type II) driver. If you do not have an Oracle Home and need to use the Type II driver, you'll need to install the Oracle Instant Client.

SQL Developer's shipped drivers

SQL Developer 4.1 ships with the Oracle Database 11g JDBC driver, `ojdbc6.jar`.

The Oracle JDBC drivers are certified for the respective currently supported databases. For example, the JDBC drivers shipped with Oracle Database 12c Release 1 are certified for Oracle Database 12c Release 1, Oracle Databases 11.1.x, 11.2.x, 10.2.x, 10.1.x, 9.2.x, and 9.0.1. As SQL Developer is certified for Oracle Databases 9.2.0.1 and above, this driver is compatible with all the current SQL Developer releases. These drivers are not certified for older, unsupported databases such as 8.0.x and 7.x.

Fixing connection errors

When installing Oracle JDBC drivers, the installer installs the JDBC drivers in the `$ORACLE_HOME/jdbc` directory. If you have an issue with the drivers, verify that you have the correct path in the `CLASSPATH`.

It is also important to ensure that your connections are compatible with the client. If they are not, you need to update your client installation. Updating your client is not related to and does not affect your database or other Oracle software installations.

Using different authentication methods

In addition to providing a choice of connection types, you also have a choice of authentication methods. As a rule, users use the standard database authentication, which is enforced with a username, a password, roles, and privileges. With security being of such importance in almost all systems today, stronger authentication methods are necessary. In many applications that work across multiple tiers, each tier is also required to provide authentication. If these authentication methods exist, SQL Developer allows users to use them as a part of the connection settings. It is not in the scope of this book to define or describe each of the authentication approaches in detail, but where possible, we will provide some background.

OS Authentication

Used more often in the past, operating system (OS) Authentication is employed to avoid logging in to both the operating system and then the database. For example, when this was first introduced, users had a secure profile to connect to Unix and then immediately connect to the database using SQL*Plus. Using OS Authentication means that a user is not required to provide the additional authentication. The database is aware of the OS connection but does not need to manage the user passwords. The action is that you'll connect to the OS and then connect to the database in SQL*Plus using **connect** / or even `sqlplus` / in the command prompt.

Security risks

If you use OS Authentication in a system, once you have logged on to your system, anyone can access your database without further authorization. Therefore, this is a potential security risk and should be used cautiously.

To set up this environment in the database, you need to create a database user using the same details as that of the operating system's user. First, you should find the OS username and then, you need to create a user in the database. If you don't know the username, then enter the following code in the SQL Worksheet:

```
SELECT UPPER(SYS_CONTEXT('USERENV','OS_USER'))
FROM DUAL;
```

You can use the **Create User...** dialog on the **Other Users** node for your **SYSTEM** connection, but it's easy to enter the syntax in the SQL Worksheet:

```
CREATE USER "OPS$AJNARAYA-LAP\AJNARAYA" IDENTIFIED EXTERNALLY;
GRANT CREATE SESSION TO "OPS$AJNARAYA-LAP\AJNARAYA";
```

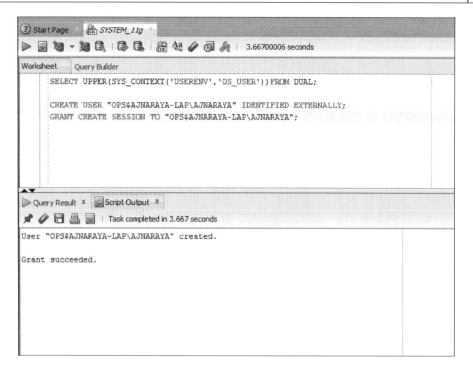

Setting the database environment variables

Note the use of the OPS$ variable in front of the username. The OPS$ value is historical and can be changed or omitted by setting the OS_AUTHENT_PREFIX database initialization parameter that controls this value. In Microsoft Windows, the username also includes the machine name.

You can use OS Authentication when you connect to a database that is local to your machine. Therefore, you're connecting and authenticated on your machine and then connecting to your local database. You can use OS Authentication to connect to a remote database. To do this, you also need to set the REMOTE_OS_AUTHENT = TRUE.

Finally, in SQL Developer, OS authentication needs to use the thick OCI driver. So, if you use OS Authentication with the **Basic** connection type, you must ensure that the thick OCI driver is used. To force the use of this driver, set the preference to **Use OCI/Thick driver**, which can be found by navigating to **Database | Advanced Parameters**.

Creating a connection using OS Authentication

Once you have created a user in the database and set the required database initialization parameters and the OCI driver preference, you can create a new connection, shown in the following screenshot:

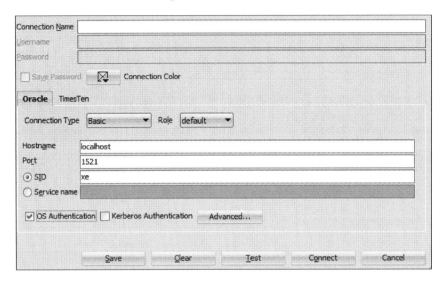

Without **OS Authentication** selected, you are required to provide the **Username** and **Password**. Once it's selected, you no longer require these values. Therefore, the fields are unavailable.

Using proxy authentication

Typically used in a three-tier environment, proxy authentication allows one connection to act as a proxy for the next connection. This can eliminate the overhead of additional authentication between clients.

To illustrate this, we need to have two users: one of them will be the actual or destination database user and the other one will be the proxy user. If we assume that HR is the actual user in this example, we need to create an additional proxy for HR. We'll allow the new HR proxy to connect to the HR schema and details without needing to know the HR schema password. To start, you need to create the new proxy user and grant the correct proxy authentication, as follows:

```
GRANT CONNECT, RESOURCE TO HR_PROXY IDENTIFIED BY ORACLE;
ALTER USER HR GRANT CONNECT THROUGH HR_PROXY;
```

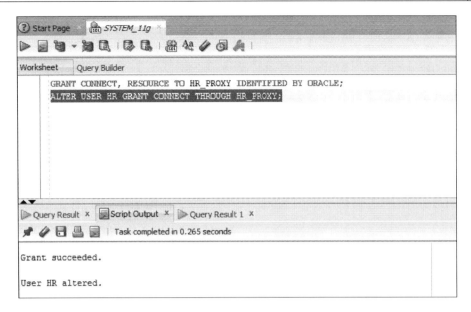

SQL Developer supports the ability to use:

- A single session with the connection
- Two sessions with the connection

In the first instance, we can use the proxy connection syntax. This is also available in a command line such as SQL*Plus in the **Connections** dialog. This syntax is `proxy_user_name[user_name]/proxy_user_password`, and this is illustrated in the following screenshot:

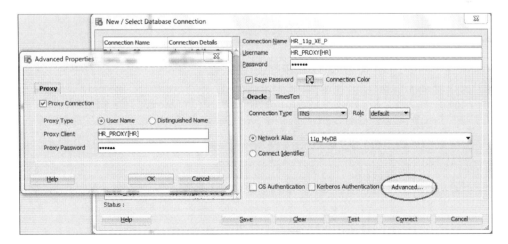

When creating this single-session connection, select the proxy **Username** and **Password** with the destination user, **HR**.

You can also use two sessions with the connection. In this case, provide the proxy user and password in the **Connections** dialog and then click on the **Advanced** option checkbox. This action invokes a new dialog for the destination user, as shown in preceding screenshot.

The preceding screenshot shows both the **Connections** dialogs, with the **Proxy Connection** checkbox selected, and the **Oracle Proxy Connection** dialog. Here, you need to only supply the **Username**; the **Password** is optional. The optional password is driven by the way you create the proxy user, as illustrated in the following two statements:

```
ALTER USER HR GRANT CONNECT THROUGH HR_PROXY AUTHENTICATED USING
PASSWORD;
ALTER USER HR GRANT CONNECT THROUGH HR_PROXY;
```

If you omit the authentication clause, then it is sufficient to use the name without the password.

In the example displayed in the previous screenshot, the **HR_PROXY** proxy user is connected to the **HR** user account and can review objects in the **HR** schema.

Using the Kerberos authentication

Kerberos is one of the strong authentication methods that are available for companies today to ensure identity security in a networked environment. It uses secret-key cryptography to store the username and password, which means that a client is required to prove its identity to the server and the server to prove its identity to the client. For more details regarding Kerberos, refer to `http://web.mit.edu/kerberos/www/` and `http://www.kerberos.org`.

SQL Developer 1.5.3 introduced the ability to connect to the Oracle database using Kerberos authentication. It is beyond the scope of this book to provide the details related to the setting up and configuration of a Kerberos server for authentication. However, this process is fully documented in the **Oracle Advanced Security** manual. For this section, we'll assume that you have a Kerberos server setup.

Implementing Kerberos authentication in SQL Developer

SQL Developer provides support for Kerberos authentication using either the thin or the thick JDBC driver. Once the Kerberos server is set up, you need to set up and access two files on the client: the Kerberos configuration file and the credential cache file. If you use the thick JDBC driver, you'll need to provide the location of these files in the `sqlnet.ora`, while for the thin driver, we'll set this up in SQL Developer.

We'll start by looking at the preferences that influence Kerberos authentication. Navigate to **Database | Advanced Parameters**. Selecting the **Use OCI/Thick driver** preference directs SQL Developer to use the thick driver, which in turn reads the `sqlnet.ora` file.

Kerberos authentication using the thin JDBC driver

The easier of the two when it comes to using them and setting them up is the thin JDBC driver, which can be done using the **Preferences** dialog, as follows:

1. Keep the **Use OCI/Thick driver** preference deselected.

2. Provide the path for the Kerberos configuration and credential cache files, as shown in the following screenshot:

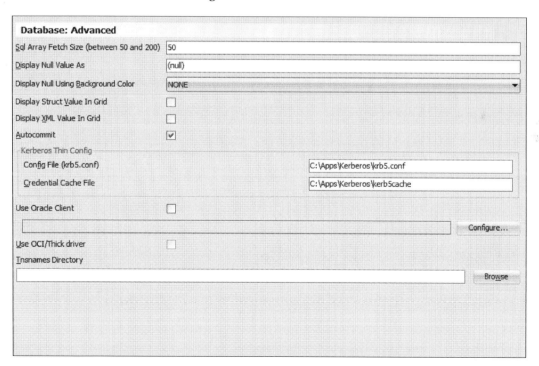

Once you have set the preference, you can create the connection. When using the thin driver, you'll need to provide a **Username** and **Password** in the **Connections** dialog, as shown in the following screenshot:

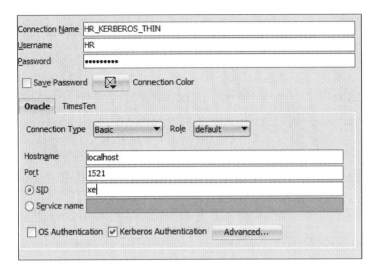

In the preceding screenshot, we selected the **Kerberos Authentication** option, which requires the username and password in this case due to the preferences that have been set.

Creating non-Oracle database connections

SQL Developer allows you to connect to and browse a non-Oracle database. Primarily available for the migration from these databases to Oracle, the connections also allow you to use the SQL Worksheet for SQL queries. More details regarding migrations and working with non-Oracle databases is described in the chapter on working with SQL Developer migrations. Here, we will focus on setting up the environment.

Setting up JDBC drivers

In order to work with the non-Oracle databases supported by SQL Developer, with the exception of Microsoft Access, you need to install additional drivers. Even though these are freely available, they do require additional license consent and as such are not shipped as a part of SQL Developer. If you do not work with non-Oracle databases, there is no need for additional drivers, and the extra connection tabs are not displayed in the **New Connection** dialog.

There are two ways of installing these third-party database drivers:

- Using the **Check for Updates** utility, which includes walking through the required license agreements
- Manually downloading and adding the drivers

Using Check for Updates

The **Check for Updates** utility provides a quick way of adding the JTDS JDBC and MySQL drivers to connect to the Microsoft SQL Server, Sybase, and MySQL databases. To run the **Check for Updates** utility, navigate to **Help | Check for Updates**. This invokes the dialog that helps you download and install the required drivers:

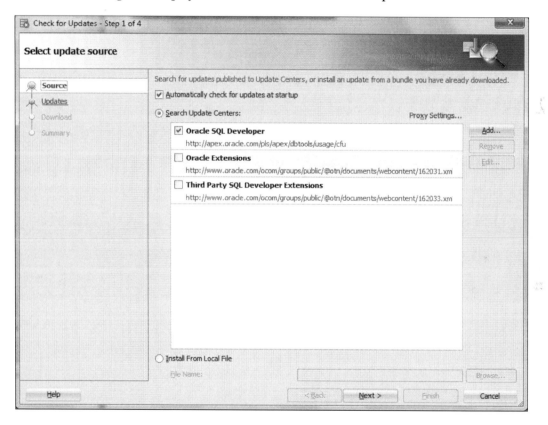

SQL Developer provides a selection of download centers. To access third-party database drivers, select the **Third Party SQL Developer Extensions** option. This center includes other non-Oracle extensions. Therefore, check only those that are required. Currently, I have only the driver updates for SVCO, Schema Visualizer, CVS, and so on, as shown in the following screenshot:

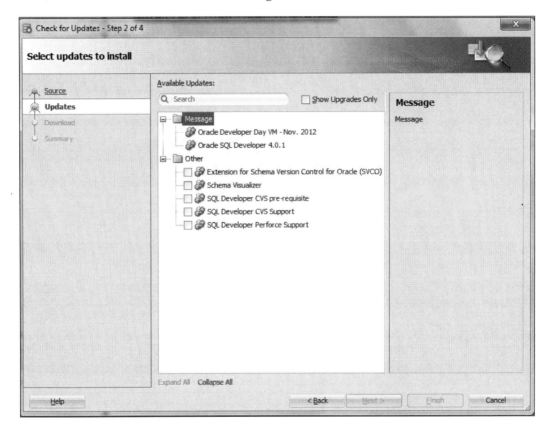

Once the **Check for Update** utility is run, restart SQL Developer. The new third-party drivers are listed in the **Preferences** dialog, which can be viewed by navigating to **Database | Extensions**.

Manually adding JDBC drivers

In order to connect to IBM DB2 and Teradata, you need to manually download and add drivers. You can use this approach to add all of your drivers, including the drivers for Microsoft SQL Server, Sybase, and MySQL.

The first step is to download the drivers to a location of your choice. In each case, you need to unzip the files and point SQL Developer to the specified JAR file. The various drivers that are available from the Internet are as follows:

- **MySQL**: Download the driver from `http://dev.mysql.com/downloads`. The required driver is `mysql-connector-java-5.0.4-bin.jar`.

- **Sybase Adaptive Server and Microsoft SQL Server**: Download the JTDS driver from `http://jtds.sourceforge.net/`. The required driver is `jtds-1.3.1-src.zip`.

- **DB2**: Download the drivers from IBM by visiting `http://www-306.ibm.com/software/data/db2/express/additional-downloads.html`. You need to include both the `db2jcc.jar` and `db2jcc_license_cu.jar` files.

- **Teradata**: Download the driver from `http://www.teradata.com/DownloadCenter/Topic9466-54-1.aspx`. You need to add both the `tdgssconfig.jar` and `terajdbc4.jar` files.

- **Microsoft Access**: No additional driver is required, as SQL Developer uses the JDBC-ODBC bridge to create the connection. The **Access** tab only appears for SQL Developer installed on Microsoft Windows.

Once you have downloaded and unzipped the files, open the **Preferences** dialog and navigate to the **Database | Third Party JDBC Drivers** node.

Irrespective of whether you complete the process manually or by using **Check for Updates**, you need to restart SQL Developer for the changes to take effect. Once this is done, the new non-Oracle database tabs appear in the **New Connection** dialog.

Summary

SQL Developer is easy to install and use. Once you have unzipped the file and started the product, you can connect to your Oracle database without downloading or needing additional files. This easy connection uses the thin JDBC driver to make the connection. In addition to this, the product supports a wide variety of alternative connection and authentication types for Oracle and non-Oracle databases. In this chapter, we reviewed the SQL Developer support offered for Oracle database connections and authentication methods. We reviewed the various drivers required for non-Oracle databases and how to set them up. Finally, we looked at ways to manage connections and folders.

In the next chapter, we'll have a look at database data modeling and how to use SQL Developer Data Modeler to create and update entity relationship diagrams as well as relational and physical data models.

9

Introducing SQL Developer Data Modeler

Oracle SQL Developer **Data Modeler** is available as an independent product, providing a focused data modeling tool for data architects and designers. There is also a **Data Modeler Viewer** extension to SQL Developer that allows users to open previously created data models and create read-only models of their database schemas. SQL Developer Data Modeler is a vast tool, supporting the design of logical entity relationship diagrams and relational models, with forward and reverse engineering capabilities between the two. It supports multi-dimensional, data flow, data type, and physical models and allows files to be imported from a variety of sources and exported to a variety of destinations.

It allows users to set naming conventions and verify designs using a set of predefined design rules. Each of these topics is extensive. So, in this chapter, we'll review a few areas, illustrating how you can use them and highlight a few key features using the independent, standalone release of SQL Developer Data Modeler. We'll include a brief review of the integration points of the Data Modeler Viewer extension to SQL Developer. The product offers support for Oracle and non-Oracle databases. In the interest of time and space, we have decided to work only with the Oracle database.

Oracle SQL Developer Data Modeler

SQL Developer Data Modeler provides users with a lightweight tool, which provides application and database developers a quick and easy way of diagrammatically displaying their data structures, making changes, and submitting the new changes to update a schema. In this chapter, we will not attempt to teach data modeling except to provide some generally accepted definitions. Instead, we will discuss how the product supports data modeling and a few features that are provided. There are a variety of books available on this subject that describe and define best practice in data modeling.

Feature overview

Data Modeler supports a number of graphical models and a selection of text-based models. The graphical models are as follows:

- **Logical**: This is the entity relationship model or **Entity Relationship Diagram (ERD)** and comprises entities, attributes, and relationships.

- **Relational**: This is the schema or database model and is comprised of tables, columns, views, and constraints. In SQL Developer Data Modeler, these models are database-independent and need to be associated with the physical model to support database-specific DDLs.

- **Data Types**: This is the model that supports modeling SQL99 structured types and viewing inheritance hierarchies. The data types modeled here are used in both the logical and relational models.

- **Multidimensional Models**: These models support fact, dimension, and summary classifications for multidimensional models.

- **Data Flow**: These models support the definition of primitive, composite, and transformational tasks.

The following support these graphical models:

- **Domains**: These allow you to define and reuse a data type with optional constraints or allowable values. You can use domains in the Logical and Relational models.

- **Physical**: This model is associated with a relational model and defines the physical attributes for a specific database and version.

- **Business Information**: This allows you to model or document the business details that support a design.

A variety of utilities tie these graphical and textual models together, which include the following:

- Forward and reverse engineering between the Logical and Relational models
- Importing from various databases
- Exporting, including the DDL script generation, for various databases
- Design rules to verify standards and completeness
- Name templates, glossary, and abbreviation files to support the naming standards

Integrated architecture

SQL Developer Data Modeler is made up of a number of layers, which have a tightly synchronized relationship. The Logical model is thought of as the core of the product, providing the starting point for any design and feeding details into other models. The following diagram shows an illustration of how the models relate to each other:

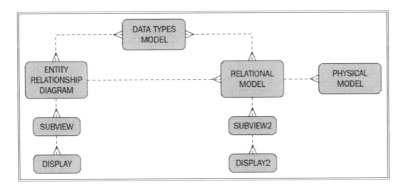

The logical ERD provides the basis for one or more relational models, and each of these feeds into one or more physical models, which are in turn used for the DDL generation. You can create separate data types model and use the defined data type in either the logical or relational models. Both relational and logical models can have multiple subviews created, and each subview can have many displays created.

Getting started

SQL Developer Data Modeler is an independent product and in the previous releases of SQL Developer, only the **Data Modeler Viewer** extension was readily available along with the SQL Developer download. But in version 4.1, the Data Modeler is integrated with SQL Developer 4.1 by default as a full product and not as a mere read-only extension.

Oracle clients and JDBC drivers

If you are designing and building a model from scratch or have access to the DDL script file to import models, then you do not need to have access to a database. However, if you want to import from a database, you'll need to create a database connection. In this case, there is no need for an Oracle client in your development environment because you can use the thin JDBC driver to connect to the database. SQL Developer Data Modeler also supports the TNS alias. Therefore, if you have access to a `tnsnames.ora` file or have other Oracle software installed in your environment, you can access the `tnsnames` file to make the database connection if and when required.

Creating your first models

The Data Modeler browser starts with empty **Logical** and **Relational** models. This allows you to start a new design and build a model from scratch, which can be either a logical model with entities and attributes, or a relational model with tables and columns. The Data Modeler also supports metadata to be imported from a variety of sources, which include:

- Importing metadata from:
    - DDL scripts
    - Data Dictionary

- Importing from other modeling tools, such as the following:
    - Oracle Designer
    - CA Erwin 4.x

- Importing other formats, such as the following:
    - VAR file
    - XMLA (Microsoft, Hyperion)

The context menu that displays the available choices is shown in the following screenshot:

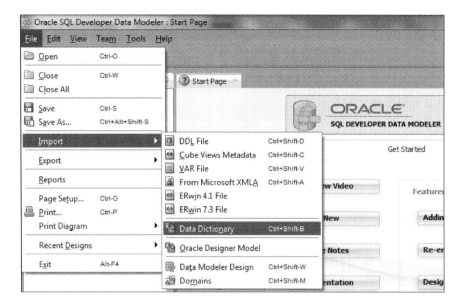

Once you have created and saved your models, you can open these or share them with your colleagues. To open an existing model, use the menu, as follows:

- **File | Open**: Browse to the location of the files, which then opens the full design with all the saved models

- **File | Recent Designs**: This opens the full design with all the saved models with no need to first search for the location

- **File | Import | Data Modeler Design**: This is more granular, offering a choice of models saved in a set of models

Recent diagrams

Navigate to **File | Recent Diagrams** to display a list of all the diagrams that you have recently worked on and saved. Using this approach saves you from needing to browse to the location of the stored files.

Importing from the Data Dictionary

There are many ways to start using this tool by just starting to draw any one of the model types mentioned. Later in the chapter, we'll start with an ERD and work our way down to the DDL scripts. In this first section, we'll import the details from an existing schema. It's a useful place to start, as the process quickly creates a model that you can investigate and then use to learn more about the tool. This may also be one of the most frequently used features in the tool, allowing anyone to quickly see a model of the data structures that underpin their database-based application.

In the screenshot shown earlier, we highlighted the **File | Import | Data Dictionary** option. Using this allows you to import from Oracle 9i, Oracle 10g, Oracle 11g, Oracle 12c, Microsoft SQL Server 2000 and 2005, and IBM DB2 LUW Versions 7 and 8.

Creating a database connection

Before you begin to import from a database, you need to create a database connection for each database that you'll connect to. Once it's created, you'll see all the schemas in the database and the objects that you have access to.

Access the **New Database Connection** dialog by navigating to **File | Import**, as shown in the following screenshot. If you have no connections, click on **Add** to create a new connection:

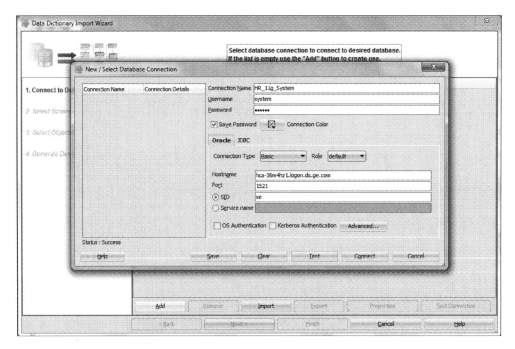

For a **Basic** connection, you need to provide the **Hostname** of the database server, **Port**, and **SID**. The connection dialog also supports the TNS alias and the advanced JDBC URL.

 Before you can add connections for non-Oracle databases, you need to add the required JDBC drivers. To add these drivers, navigate to **Tools | General Options | Third Party JDBC Drivers**.

Using the Import Wizard

Once you have a connection created, select the connection and continue using the dialog by clicking on **Next**. You can select more than one schema during an import. In the following example, we have selected two schemas, which results in three diagrams: one central model with all the imported tables and views, and two subviews. When importing, a separate subview is created for each schema that you select, and all the imported objects are displayed in that schema (this is not the only role for subviews, and we'll expand on this later in the chapter):

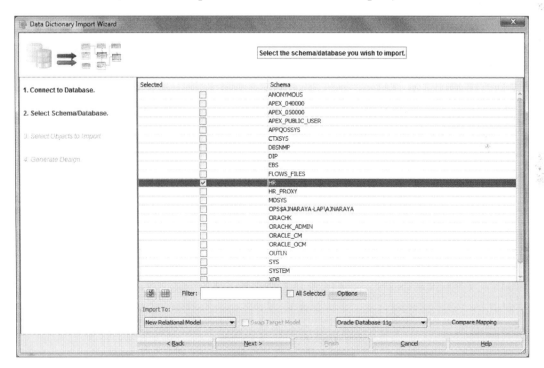

In the **Import Wizard** that's displayed, there is a set of checkboxes and buttons below the listed schemas. By selecting **All Selected**, the screens that follow will have all instances of all the objects that were automatically selected. Depending on what you are planning to import, it is often easier to keep that deselected and then use the **Select All** button on each object type tab:

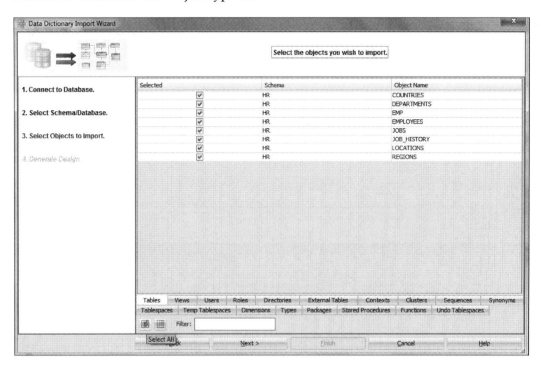

Once you have selected the schemas, you can select the individual objects. **Tables** and **Views** are placed on the central Relational model and onto the respective subviews for each schema. All other objects, such as **Roles**, **Users**, and **TableSpaces**, are maintained in the Physical model listed in the object browser.

A summary of the objects that need to be imported is displayed, and you are offered the choice of the model destination. The default destination is HR_11g_System. The choice given here is needed for second or any subsequent imports. For these, you need to decide whether you'll want to merge the objects into an existing model or create a new model.

To create the initial model, complete the dialog and select **Finish**. Each time you import a set of database objects, a log file of the completed activity is created, which tallies with the number of statements and errors. It is worth saving the log files so that they can be used for troubleshooting later.

Importing multiple schemas from **Data Dictionary** creates a central Relational model and a subview for each of the imported schemas.

Reviewing the results

Once the import is complete, the main Relational diagram opens:

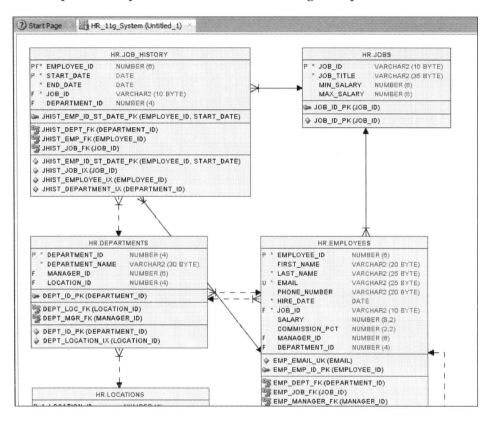

The preceding screenshot shows a few tables imported into the Relational model. To see the initial subviews created for each schema that was made, expand the **Relational Models** node and then the **SubViews** node. Right-click on one of the schema subviews listed and select **Show Diagram**.

Working with diagrams and their components

You can waste away many hours laying out the elements on a diagram. Therefore, this aspect of modeling can be time-consuming. However, a model serves as a documentation and a communication device. Therefore, taking time to ensure that it is well annotated and clearly designed is important. Most of the controls for the models are on the context menu, allowing you to modify individual aspects of the diagram. The context menu changes depending on whether you have an object or line selected, or you're just clicking in the open space. You can also set general defaults by navigating to **Tools | Preferences | Data Modeler**. In this section, we'll look at the various options available when working with the diagrams.

Formatting the elements

Before moving a relationship line, entity, or table, you can dramatically change the impact and readability of a large diagram just by changing the colors. This is readily demonstrated when importing from two or more schemas. Using the previous example where we imported from two schemas, open one of the subviews and select all the tables. With the objects selected, invoke the **Format Object** dialog using the context menu:

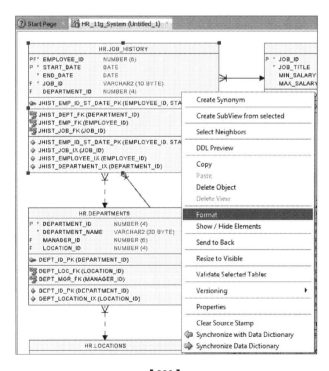

Controlling the layout

When working with a large number of items in a model, it's important to keep the layout organized. A variety of tools to help with the process are explained in the following sections.

Adjusting the level of detail displayed

Change the amount of detail displayed in a table (or entity) using the **View Details** menu. It is invoked with a right-click on the white space of a diagram. The **View Details** menu has options to display:

- All Details
- Names Only
- Columns
- Datatype
- Keys

Adjusting the width and height across the model

If you have a large diagram and want to see how tables or entities relate to each other, you can create a more compact model using a display without impacting the main model. This can be done by setting the details to display only the name and then resizing and repositioning the objects.

In the following screenshot, we have set the model to display only the name of the tables. Create a more compact diagram by resizing one of the tables to a more fitting set of dimensions, select the rest, and then resize them all to the same width and height:

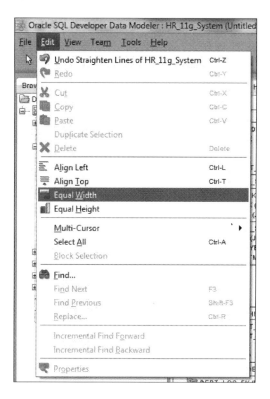

Analysis, design, and generation

Some developers like to have a clear separation between the logical analysis and physical design of an application system. SQL Developer Data Modeler supports this separation of tasks and also supports the synchronization of metadata between these. This means that you can start new application development with a logical model without needing to think about the physical implementation details. Once you have completed the analysis, you can then transform the entities to tables and work on the physical implementation. SQL Developer Data Modeler also allows you to work on the relational model with its tables, views, and constraints without needing to consider the physical detail. Without the physical detail, you can create a relational model that is database-agnostic. Then, for a single relational model, you can create multiple physical implementations and generate different DDL for each of these.

In this section, we'll start with a logical model, transform this to a relational model, and then look at the physical details before generating the DDL.

The flow of work

While some believe that the only way to start data modeling is with conceptual analysis, others believe that this extra layer of work is not necessary. Therefore, they skip the high-level conceptual analysis and start by building the data model. SQL Developer Data Modeler supports these alternatives and provides the option to synchronize these models.

Starting with analysis (top down)

This is often considered to be the most traditional approach to database design and generation and falls into the waterfall approach of strategy, analysis, design, and generation. The mindset behind this approach is that the more work you do up front, the better. Early changes to the design are less costly than they are likely to be later on. Liken this to building a house. If you plan to change the position of the bathroom while the house is still in the drawing and architectural phase, it's much less costly than planning to move it once the building work has begun. The further down the line the changes are requested, the more costly the decision.

The flow of work in this approach is to build the logical model, set standards and build the glossary, and then transform or forward engineer it to the relational model. Once you have the relational model, review and make adjustments as required. At this stage, you can add extra columns, rename columns or tables, and add constraints. Once the relational model is sound, you can create the additional physical detail as needed. Generate the DDL and review the scripts when the relational and physical models are complete.

Importing existing models (bottom up)

If you already have an application built, the database will be in place. Being able to visualize the model allows you to view and extend the mode or migrate the details to a new database. Starting with the schema supports migrating to new environments or upgrading applications. In the current climate, consolidating applications is important. Therefore, being able to review the models for these existing applications means that you can make decisions before embarking on updates.

Building the relational model

Some teams want to model their databases but feel that the ERD is an unnecessary layer. Therefore, they start by building a schema model. At this level, you are building tables, columns, and constraints. You can start by importing tables from an existing database and then augment them by adding new tables and modifying the imported tables. This is a valid approach to modeling, but it does mean that you are already thinking about the implementation details when you start designing.

Logical models

A logical ERD is made up of entities and attributes. You can identify unique identifiers and relationships between entities. You are not tied down to the implementation details at this point. Therefore, you can create a many-to-many relationship or supertypes (if they support the business requirement). In essence, you are using an ERD to capture the business needs:

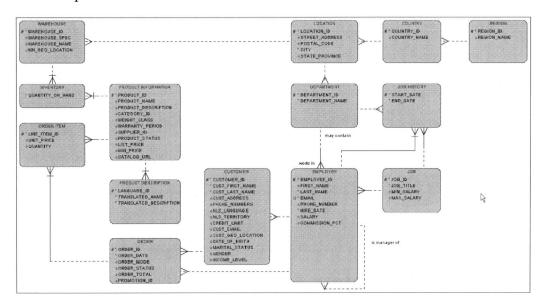

Creating an ERD

Select the **Logical** node in the object browser and select **Show** from the context menu to create or open a blank page for your logical model.

To start creating the model, use the set of buttons on the toolbar, as shown in the following screenshot. The button is "sticky" by default. This means that you can draw an entity, which invokes the property dialog. Then, on closing the dialog, you are immediately ready to draw the next entity without needing to select the button again:

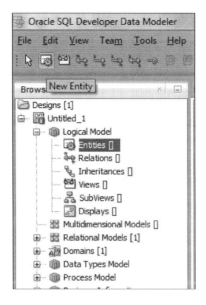

Creating entities

As soon as you have drawn the shape, the **Entity Properties** dialog is invoked, allowing you to populate the details.

You can provide a broad spectrum of details for each entity, including documentation details, such as change request details and comments.

General entity properties include adding synonyms and abbreviations. Synonyms are for documentation purposes and can be a part of your glossary. They are not database synonyms.

Singular entity names and plural table names

Typically, entity names are singular and table names are plural. Some products allow you to set this plural value under the entity properties, and the plural value is then used when engineering to create the table. You can use the **Preferred Abbreviation** field for this purpose in SQL Developer Data Modeler. If you want to use the preferred abbreviation, you will also need to set the **Use preferred abbreviation** in the forward engineering **General Options** dialog.

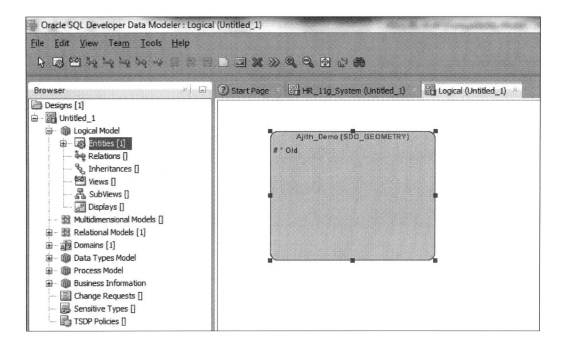

Adding attributes

Once you have entered the main details for the entity, you can add the required attributes. In the following screenshot, you can see the basic requirements for each attribute, such as setting the data types and the unique identifier properties. To add more details to each attribute, click on the **Properties** button or double-click on the required attribute:

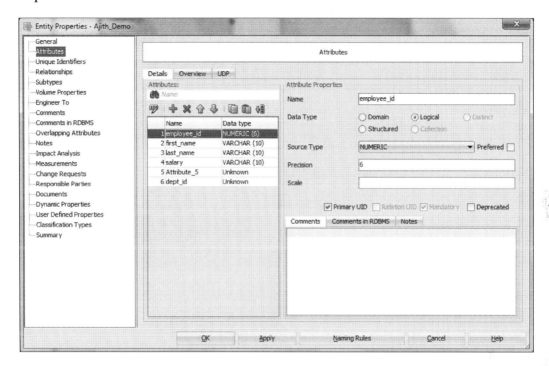

Working with relationships

The **Entity Properties** dialog includes a **Relationships** node with a list of all the available relationships. Double-click on the name of the relationship to drill down to the detail. The **General** detail is useful when you need to review, as shown in the following screenshot. If you reverse engineer the details from a relational model, the name on the source and the target are blank. Completing this detail and displaying it on the model is very useful for later documentation when using the model as a discussion point:

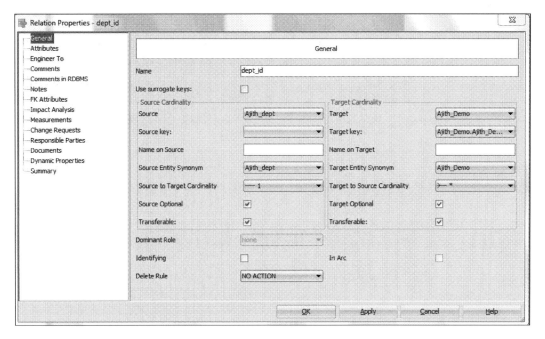

In the earlier section on syntax, we mentioned the **Cardinality**, **Optional**, and **Identifying** properties on the diagram. These properties are set in this dialog.

You can invoke the same dialog by selecting the relationship in the diagram and invoking the **Properties** dialog.

 To display the relationship names on the model, navigate to **Tools | General Options** and go to **Diagram | Logical Model** to set the display property to **Show Source/Target Name**.

Creating constraints, domains, and setting default values

A domain is a defined data type that may have associated valid values. By defining domains, you can reuse them throughout the model, thus providing consistency to the model. For example, you can create a Yes/No domain and set the data type and associate valid values to Yes and No. Once this is created, you can associate it with all the columns or entities that use the Yes/No values. Domains need not be associated with valid values. Instead, you can just set the data type and then apply the domain to columns or entities. You can work with domains and default values independent of the ERD or Relational models. If you set these at the attribute level and then forward engineer, the detail is carried forward to the tables and columns. However, these can be easily added directly to the columns.

Working with domains

When setting data types for attributes or columns, you have a choice of categories, such as:

- Domains
- Logical
- Distinct
- Structured
- Collection

The most common category from the aforementioned ones is the **Logical** type, where you can set the type and scale for the data type. When working with a large number of entities and attributes, using domains is more efficient, as any changes made to the domains are propagated to all the columns or attributes that use them. SQL Developer Data Modeler provides a default domains file. All the domains that are added to this file are available for all the designs that you work on. Alternatively, you can create a domains file that can be used with specific designs.

A user-defined distinct type is a data type derived from an existing logical type, defined under **Tools | Data Modeler | Types Administration**. A distinct type shares its representation with all default data types, but is considered to be a separate and can also be named as per our choice. Structured types are supported as named user-defined composite. A structured type can be defined based on a basic data type, a distinct type, another structured type, or a reference to structured type, or it can be defined as a collection type. Collection types represent arrays or collections of elements (basic type, distinct type, structured type, or another collection). You can create new collection types or edit the properties of existing collection types.

Creating domains

Navigate to **Tools | Domains Administration** and create your own new domain by clicking on **Add**. This action adds a new domain to the default domains file. When adding domains, provide the name and the **Logical** type details and add the details such as size and precision. You can also remove or modify domains using this dialog, as shown in the following screenshot. The changes that were made here are maintained separately from your design. Therefore, you can enforce standards across designs:

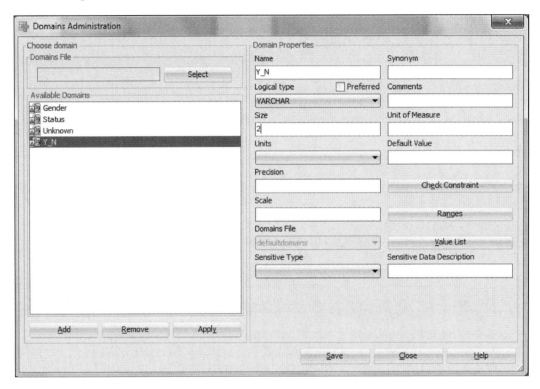

You can create a separate domains file that is associated with your design by clicking on the **Select** button in the **Domains Administration** dialog. This action allows you to create or open a separate domains file. Once it's created, add new domains to the file as previously described. To use these domains in a design, navigate to **File | Import | Domains**. When you save the design, these domains are then saved with the design.

Using domains to implement check constraints

Domains offer more than just providing standard data types. They can also contain valid values and thus allow you to use the domain to:

- Implement a check constraint
- Enforce a range of values
- Provide a set of valid sets

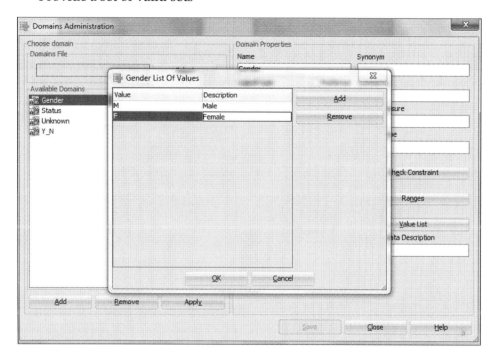

In the preceding screenshot, we added a value list. When adding check constraints to domains, you can add constraints specific to a database version, or you can choose to create a generic constraint, which will be applied to any database that you choose.

Introducing forward and reverse engineering

SQL Developer Data Modeler supports forward and reverse engineering. These transformation tools support:

- Forward engineering from an ERD to a new or an existing relational model
- Reverse engineering from a relational model to a new or an existing ERD

When engineering to an existing model, you can choose whether you want to include or exclude changes made in the different models.

Forward engineering

SQL Developer Data Modeler supports multiple relational models for each logical model. Irrespective of whether you are starting with a logical model, or the logical model is derived from an existing relational model, you can forward engineer to a new relational model. Create an empty relational model by selecting **New Relational Model** from the **Relational Models** context menu in the object browser. This automatically opens a new blank relational model. Open the **Logical** model and select the **Engineer to Relational Model** button (»):

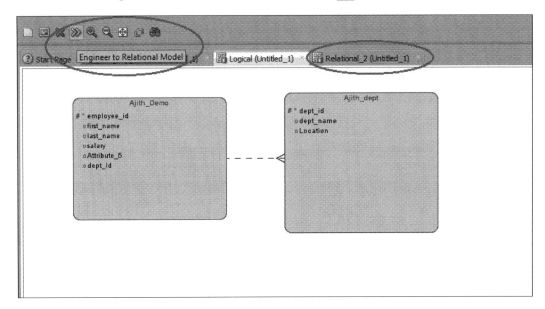

Once the dialog opens, you can use the drop-down list of relational models to determine which model you want to update or create, as follows:

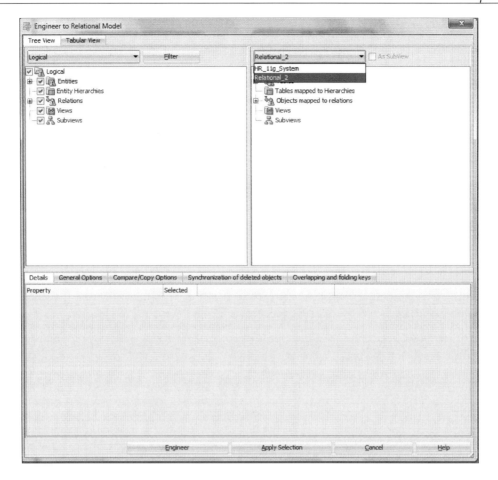

Reverse engineering models

This is the reverse action of the previously described forward engineering option. In this case, you use a relational model to create or update a logical model. If you already have a model, the decisions that you need to make revolve around layout, and the adding, deleting or updating of items. Reverse engineering relational to logical models is very useful when you are doing a "bottom-up design". In other words, you have imported the table definitions from an existing script or data dictionary. Once the relational model has been created and refined, reverse engineer the model to create a logical **Entity Relationship Diagram**.

Creating relational models

The relational model is made up of tables and views with their columns and relationships. The details for these items are listed in the object browser under the **Relational Models** node. These are also the only details that are displayed in the diagram, as shown in the following screenshot. Details such as tablespaces, triggers, or physical properties are listed in the physical model:

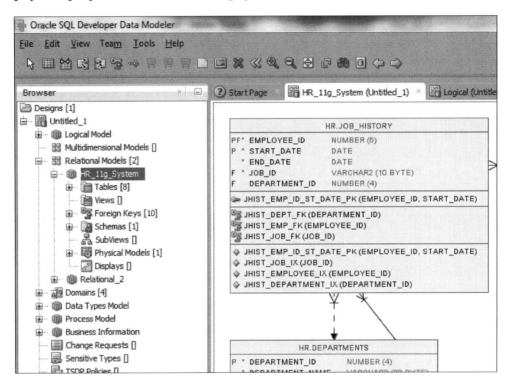

Building the physical model

The physical model is the source for the DDL scripts. Therefore, it contains many more details than are available on the diagram. If you start from the logical model and engineer forward to the relational model, you'll need to start building the physical model from scratch. It will initially only be populated with the details in the relational model. If you are working from an existing database model, then importing the schema also imports the physical model.

SQL Developer Data Modeler supports multiple physical models for each relational model. This is useful if you want to build different DDL scripts for different databases (for both Oracle and non-Oracle databases) or the test, development, and production databases in Oracle. In the next section, we'll look at ways to:

- Import a schema from the Data Dictionary
- Create a new physical model

Importing a schema from the Data Dictionary

Importing from a database connection imports objects such as tables, columns, and views and places them in the relational model diagram. You can also import physical properties such as tablespaces, roles, and directories. These details are listed under the physical node in the object browser. The **Data Dictionary Import Wizard** lets you select the objects and object types that you can import, as shown in the following screenshot:

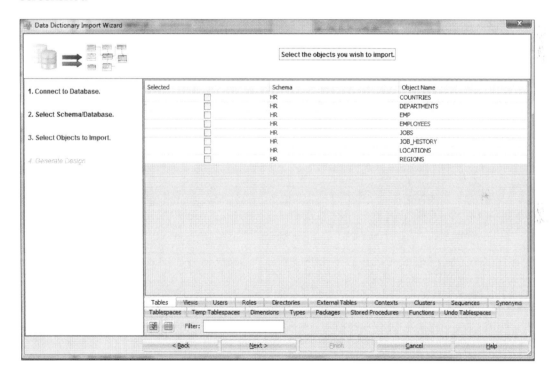

Generating the DDL

All of the preceding work culminates in producing the DDL scripts to create or update a schema design. Invoke the **DDL Generation** dialog by navigating to **File | Export** and then, select the model of your choice. You can also click on the **Generate DDL** button in the toolbar to invoke the **DDL File Editor** dialog.

With the correct database selected, click on **Generate** to invoke the **DDL Generation Options** dialog:

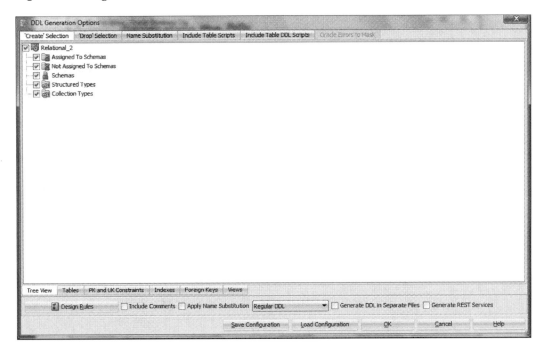

By default, all objects are marked for generation. Thus, you can work through the lower tabs and remove the items that you don't want in the DDL.

Use the **Tree View** tab to generate a DDL for a specific schema or for any of the objects that are not assigned to the users, as shown in the following screenshot. For example, if you have associated various objects with the HR schema in the physical model, then you can generate all the DDLs for the HR schema. To generate schema-specific DDL, select the **Assigned to Users** node in the tree and expand the required user; in this case, it's HR.

The top set of tabs drives additional text within the scripts. We mentioned naming standard templates and resetting object prefixes earlier; here we have another opportunity to switch the names, either for certain object names, or to switch out a prefix and replace it:

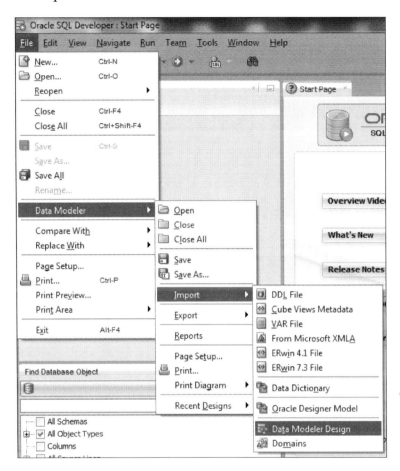

Creating a new model

The **Data Modeler Viewer** extension to SQL Developer also allows you to create models of the tables, views, and constraints in the database connections that you have access to. To create a new model, expand the database connection in the **Connections** navigator and then, select the tables that you want to include in a diagram. Drag the selection on the relational model.

Summary

In this chapter, you had an insight into the features offered by SQL Developer Data Modeler. Data Modeler provides a number of graphical and textual modeling tools for Logical, Relational, and Multidimensional models. We looked at how to create Logical and Relational models and how we can import models from the Data Dictionary or create models from scratch. We looked at forward and reverse engineering, how to build a physical model, and generate the DDL.

The subject of data modeling is vast, and this chapter only introduced some of the many and varied features available in SQL Developer Data Modeler. Whether you are a data architect, or updating an existing design, you can use SQL Developer Data Modeler to build an entire Entity Relationship Diagram or update schema models and generate DDL scripts.

In the next chapter, we'll discuss SQL Developer's extensible framework and look at how we can create user-defined extensions and use XML with embedded SQL and PL/SQL to add features to a SQL Developer environment.

10

Extending SQL Developer

Oracle SQL Developer is written using a Java framework, provided by Oracle JDeveloper. This underlying integrated development environment is commonly referred to as the JDeveloper IDE, or more recently, the **Fusion Client Platform (FCP)**. The framework provides the underlying structure onto which developers of both Oracle JDeveloper and Oracle SQL Developer add their features. This framework is extensible and is available to development engineers and end users to add functionality. The nature of these extensions can range from including a single XML report, to adding complex Java extensions bundled as JAR files. In this chapter, we'll look at the range of support available for adding XML extensions, a task that is easily within the reach of any database developer with SQL and PL/SQL skills. While it is considered beyond the scope of the book to include information on building a Java extension, we will discuss working with existing Java extensions.

Introducing extensibility

Extensibility, in terms of software development, means that the software can have components added without impacting or having to change the underlying code. Moreover, the underlying code provides "hooks" within the infrastructure, specifically designed to make for the addition of new components, thus allowing developers to add new or alternative capabilities not provided by the product.

Extensibility in SQL Developer

The FCP is designed to allow users to build Java extensions that can be added to either JDeveloper or SQL Developer. You can build large complex features using Java. The **Migrations and Versioning** support within SQL Developer are examples of this, and there are external customers building Java extensions.

SQL Developer provides an additional infrastructure with code "hooks" for adding items using only XML with embedded SQL and PL/SQL. The extra item types that you can add are as follows:

- Display editors
- Context menus
- Reports
- Navigator nodes

We will review these XML extension types and consider various examples to illustrate them.

Who builds extensions?

With the ability to support both XML and Java extensions, there is the opportunity to support different extension-building audiences. XML extensions are typically used by developers well versed in SQL and PL/SQL. These are database developers and DBAs who use tools and command-line interfaces to access the database. The extensions they build are often shared within a team or the company. Java extensions are more often developed by development teams in Oracle, Oracle Partners, and by other Java literate developers and engineers. **Oracle TimesTen** and the **Versioning Navigator** are Oracle-developed Java extensions, built by different teams and shipped as part of SQL Developer. Java bundled extensions, which could be a combination of XML and Java, lend themselves to be viable as commercial entities. There are a few public Java-based user-defined extensions; some are commercial and some are freely available.

Why extend?

Software products do not always provide the full functionality you need in your development environment. Being able to add a few additional components to those that are already provided means you can augment your environment with features that are specific to your needs. With SQL Developer extensions, you only need one person in the team to create the extension(s), which can then be shared. So, create an enhanced, yet company standard tool. The kind of missing functionality might be that grey area between being a developer and DBA.

SQL Developer XML extension types

In this next section, the extensions described focus on XML extensions and can be added by anyone who has a good grasp of SQL and PL/SQL. Although the documents we create are written in XML, they conform to a set of **XML Schema Definition (XSD)** standards, which you can think of as templates. For all the extensions added, whether you create Java extensions bundled as JAR files or XML extensions and add them individually or bundled as JAR files, you need to restart SQL Developer for the additions to take effect. In this next section, we'll look at the different types of XML extensions you can create in SQL Developer. We'll start with the easiest, progressing to the more complex.

Adding an XML extension

Regardless of the XML extension you are adding, you add the files to SQL Developer in the same way. They are either as individual files or bundled as JAR files. When adding a single file or a few files, it's easier to add them individually.

> To add a single XML file as an extension, select **Tools | Preferences**, expand **Database | User Defined Extensions**, and click on **Add**. Add the extension details and restart SQL Developer

If you have a large number of files, then it's easier to bundle them in JAR files and add the files. This is more efficient, however, you need a certain level of Java knowledge to create the JAR file, and so we'll add them individually. We will show you how to add Java extensions later.

Sharing user-defined reports

The most straightforward of all extensions to create is the shared reports extension. Once you have created a set of your own reports, use the context menu to export them to an XML file. You can export reports at any level in the **User Defined Reports** section. You can select one of the following:

- The top-level **User Defined Reports**—this exports all sub-folders and reports
- Any subfolder—this exports all sub-folders, if there are nested folders, and reports
- Any report—this exports the selected report only

Regardless of the level you select, invoke the context menu and select **Export** (as shown in the following screenshot). Provide a report name and the file location:

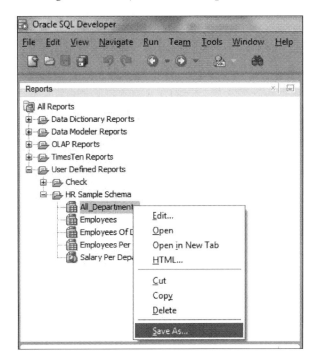

When creating reports, SQL Developer creates the XML file in the correct format. Therefore, in order to create the XML file for shared reports, you only need to worry about creating the initial reports, using the **Create Report** dialog for assistance. Once you have exported the reports to an XML file, and you can create one or many files, move them to a central file or web server to be made available for more general use.

To include the shared reports, open the **Database | User Defined Extensions** preference and click on **Add Row**. Select **REPORT** from the drop-down list for the extension type, and browse to locate the XML file, as shown in the following screenshot:

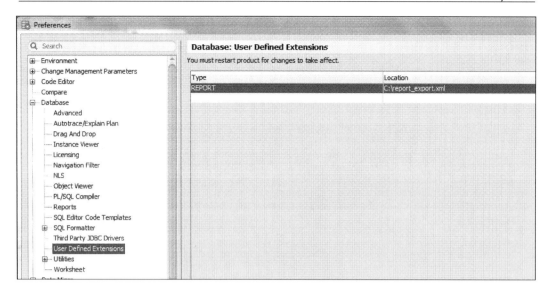

By sharing reports, you can achieve the following:

- Save time and resources by having only one or a few team members create the reports and then share them with the group

- Use the best skills for the job by using those developers with the most knowledge of the Data Dictionary or of the application you are working with

- Use those best skilled at writing well-tuned SQL queries that others can take advantage of

Once the new file location has been added, restart SQL Developer. A new **Shared Reports** folder will display in the **Reports** navigator. These reports, like those in the **Data Dictionary Reports** node, are not updateable. To review or edit the SQL, you can copy and paste them into a new report in the **User Defined Reports** node, or run the report and copy the SQL to the SQL Worksheet once run.

Another advantage of shared reports is that the next time you re-start SQL Developer, you pick up any updates to the existing reports or new reports added to the centrally stored file.

Adding display editors

Adding display editors is a little more involved than adding shared reports, because you need to create the XML file yourself. You invoke a set of display editors each time you click on an object in the **Connections** navigator. The set of view display editors is highlighted in the following screenshot:

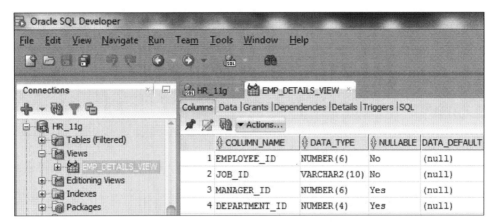

The contents of these display editors are the results of queries run against the data dictionary. For example, to get the kind of detail in the **Triggers** or **Columns** display editors shown in the previous screenshot, you can write queries against the **USER_ TRIGGERS** or **USER_TAB_COLUMNS** dictionary views. For more detail, you need to write more complex queries, possibly joining many dictionary views.

Examples of display editors

The list of examples is potentially long, and we offer a few here only to give you an idea of the kind of content you can add. Naturally, any additional displays that you add will depend on your areas of focus.

Include subpartitions

If you work with partitioned tables, you can add a user-defined extension to display the subpartition's details.

Use restricted queries

You can create editors that focus on a feature, for example, by creating display editors that display only the disabled constraints or triggers of a certain status.

Add display editors for new navigator nodes

If you create a new node in the **Connections** navigator, such as adding a Tablespaces, Dimensions, or a new Projects node, then you need to add the full set of display editors that define the objects you have listed.

Building the XML file for a display editor

Taking the idea of adding a subpartitions display, consider the following piece of code:

```
<displays>
  <!-- OverView -->
  <display type="editor" style="null" enable="true"
          class="Oracle#SUBPARTITION" objectType="TABLE">
    <name><![CDATA[Subpartitions]]></name>
    <query>
      <sql>
        <![CDATA[Select * FROM USER_TAB_SUBPARTITIONS WHERE
                TABLE_NAME = :TABLE_NAME]]>
      </sql>
    </query>
        <CustomValues>
        <TYPE>horizontal</TYPE>
        </CustomValues>
  </display>
</displays>
```

By saving this code to an XML file, and then hooking that file into SQL Developer, you add another display editor to the set already defined for tables.

The structure for each display editor you add is the same. The first CDATA entry highlighted previously is for the title, displayed in the display editor tab. The second CDATA entry highlighted is the SQL query, which provides the content. The results of the new display editor are shown in the upcoming screenshot. Notice that the new editor is added at the end, after the SQL editor. Notice too that in the example, the table name is unnecessarily included in the list. Here, we have used a simple Select * FROM ... query. Even for a simple query, just by specifying the columns in the select statement means that you can control the columns that display and avoid the unnecessary additional columns; in this case, the table name.

The example we have included is basic and is sufficient to add in additional display editors. If you are familiar with XML, then you'll want to see the **XSD**. The **XSD**, or **XML Schema Definition**, provides the syntax and structure of the way the elements should be defined in the XML file.

The structure of the display editor conforms to an **XSD** called `displays.xsd`. The `displays.xsd` includes a `query.xsd`.

The SQL query you include in the XML file can be as simple as `SELECT * FROM <a data dictionary view>`, or a more complex query, joining multiple dictionary views.

Once you have created the XML file, save it to a file or web server location of your choice and open the **User Defined Extensions** preference. Click on **Add Row**, select **EDITOR** from the drop-down list for the extension type, and browse to locate the XML file, as shown in the following screenshot:

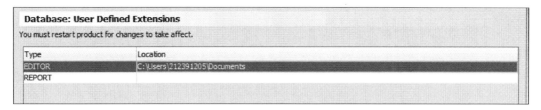

 Group display editor topics into a single file

Instead of creating multiple individual XML files for each display editor, add all of the code for the display editors for a single object into one file. For example, create an `ExtraTableEditor.xml` file with all of the additional table related display editors.

Working with context menus

Throughout SQL Developer, a right-click on the mouse invokes a context-sensitive menu. The menus in the **Connections** navigator are all DDL commands that provide actions such as dropping, adding, and setting privileges. For example, if you select a table and invoke the context menu, you can drill down to the **Drop** menu, as shown next:

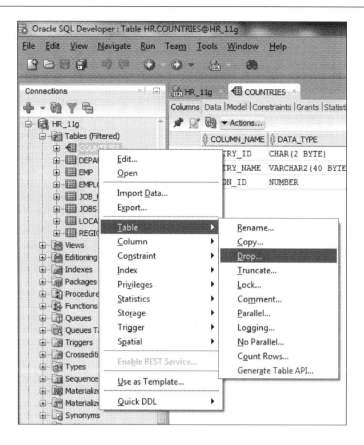

Selecting the menu item invokes the dialog with two tabs. The pieces that are consistent for each of these context menu dialogs are the three buttons, **Help**, **Apply**, **Cancel**, and the two tabs, **Prompts** and **SQL**. The initial **Prompts** panel also displays the context you are in, the schema name (displayed as the **Owner**), and the selected object name. In the example shown in the following screenshot, we have selected a table, and so the **Name** displayed is that table name:

You can add these extra context menus at various levels in the **Connections** navigator tree, such as at the connection, object node, or instance level, so the name displayed depends on the node you have selected.

Adding a context menu to the connections menus

You can add the option to compile the schema currently selected. Consider the following piece of code:

```xml
<?xml version="1.0" encoding="UTF-8"?>
<items xmlns:xsi="http://www.w3.org/2001/XMLSchema-instance"
                 xsi:noNamespaceSchemaLocation="dialogs.xsd">
  <item type="CONNECTION" reload="true">
   <title>Compile Schema</title>
   <prompt type="confirm">
     <label>Confirm to compile all in the schema.</label>
   </prompt>
   <sql>
      <![CDATA[BEGIN DBMS_UTILITY.COMPILE_SCHEMA
         (:OBJECT_OWNER); END;]]>
      </sql>
   <help>Compiles all the objects in the schema. </help>
  </item>
</items>
```

This adds a new context menu when you right-click on the connection. It invokes a dialog with two tabs: the first with all of the details of the action about to take place, and the second displays your SQL or, in this case, PL/SQL code. You can include help text and a confirmation dialog to follow the action.

As mentioned earlier, if you are familiar with XML, there is an XSD file to assist with the development of the XML file structure.

 The structure of the context menu conforms to an XSD called `dialogs.xsd`.

Passing parameters

In the previous example, we only passed a single parameter: the object owner name. You can create context menus and provide empty fields, checkboxes, or drop-down lists, which allow the user to have more control over the SQL executed. In the **Drop** table example illustrated at the start of this section, the checkbox allows the user to include the **Cascade Constraints** option.

To provide the user with a fixed list of values, add the static list options after the
`<title>Compile Schema</title>`. The code is shown next:

```
<prompt>
  <label>Compile All </label>
  <value><![CDATA[STATIC:TRUE:FALSE]]></value>
</prompt>
```

Once you start passing in additional parameters, you can use them in the SQL
as follows:

```
<sql>
    <![CDATA[BEGIN
       DBMS_UTILITY.COMPILE_SCHEMA('#OBJECT_OWNER#', #0#);
       END;]]>
</sql>
```

Here, the parameter is referred to by the value, #0#. You can pass a number of
additional values to the SQL statement, referencing each in turn by using the
values #0#, #1#, #2#, and so on.

You will see the result of our code, including the drop-down list. Notice that we do
not need to code for the **Owner** or the **Name** values displayed. These are exposed in
the dialog through the extensions framework. If you do not see them, no connection
has been made.

Creating a utility using context menus

The extent of what the context menu does is up to you. You can create a simple menu
to drop or rename an object, or you can create more complex menus. You don't need
to limit yourself to a single command either (whether basic or complex). Instead,
you can bundle a set of commands to create a small utility, like the **Normalize** menu,
provided by SQL Developer.

The context menu is available off **Columns | Normalize**, when you select a table.

In the dialog previously displayed, you can see that the code requires four free form values to be added, and one selected from a drop-down list.

This little utility is very useful if you have imported a spreadsheet to create a new table populated with that data. Invariably, there are redundancies and the table is better suited to be split into two or more. You manually need to create a new table and move the duplicate values to the new table, populating a **Primary Key** automatically while you do so. Then, you need to create a **Foreign Key** constraint to link the two tables. This utility does all of the steps, wrapped in PL/SQL.

In the code shown in the following screenshot, you can see a subset of the code, displaying the steps that you need to follow when carrying out the process manually:

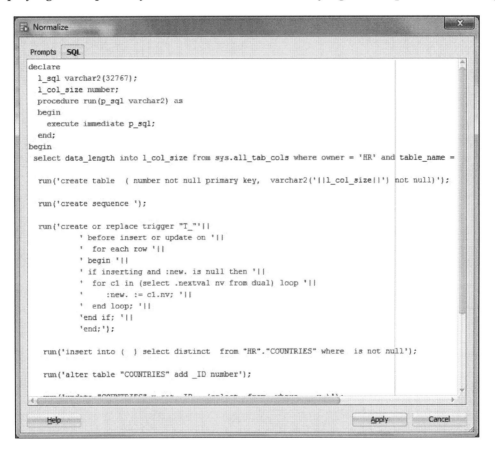

Including the user-defined extension for context menus

In the same way as you have done for the previous examples, once you have created the XML file, save it to a file or web server location of your choice and open the **User Defined Extensions** preference. Click on **Add Row** and select **ACTION** from the drop-down list for the extension type, and browse to locate the XML file, as shown in the following screenshot:

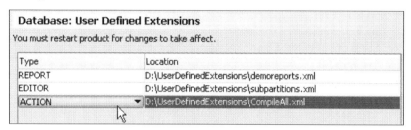

In this case, the code adds an extra menu item in the **Connections** context menu.

When adding context menus in the **Connections** navigator, you can add individual menus, or a menu with a number of submenus. There are many such menus in SQL Developer, such as the **Column** context menu with its set of submenus. To include a collection of context menus for one node, add all the pieces of XML code into the same file.

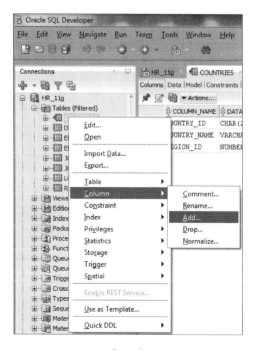

Adding new nodes to the Connections navigator

The last of the XML user-defined extension types available in SQL Developer is the **Navigator**. The name is a little misleading because the "**Navigator**" user-defined type allows you to add a new node into the list of currently available nodes in the **Connections** navigator. Currently, these nodes are predominantly made up of Data Dictionary object types such as **Table**, **View**, and **Index**. The list includes the **Application Express** node that allows you to browse the detail of your Oracle Application Express applications. In this case, you are browsing the metadata that defines the application.

You can add nodes for database objects that are not yet supported in the navigator, such as tablespaces, or you can add new nodes to browse external application metadata stored in database repositories. For example, you can create an Oracle **Designer** node to query the Oracle Designer Workareas. Alternatively, you can add a node to query instance data in applications.

Including user-defined extensions for a navigator node

Adding extra nodes to the **Connections** navigator is a little more involved than for the preceding examples. You still create a single file, and in the same way as you have done for each of the previous examples, once you have created the file, save it to the file or web server location and open the **User Defined Extensions** preference. Click on **Add Row**, and in this instance, you should select **NAVIGATOR** from the drop list for the extension type and browse to locate the XML file.

To investigate this example, we'll break up the file and code into sections and then build it up in phases. You can start by creating the skeleton, adding it into SQL Developer and restarting the product. Then, you only need to refresh the navigator by restarting SQL Developer after any additional changes to the XML file.

Updating the navigator extension

You will not be able to save changes to the XML file while SQL Developer is still open. Include the XML skeleton and then close and reopen SQL Developer. Close SQL Developer each time you want to update and save the XML.

In the following screenshot, a number of additional nodes have been added. The new nodes are added above the shipped nodes, which are sorted by typical usage priority:

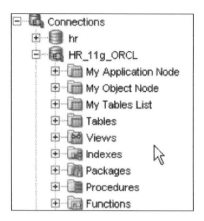

Adding a new tree to the navigator

The structure that you generally want to replicate in the tree is a top-level node (for example, **Tables**), and after that, you want to display the list of tables. Next, we have the columns that are associated with each of those tables. Using this example, we have the following structure:

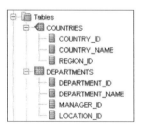

Extrapolating from the previous structure, which you know, call the **Tables** node Level 1, the actual table listing Level 2, and the columns Level 3:

- `Tables`: This would be Level 1
- `COUNTRIES`: This would be Level 2
- `COUNTRY_ID`: This would be Level 3
- `COUNTRY_NAME`: This would be Level 3

Once again, there is an XSD file to assist with the development of the XML file structure.

 The structure of the navigator node conforms to an XSD called `navigator.xsd`. The `navigator.xsd` also calls the `query.xsd`.

To add a new top-level folder, consider the following code:

```
<?xml version="1.0" encoding="windows-1252" ?>
<navigator RESOURCE_FILE="oracle.dbtools.raptor.navigator.
OracleNavigatorResource"
  xmlns:xsi="http://www.w3.org/2001/XMLSchema-instance"
  xsi:noNamespaceSchemaLocation="navigator.xsd">
  <objectType connType="Oracle" id="MyApplication"
    weight="50.0" includesSyns="true">
    <folder> <!-- level1 -->
      <icon RSKEY="TABLE_FOLDER_ICON" />
      <label RSKEY="My Application Node" />
      <queries> <!-- level2 -->
           <query minversion="8">
        <sql constrained="true"><![CDATA[]]></sql>
        </query>
      </queries>
    </folder>
  </objectType>
</navigator>
```

The only piece you are really interested in changing is the label, which is the name of the new **Connections** navigator node that you are creating. The other value that you can change when creating your own copy of this file is the `id`. It is a good idea to keep this `id` as descriptive as you can.

There is currently no query listed in the **CDATA** section. Therefore, if you add this code and open SQL Developer, you'll only get the new node; there is no tree of objects below the node, and so, no detail of any interest at this stage. To list the elements under that first node, you need an initial query. The example we use here is trivial (to illustrate the concept) and does not take into account other objects that you might want listed, or even any privileges.

In addition to including a SQL query to populate the list, you also need to add a `<columns>` section. This references the columns in the query. Notice that the following query includes an alias, which is referenced in the `<columns>` section. The following code listing is just that portion of the full file that lies between the `<queries>`...`</queries>` tags in the previous section of code:

```
<queries> <!-- level2 -->
  <query minversion="8">
   <sql constrained="true">
   <![CDATA[SELECT TABLE_NAME NAME FROM TABS]]></sql>
  </query>
  <columns>
    <column filterable="true" sortable="true" id="NAME">
      <colName><![CDATA[name]]></colName>
    </column>
   </columns>
 </queries>
```

Once again, you have an `id` field; in this case, `id="NAME"`. It is a good idea to keep these `id` values meaningful, as they can be used as bind variables for future sub-nodes or to link to the display editors.

To finish off that node, you still need to add the icon detail. Add this detail to the file below the `</folder>` tag, as shown next:

```
<node> <!-- level2 details -->
  <icon RSKEY="OracleIcons.TABLE" />
</node>
```

In this example, we are referencing the icons shipped as part of SQL Developer. The icons are available in the `\sqldeveloper\sqldeveloper\extensions` folder, in the `oracle.sqldeveloper.jar` file. If you browse this file, you can see the images are in the folder structure, `/oracle/dbtools/raptor/images/`, which you can reference as follows:

```
<icon RSKEY=" /oracle/dbtools/raptor/images/snippets.png" />
```

Instead of using the shipped SQL Developer icons, you can create your own set in a JAR file, and add these as a Java extension.

The output of what we have achieved until now is shown next. Notice that there is a list of tables based on that SQL query, but we don't have any columns, which would complete this node in the navigator:

To complete the node, you need to add the third-level query. The structure here is as before, using the same queries and columns tags as shown here:

```
<queries>
  <query>
    <sql> </sql>
  </query>
  <columns>
  </columns>
</queries>
```

This third level is included in the second level's `<node>` details, with the extra code shown as follows:

```
<node> <!-- level2 details -->
  <icon RSKEY="OracleIcons.TABLE" />
  <childType id="Level3"> <!-- Level3 -->
  <icon RSKEY="OracleIcons.COLUMN" />
  <queries>
     <query>
      <sql> SELECT COLUMN_NAME FROM USER_TAB_COLUMNS
            WHERE TABLE_NAME = :PARENT_NAME
      </sql>
     </query>
    <columns>
      <column filterable="true" sortable="true" id="NAME">
      <colName><![CDATA[column_name]]></colName>
      </column>
    </columns>
     </queries>
  </childType>
</node>
```

Notice how this SQL now includes the bind variable to ensure that you only get the required detail records. In this case, we have not used an alias in the query, so we need to ensure that the full column name is referenced in the `<column>` section.

The addition to this `<node>` detail results in the output shown in the following screenshot:

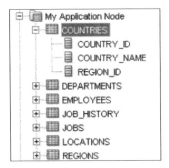

You have now reached the point where you can return to the start of this chapter and add all of the display editors and context menus for each of the nodes as required.

Working with extensions

Whether you create your own extensions or use SQL Developer out of the box, you are taking advantage of the product's extensibility when you use the features. In this section, we'll consider the additional external extensions that are available, and how you can work with them.

Controlling existing extensions

You can add or remove Java extensions using the **Extensions** preferences. Oracle TimesTen, Migrations, and the version control support are all extensions designed and shipped with the product. You can see these extensions listed in the **Extensions** node.

Adding in new Java extensions

You can add new Java extensions using the **Check for Updates** facility. There are a number of options, which are listed next:

- Check for Updates—**Use the Update Center**
- Check for Updates—**Install from Local File**

In the first instance, developers outside of Oracle who have created a Java extension can approach Oracle to have these included in the **Check for Updates** facility. If you want to use these extensions, then invoke the wizard, select **Search Update Centers**, and include the **Third Party SQL Developer Extensions**. The third party database drivers are also included in this selection.

If you have a Java extension internally, you can also add a link to your own update center by selecting **Add** and then providing the URL of the location of your file.

Using the **Check for Updates** wizard, you can install Java extensions that you or someone else has developed and provided you with the file. For example, your own icon image bundle. Here, select **Install From Local File** and browse to locate the zipped bundle.

All of your additional Java extensions are listed together with the shipped extensions in **Preferences | Extensions**. In the following screenshot, the JTDS JDBC driver is one that was added using the **Check for Updates** facility:

Removing extensions

It doesn't matter whether these are shipped extensions or ones that you have added using **Check for Updates**, you can remove any of them by deselecting the extension in the list and restarting SQL Developer.

Delete the link to the XML file to remove any of the XML extensions that you created, and include in the **User Defined Extensions** preference.

If you are adding or removing extensions, whether Java or XML, you need to restart SQL Developer for the changes to take effect.

Sharing extensions

The real advantage of the extensible environment is that you only need a few members in the team to create the extensions, whether they are Java or XML, and then share these within the group. To share extensions, you can store them on a shared file server or on a hosted web server. In either case, any changes made to the XML files will be reflected in your product the next time you start it.

Summary

In this chapter, we reviewed the ability to extend SQL Developer by adding XML-structured, user-defined extensions. The structure of SQL Developer means that you can also take advantage of any Java-developed extensions available. User-defined extensions give you the flexibility of adding small or larger utilities to augment the tool's capabilities. Sharing extensions within a team means that you can use the new functionality without having to define it yourself.

In the next chapter, we'll take a look at the integration of SQL Developer and Oracle Application Express. This is an example of another team within Oracle taking advantage of the extensibility and creating a new node in the Connections navigator, much as we have discussed in this chapter.

11
Working with Application Express

SQL Developer provides an access point to Oracle Application Express for browsing, monitoring, and managing your applications. Using SQL Developer, you can browse and review application data in the same way that you browse and review any other schema data using the **Connections** navigator. SQL Developer also provides administrative utilities, such as being able to rename or deploy applications. Also, using the PL/SQL coding and SQL tuning capabilities, you can test and tune pieces of code to enhance the performance of the application. In this chapter, we will show you how to connect to Application Express, browse your applications, review some of the administration utilities, and use the SQL Worksheet to refactor PL/SQL code.

Setting the scene

To derive any benefit from this chapter, you need to have an Application Express environment set up. If you are already a regular user of Application Express, you can follow these examples using your own applications. In this case, you can skip the section on *Setting up in Application Express*, which is about creating a workspace and schema for the examples that follow. Alternatively, you can follow the preparation setup steps provided next to create an example that you can delete later.

If you are new to Application Express, you can still take advantage of the combination of the two tools and the details in this chapter. Before you start, it is recommended that you visit the *Getting Started* section on `http://apex.oracle.com`

(`http://www.oracle.com/technetwork/developer-tools/apex/overview/index.html`). The site provides a number of useful links to help you get Application Express set up and to familiarize yourself with the environment.

To understand the examples we use in this chapter, you need access to the following:

- Create a new workspace and schema in Application Express. This action also creates the default sample application we refer to. The database schema created is the one that we connect to using SQL Developer.

- Create an Application Express user. This is the user that we use to connect to Application Express to edit and update the sample applications.

- Import and use one of the packaged applications available for download from the Application Express site, `http://apex.oracle.com/i/index.html`, or from the Oracle Technology Network.

The details on how to do this is provided in the next section.

Setting up Application Express

For most of this chapter, we'll work in SQL Developer. There are sections that require you to work in Application Express, such as this first one, where you set up your Application Express environment.

Creating a workspace and database schema

Invoke Application Express using the administrator login and select **Manage Workspaces**. You can either invoke the **Manage Workspaces** page and select **Create Workspace** or access the **Create Workspace** pages from the front panel, as shown in the following screenshot:

The wizard guides you through the steps of creating the workspace and schema. Creating a new workspace also creates the default sample application for the schema associated with the workspace. It is this schema and application that we will use in the examples that follow.

In the example shown in the previous screenshot, we created a workspace called SampleWorkspace and a new database schema called SAMPLE.

Creating an Application Express user

You can, at this point, use SQL Developer to connect to the database schema and view the details of the sample application created. However, later in the chapter, we'll return to Application Express to edit an application, and for that you'll also need an Application Express user who can access the workspace, modify, and run the application.

To create an Application Express user and associate it with one or more workspaces, use the **Manage Developers** and **Users** page, accessed from the main **Manage Workspaces** page, as shown in the following screenshot:

Click on the **Create** button to invoke the **Create/Edit User** screen and add your new user details to this. In the next screenshot, we show the part of the page with the initial details populated. Use this user to connect to Application Express and edit the applications in the workspace.

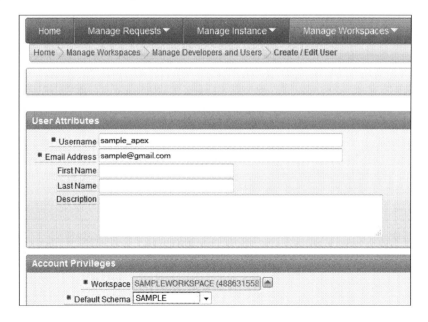

Browsing applications in SQL Developer

The rest of the chapter is about working with, and accessing applications from within, SQL Developer. So, unless otherwise directed, assume that the instructions refer to working in SQL Developer. The section starts with creating a connection and browsing applications.

Creating a connection in SQL Developer

To view both the schema objects and the applications owned by the schema, create a new database connection in SQL Developer for the Application Express schema, as shown in the following screenshot:

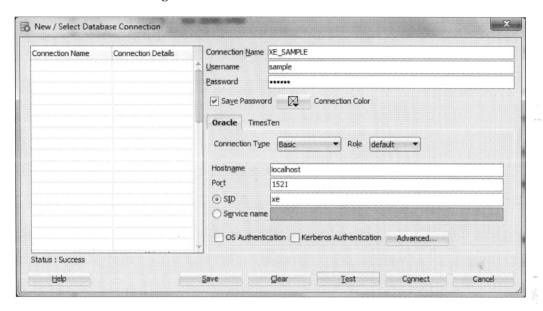

Browsing and working with schema objects

In addition to viewing the applications, you can use SQL Developer's **Connections** navigator to review schema objects such as tables, views, and indexes, in the same way as you have browsed, created, and updated any other database schema objects. Application Express provides an SQL **Workshop** (similar to SQL Developer's SQL **Worksheet**) to create, edit, and update database objects. You may prefer to use SQL Developer for these activities when working with Application Express.

The next screenshot shows the tables used in the sample application. SQL Developer provides easy access to browse and query these tables and the data they hold.

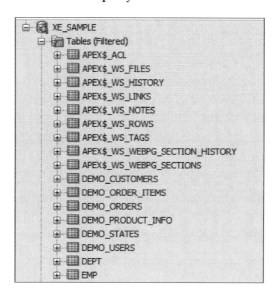

Browsing the applications

Expand the **Application Express** node in the **Connections** navigator and select the **Sample Application**. As you select the application, a selection of display editor tabs reveals the application details, including pages, LOVs, and items. This top-level set of display editors includes the scripts to install, reinstall, and upgrade your applications. The following screenshot shows an example of the SQL script for an application called **Sample Application (101)**:

There is also an SQL display editor, just as there is for other objects in the **Connections** navigator. In this case, it contains the full SQL script of the application.

Using SQL Developer, you can not only review the details of your application quickly and easily by clicking through the display editor tabs, but also compare these details across applications, as shown in the next screenshot. When comparing, you can do the following:

- Select the detail you want to focus on, such as the **Pages** or **Tabs** display editors, and then click down through the list of applications in the **Connections** navigator, taking a look at the details of each as you go.

- Use the **Freeze View** pin to freeze one application and then open the next. By tiling the applications, you can compare values across applications.

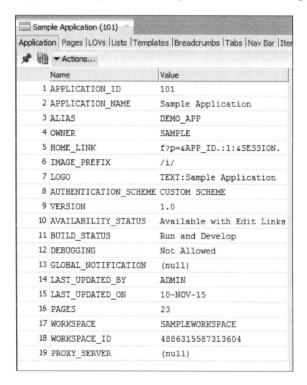

Drilling down into lists of values

Some of the display editor tabs have a set of detail records for each of the master records returned. The **list of values** (**LOV**) display editor is one of these. You'll notice that each **LOV_TYPE** is either **Static** or **Dynamic**. The detail records for these are displayed in either a **Query** or **Static Values** report. In the following example, the **CATEGORIES** list of values in the sample application is selected, and the list of static values is displayed in the **Static Values** report:

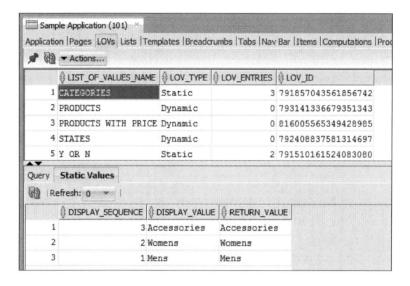

You can't use SQL Developer to update these values, but you can use it to quickly review and decide if there are incorrect or missing values, and then use Application Express to update the values.

Focusing on pages

Each of the pages displayed in the **Pages** display editor is also listed in the **Connections** navigator under the application node. Each page has its own set of display editors describing the page and providing detail on aspects of the page, including items, regions, and buttons.

If you select each page in the **Connections** navigator in turn and review the resulting page detail, you'll see that there are high-level page summary changes, detailing the number of buttons, items, and regions defined for each page. To get more details about each of these objects, select the appropriate display editor. In the following screenshot, the **Buttons** display editor shows the details for the buttons on the **Customer Details** page:

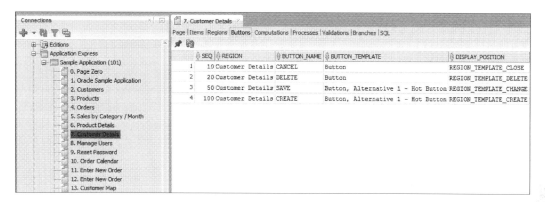

Mapping objects from SQL Developer to Application Express

While reviewing your application in SQL Developer, you may want to make modifications to some of the objects in Application Express. Consider again the example shown in the screenshot above, where a list of buttons is displayed. You can also look back at the previous example, where a set of LOV static values was shown. Each of these is an object defined in Application Express, and you need to know where to find each object in order to update it. Invoke your Application Express environment and edit the **Customer** Details page.

Notice that each grouping on the Application Express page has a matching area in SQL Developer:

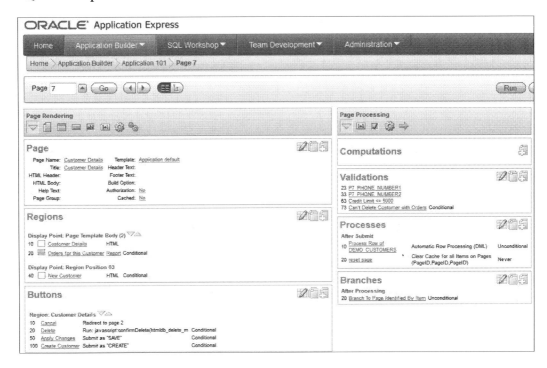

Use Application Express to update any objects in the application and then refresh the view in SQL Developer.

Tuning SQL and PL/SQL code using SQL Developer

Not only can you use SQL Developer to review the details about the objects you create in Application Express, you can also use it to see the source code. Consider the **Regions** display editor for Page 1, **1. Oracle Sample Application**, as shown in the following screenshot:

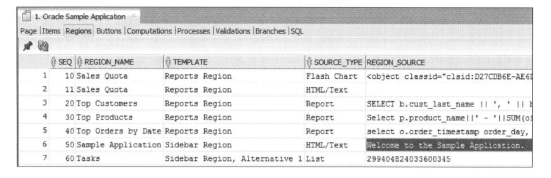

The regions on this page are derived from different source types. For example, the **Sample Application** region has a **Source Type** of HTML/Text. You can copy and paste this into a text editor, or even an HTML editor, and refine the text before pasting it back into the application using Application Express. It becomes more interesting when this region source is SQL or PL/SQL, because you can use SQL Developer to review, test, and even tune the code.

Working with Region Source SQL

You can select and copy the SQL code into the SQL Worksheet and then tune it as you would any other piece of SQL code. Using the same Page 1, **1. Oracle Sample Application** in the example in the previous screenshot, select the **Region Source** for the region, **My Top Orders**. This is a SQL query. To select the code, click to highlight the value. *Ctrl+C* copies the code, and you can then paste it using *Ctrl+V* into the SQL Worksheet. Alternatively, double-click on the field to expose the edit button, which when clicked invokes a new window displaying the full text. Now, you can use *Ctrl+A* to select the text and *Ctrl+C* to copy it. Cancel the window and then use *Ctrl+V* to paste the code into the SQL Worksheet. You need to remove the word, CLOB, which precedes the text.

Once you have completed the copy and paste, you'll have the SQL in the SQL Worksheet, and you can run it just as you would any other SQL. Often, the Application Express SQL includes bind variables, as this example does. In this case, use the **Run Statement** (*F9*) to be prompted for the bind values.

Tuning with Explain Plan

Once you have the SQL code in the SQL Worksheet, you can execute the **Explain Plan** (*F6*) to review the code. The following screenshot displays the code and plan details:

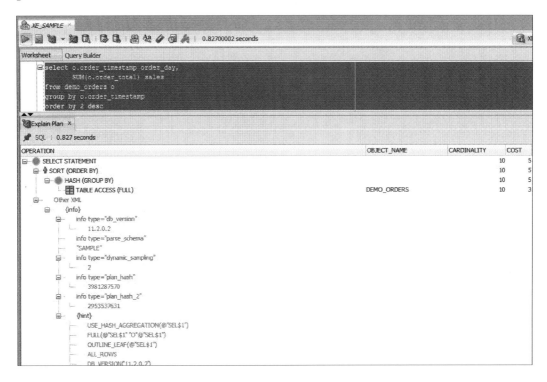

It is beyond the scope of this book to delve into tuning code using the results. However, SQL Developer does provide an extensive list of **Optimizer Hints** in the **Snippets** dialog, which you can drag into the query. Once you have added the **Optimizer Hints**, you can re-run the plan and compare the differences. Adding in **Optimizer Hints** is not a solution for tuning SQL, and it is recommended that you read some of the documentation on tuning and writing queries that is available online. If you have updated the SQL query, you need to return to Application Express and edit and replace the query.

Working with PL/SQL code

While the SQL queries in Application Express applications may be straightforward, developers sometimes create anonymous blocks when adding PL/SQL code. Certainly, tuning SQL is important to an application, but reducing the calls to anonymous blocks in any application is also very important. Anonymous blocks are compiled at runtime, thus placing unnecessary overhead on the application. If you can identify and replace anonymous blocks with compiled procedures, you can significantly improve the performance of an application since the application calls compiled code.

Consider Page 12, **12. Enter New Order**. To work with the PL/SQL code, first edit, select, and then copy the PL/SQL block to the SQL Worksheet, as previously described for the SQL query. The PL/SQL code that is now pasted on the SQL Worksheet is shown in the following screenshot:

```
declare
    l_customer_id varchar2(30) := :P11_CUSTOMER_ID;
begin


    -- display customer information

    if :P11_CUSTOMER_OPTIONS = 'NEW' then
        l_customer_id := :P18_CUSTOMER_ID;
    end if;
for x in (select * from demo_customers where customer_id = l_customer_id)
    loop
    htp.p('<div class="demoCustomerInfo">');
    htp.p('<strong>Customer:</strong>');
    htp.p('<p>');
    htp.p(htf.escape_sc(x.cust_first_name) || ' ' || htf.escape_sc(x.cust_last_name) || '<br />');
    htp.p(sys.htf.escape_sc(x.cust_street_address1) || '<br />');
    if x.cust_street_address2 is not null then
        sys.htp.p(sys.htf.escape_sc(x.cust_street_address2) || '<br />');
```

This is an anonymous block. SQL Developer provides the facility to refactor to PL/SQL code and extract a procedure. To create a PL/SQL procedure from the anonymous block, select the full PL/SQL text, and use the context menu to invoke the **Refactoring** menu. Click on **Extract Procedure...** to invoke the **New Procedure** dialog. You need to provide a name and ensure that the procedure is stored as shown in the following example:

You can edit the code in the **Confirm Running** SQL dialog. Some anonymous blocks expect a bind variable, and so when you refactor the code and extract a procedure, you'll need to take this into account. We prefer to review the code in the PL/SQL **Code Editor**. To do this, accept the default code. This is now available for later review.

Once you have refactored the code, you can browse this code in the **Connections** navigator. To see the new procedures, expand the **Procedures** node, and using the previous example, reveal the new stored procedure, named PlaceOrder. Notice that the Application Express bind variable has been replaced by a declared variable and that the refactored code includes the required input parameter, as shown in the following screenshot:

```
create or replace procedure PlaceOrder(p_P11_CUSTOMER_ID IN NUMBER
    ,p_P11_CUSTOMER_OPTIONS IN VARCHAR2
    ,p_P18_CUSTOMER_ID IN varchar2
    ,p_app_session IN VARCHAR2
    ) as
    l_customer_id varchar2(30) := p_P11_CUSTOMER_ID;
begin

if p_P11_CUSTOMER_OPTIONS = 'NEW' then
  l_customer_id := p_P18_CUSTOMER_ID;
end if;
```

Replacing the anonymous block in Application Express

Once you have refactored the code in SQL Developer, you can replace the anonymous block in the Application Express environment. Return to Application Express using the Application Express user created earlier and edit **Page 11**. The following example shows the Regions area in Application Express, with the Order Header PL/SQL region selected:

Replace the region source with placeorder (:P14_ORDER_ID) and select **Apply Changes**. To verify that the code has been correctly handled, run the application and place a new order for an existing customer. If you have replaced the code correctly, there will be no errors when you add the order.

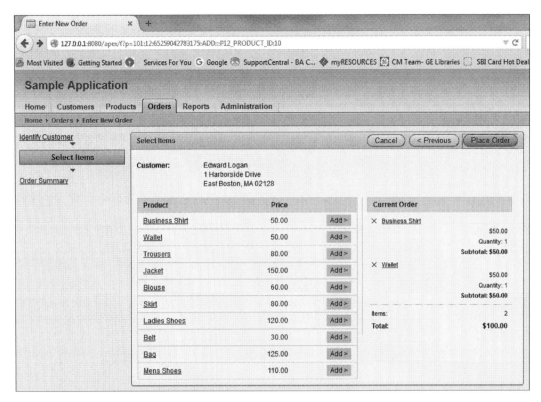

In SQL Developer, if you review the updates, you'll see that the anonymous PL/SQL block is now replaced with a call to a compiled procedure.

Improving performance of Application Express applications

Use SQL Developer to refactor any anonymous PL/SQL blocks and replace these with calls to compiled procedures.

To learn more about compiling and debugging PL/SQL, refer to *Chapter 2, Working with PL/SQL*, the chapter focusing on those topics.

Managing applications in SQL Developer

SQL Developer also provides the abilities needed to manage applications by offering a variety of administrative utilities. In this next section, we look at importing, modifying, and deploying applications.

Importing applications

The Application Express home page, `http://apex.oracle.com`, has a link to a long list of packaged applications. These are ready-built and functional applications that you can download, import, run, review, and also edit. They are useful as starter applications, and they also provide examples of code and techniques.

To learn more about importing applications, download and unzip one of the packaged applications, or you can follow the steps by importing one of your own applications. To import a new application, select the Application Express node in the **Connections** navigator and click on **Import Application** using the context menu. You need to select an SQL install script to import. Once you have the file, you can set the import options as shown in the following screenshot:

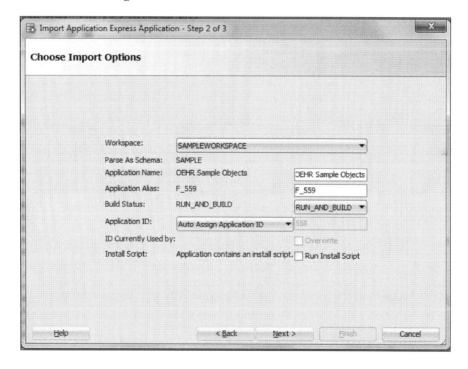

You can select the workspace that this application is imported into. You can also change the following:

- The name and alias of the application.
- The application ID. Although this is automatically assigned by default, you can control it.

Be sure to select the **Run Install Script** checkbox to install the application in your chosen workspace.

Modifying applications

You can change the name and alias of an application using the **Modify Application** context menu.

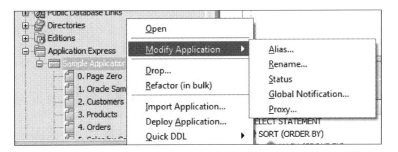

In addition, this menu offers additional options, such as being able to send out a global notification. The **Modify Application** menu is displayed in the previous screenshot with the **Global Notification...** option selected. Once selected, you should supply the message that you want to send to the users.

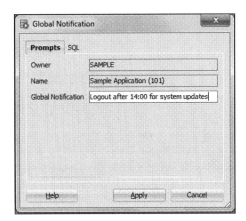

When created, a global notification appears on all the pages of an application and is visible to all of the users who start up or access the application, as shown next for the sample application:

You can also set the status of the application, which is useful when you need to carry out maintenance on the application and have a few users accessing the application simultaneously. The choice of status options are as follows:

- Available
- Available_w_edit_link
- Developers only
- Not available

Deploying applications

This facility allows you to deploy a completed application to another schema from outside of Application Express. This is useful when you are working on an application in a "sandbox" environment and you want to move it, say, to test or production schemas. When deploying an application to another schema, this new schema must have access to a workspace in Application Express.

Controlling services

SQL Developer offers users the ability to start and stop the embedded PL/SQL gateway for Application Express (which is shown in the following screenshot). You may not have access to do this in a large shared environment, but it can be useful in a test setup.

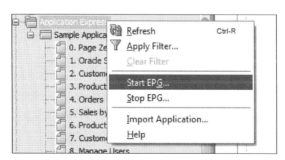

Starting and stopping the embedded PL/SQL gateway

Start and stop the embedded PL/SQL gateway from within SQL Developer. Select the Application Express node in the **Connections** navigator and select **Start EPG** or **Stop EPG**.

Reporting on applications using SQL Developer

SQL Developer includes a set of Application Express shipped reports. You can find these under the **Data Dictionary Reports**. Most of these reports, such as the **Applications** and **Pages** reports, provide the same detail that is available in the **Connections** navigator as described earlier, using a slightly different layout.

The reports also include a Workspace report, which is a Master/Detail report on the different aspects of a workspace. This report provides details on the different applications in the various workspaces that a schema has access to and also on the applications in each respective workspace. The details shown in the following screenshot reveal that this schema has access to a number of workspaces and that the packaged application workspace includes a number of applications:

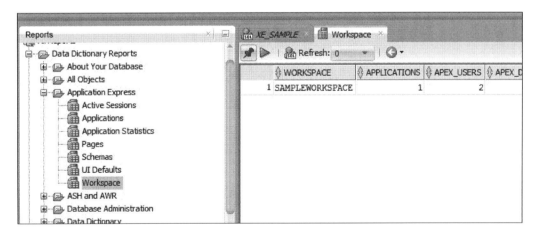

Summary

In this chapter, we reviewed the many aspects of using SQL Developer and Application Express together to provide a strengthened working environment. By supporting Oracle Application Express, SQL Developer offers additional support to an Application Express developer who is working with, and managing, a large number of applications or who writes a lot of extra SQL and PL/SQL code to support the applications.

The next and final chapter is about working with non-Oracle databases and migrating database objects and data to Oracle. We'll show the tight integration of SQL Developer and the migration features available when working with and browsing non-Oracle databases and then using the migration utilities.

12
Working with SQL Developer Migrations

Oracle SQL Developer Migrations is an integrated feature of Oracle SQL Developer that's used to migrate from some of the popular non-Oracle databases to Oracle. It provides users with a basic migration wizard (for small, less complex migrations) and an interactive migration alternative, where the stages of the migration are separated, allowing users to make changes to the objects and code at each stage. SQL Developer Migrations supports the migration of most database objects depending on the database in question (including procedures, functions, and the data in the tables) to Oracle. In this chapter, we'll look at preparing the SQL Developer environment, preparing the required Oracle database repository, and the steps involved in the migration process. Refer to `http://apex.oracle.com` for more information.

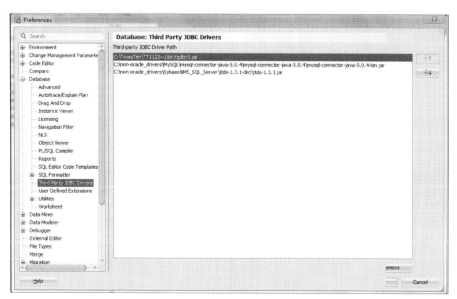

Migrating a database requires careful planning and preparation. In this chapter, we'll review the tool support for a migration, while not discussing the additional work required when planning and preparing for a migration. We will not list the reasons for migrating from one database to another or the advantages of one database over another. We'll make the assumption that these decisions have been made.

Introducing SQL Developer Migrations

Oracle SQL Developer's Migrations feature supports the conversion of tables, views, triggers, stored procedures, and other objects from non-Oracle (third-party) databases to Oracle database equivalents. Once the objects are converted to Oracle, the data can be copied from the source to the target database. The extent of what is converted depends on the third-party database in question. For example, not all migrations support the migration of procedures and functions.

An overview of the migration process

SQL Developer offers users a choice when converting from a third-party database to Oracle by offering the following alternatives:

- A quick migration wizard
- Interactive migration

For both approaches, SQL Developer Migrations provides a phased approach to migrate from a third-party database to Oracle. Initially, the tool queries the source database, and the captured metadata is written to an Oracle repository. The next phase is the conversion of objects to Oracle metadata. Once converted, the Oracle metadata is used to generate the DDL for execution in the target database. The final phase is to copy the data from the source database to the target database.

If you use the migration wizard, the entire process flows from the beginning to completion with no chance to make adjustments before completion. This is typically used for smaller, less complex migrations. If you use the interactive approach, you can make adjustments (such as deleting or updating objects) after each phase is complete. We'll look at the details of these phases later in the chapter.

Offline or online migration choices

The quick migration wizard requires a direct connection to the database being migrated, while interactive migration allows you to make a direct connection to the source database or migrate from files. There may be a multitude of reasons for not wanting to directly access the database, and so, using files as a source can be very useful. Using files as a source can have the following results:

- You have a point in time when files are created. If the source database is still actively in use, you know the point in time that the objects are migrated.

- You don't need to grant additional database access to the source database to users working on the migration.

Interactive migration follows the same approach for a direct or offline migration, with the exception of how you start off the migration and load the data at the end.

Supported third-party databases

SQL Developer Migrations supports browsing and migrating from the following databases:

- IBM DB2 LUW: 7, 8, and 9
- Microsoft Access: 97, 2000, 2002, 2003, and 2007
- Microsoft SQL Server: 7, 2000, and 2005
- MySQL: 3, 4, and 5
- Sybase Adaptive Server: 12 and 15
- Teradata: 12

Setting up your environment

There are a few one-off setup steps that you need to complete before you can use Oracle SQL Developer to browse or migrate from other databases. Before you can create a connection to a database such as MySQL, you need to set up the required database driver for the database. Once you have the drivers installed, you can create the database connections as you do for an Oracle connection. If you plan to migrate to Oracle, you'll also need to set up a migrations repository. In this section, we'll review the options available for the setting up of the additional database drivers, creating the database connections, and managing the migration repository.

Setting up JDBC drivers

Due to additional licensing requirements, Oracle SQL Developer does not ship the JDBC drivers required to connect to IBM DB2, Microsoft SQL Server, MySQL, Sybase, and Teradata. To connect to any of these databases, whether for browsing or migration purposes, you need to download additional drivers and set up SQL Developer in order to access the drivers. This setup is not required for Microsoft Access as it uses the JDBC/ODBC bridge. For a detailed explanation on downloading and setting up the required third-party drivers, refer to *Chapter 8, Database Connections and JDBC Drivers*.

Every downloaded driver will have a driver binary JAR file to a location on your machine. The driver binary JAR file is typically a separate JAR file located inside the downloaded archive file. The extracted JAR file should be used to import the extension into our SQL Developer environment:

1. In SQL Developer, navigate to **Tools | Preferences...**.
2. Expand the **Database** option in the tree on the left-hand side.
3. Click on **Third Party JDBC Drivers**.
4. Click on **Add Entry...**.
5. Navigate to your third-party driver JAR file and choose **OK**.
6. Use **Check For Updates** to configure JDBC drivers.

Once you have set up the drivers, the connection dialog changes to include the additional tabs for the database drivers that you have added, as shown in the following screenshot:

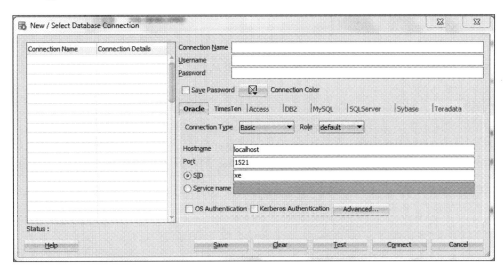

Creating third-party connections

You are now ready to create connections. Each of the connection tabs requires slightly different details. For example, in SQL Server, once you have entered **Hostname** and **Port**, click on **Retrieve database** to connect to and access the list of available databases:

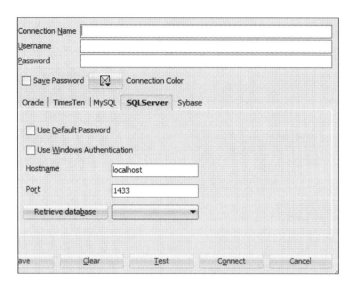

By contrast, the Microsoft Access connection requires only the MDB file access. Setting up connections for supported third-party databases is discussed in *Chapter 8, Database Connections and JDBC Drivers*.

For each database, create the connection, save the password (optional), and test the connection. The **Save** and **Connect** buttons save the created connection, while **Connect** closes the dialog and makes the connection.

Accessing non-Oracle databases

You can browse any of the non-Oracle databases in the same way that you can browse any Oracle database connection. The features that are available differ depending on the database you connect to. You can browse the objects and their details and review the data. The context menus for these objects are migration-specific and do not support any DDL.

Browsing database objects

In the preceding example, we created a database connection to Microsoft SQL Server, as shown in the previous screenshot, using the Microsoft SQL Server database.

Select and expand the database connection. Expand the **Tables** node and select a table in the list. The details for **Columns**, **Keys** (for **Primary** and **Foreign** keys), **Indexes**, **Constraints**, and **Triggers** are all displayed. There is also a data display editor that's used to browse the instance data:

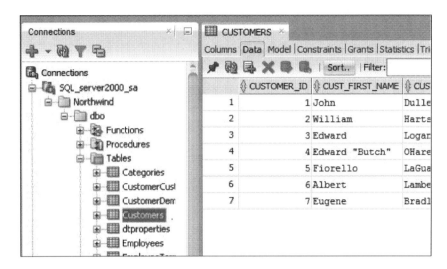

This level of detail differs for each database type. For example, when connecting to MySQL, the set of display editors includes the column, index information, and constraints. All third-party connections display data in tables, and some support the ability to export data to various formats. The main difference between non-Oracle database connections and Oracle connections is that non-Oracle connections are read-only views of the database objects and data, while Oracle connections provide context menus to execute DDL and DML.

Managing the repository

SQL Developer Migrations uses a database repository to collect, store, and transform the metadata during the migration process. The repository is used only during the migration process, which can be discarded once complete.

Setting up the repository owner:

Using either the SQL worksheet or the **Create User...** context menu for other users, create a new Oracle database user with role and system privileges, which include the following privileges:

- Resources
- Creating a session
- Creating a view

Once you have the new user set up, create a new database connection for that user.

Creating the repository

By navigating to **Tools** | **Migration**, you can manage all aspects of your repository, including creating, truncating, and deleting. Initially, select **Create Repository...**:

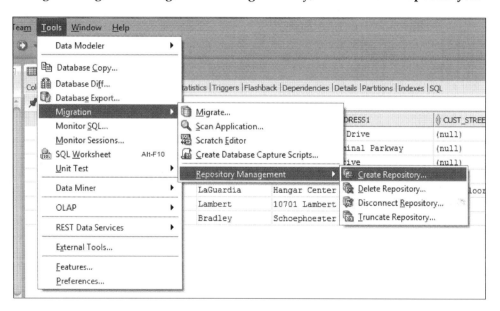

This builds an Oracle database repository with the following components:

- 37 tables with required primary keys, indexes, and triggers
- Nine views
- Four packages

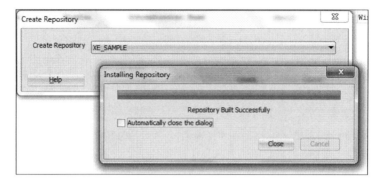

Creating the repository is not a long process, with the progress tracked in a pop-up dialog that displays the current activity.

Associating a repository with a user

At any stage, in order to connect to a previously created repository, select **Associate Migration Repository** from the context menu. This **Associate Migration Repository** menu option performs a number of activities:

- Associating the user with an existing repository set up for that user
- Updating a repository created in an earlier release of SQL Developer
- Creating a new repository for the user if one does not exist yet

If you have a number of migration repositories, you can select and set the current repository using **Select Current Repository…**.

As soon as you have a user connected or associated with the repository, two new windows open. These windows are as follows:

- Captured models
- Converted models

If the windows do not open, you can open them manually from the **View** menu. These windows will display a list of the captured or converted models you have previously worked with unless you delete or truncate the repository between migrations.

Planning database connections

Before you start the migration, you should set up two additional database connections: one for the source database and another for the target database. These connections are no different from the connections you have created previously, but you should give some thought to the database schemas you are going to use.

Setting up the source database connection

The database you are migrating from is known as the source database. You need to create a connection to this database. SQL Developer Migrations uses **Least Privilege Migration**. This means that any user can migrate database objects and data to an Oracle database. However, the migration only reads and migrates those objects that you have access to depending on your privilege level.

Create a database connection, as described in *Chapter 8, Database Connections and JDBC Drivers*, using a schema that owns the objects you want to migrate.

Setting up the target database connection

When migrating to Oracle, you need to create a database connection to a schema that will hold the new database objects. This can be an existing or new schema. If you use an existing schema, you should ensure that no conflicts will arise due to the objects already in the schema. If you create a new schema, you need to ensure that the schema has the following privileges:

- Resources
- Creating a session
- Creating a view

Moreover, if you're performing a multischema migration, this is the main Oracle schema that is used to create the additional target schemas, and so it needs the following additional privileges:

- Creating a user
- Altering any trigger

 We recommend that you set up source and target database connections before you start the migration.

Migrating

Now you're almost ready to start the migration. The last step is to decide on the approach you'll use for the migration. For a quick review or prototype or when migrating a small, straightforward database, the **Quick Migrate** option is ideal. Alternatively, you can use a more interactive approach and step through each phase of the migration. We'll review both approaches in the next section.

Using Quick Migrate

Quick Migrate is a wizard-driven dialog that follows seven steps:

1. You can start **Quick Migrate** from two areas: either by navigating to **Tools | Migration** or from the context menu of the source database connection you are planning to migrate (as shown in the following screenshot). Either action invokes the same **Quick Migrate** dialog. If you start the wizard from the context menu of the source database connection, the first page of the wizard will already be populated with the source database connection.

2. The next step is to select **Target Connection**. As you can see in the following screenshot, this step reminds you about the required privileges and offers you the opportunity to set up a new target Oracle database connection if you do not have a created one already:

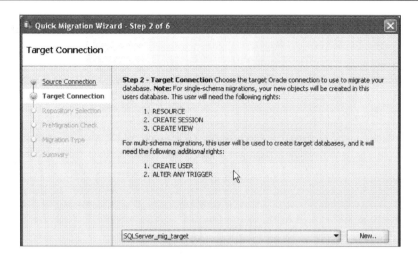

3. Create source and target connections before starting.

> If you start **Quick Migrate** without having connections to the source database or the schema in the target database, you can create these new connections from within the dialog. We recommend that you set up all of the connections you'll need before starting the process.

4. Select the repository you plan to use during the migration. If you have only one repository, it will be in the drop-down list. If you have more than one repository, then the repository that you last associated your repository user with will appear here first. At this stage, if you have no repository, the dialog is a little different, looking more like the screenshot shown in step 2. You have the option of creating a repository here. This repository is created at the start of the migration, and you can have it removed on completion.

5. This is the premigration step, and it gives you the opportunity to check whether all of the required privileges and connections are valid. If you are not working on a multischema migration and have not assigned additional privileges, you get a privilege warning, as shown in the following screenshot. This does not affect a single user migration.

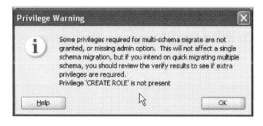

The result of the checks should be a success status for all but the multischema privilege test, which fails for single schema settings, which is okay:

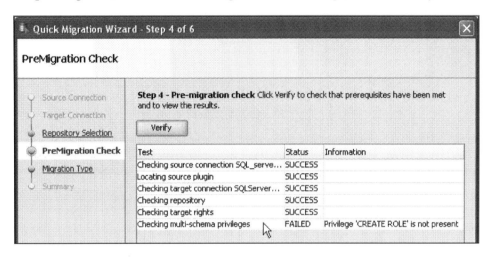

6. In step 6, you can select the type of migration, as follows:

    ° Migrating tables only

    ° Migrating tables and data

    ° Migrating everything

    These are self-explanatory, except the last option possibly, where *everything* includes the additional structures in the schema, including the procedural code, which is translated to PL/SQL in Oracle.

7. This is a summary of the source and target connections, the repository you are using, and the type of migration you're about to use:

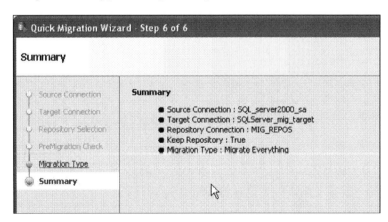

The migration

This follows the five phases mentioned earlier in the chapter:

- **Capture**: Writes the metadata to the repository
- **Convert**: Converts the metadata to the Oracle metadata
- **Generate**: Generates DDL scripts based on the metadata
- **Build**: Executes the scripts to create new objects in the target schema
- **Data Move**: Copies the data from the source to the target database

Once the process is complete, you can review the steps in a tabbed window. The upcoming screenshots show three points of the migration.

The first screenshot of the migration is towards the end of the first phase. You can see the types and tallies of the objects being migrated. Note that you can elect to automatically close the dialog on completion. This is true for many of the migration dialogs. For the **Quick Migration** wizard, we recommend that you leave it deselected. This way, you can review all of the phases of the migration when the wizard completes them before the dialog closes.

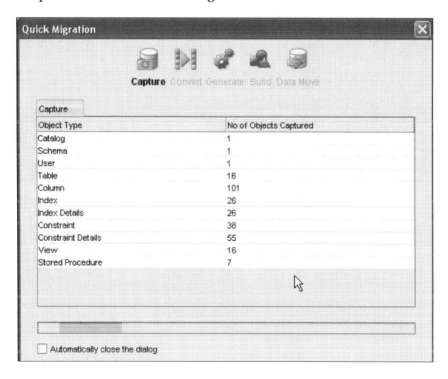

If the migration appears to have completed at any point, check the icons at the top of the window. These icons indicate the progress of the migration and should be highlighted if the migration has finished successfully.

The tail end of the **Capture** phase is shown in the preceding screenshot. Here, you see that the **Capture** icon has color, and there is also a **Capture** tab, indicating that the phase is now complete.

The next screenshot shows the final stage of the migration where the data is being moved to the target database. You can see that the all other phases are complete, and their tabs are now ready for review. What's also significant is that the data is not moved to the tables sequentially, but it's moved using threads instead so that much of the data is moved at the same time.

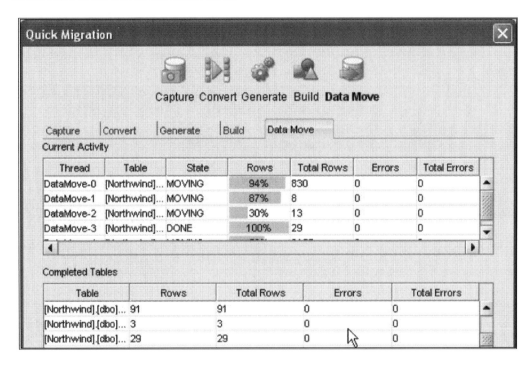

 Data Move is a misnomer. The data is copied from the source to the target database. None of the artifacts or data in the source database are affected in any way by the migration.

Verifying the results

Once the migration is complete, all that remains for you to do is verify the data. You can expand your connection and review the objects and the data created by browsing them as you would in any other Oracle connection that you have created.

The captured and converted metadata is still in your repository, and so you can return to the metadata that resulted from **Quick Migrate** and make some fine-grained adjustments. In the next section, we'll review the individual steps of the migration. Therefore, you can return to the metadata that resulted from Quick Migrate and make some fine-grained adjustments.

Reviewing the logs

When running a migration, the details of any issues or information are tracked in the **Migration Log** window. If you don't see a log window, go to **View | Log** to display it. Many entries are informative, while others show errors. The screenshot that follows shows the Microsoft SQL Server log and the Sybase migration log:

In the log displayed in the previous screenshot, we expanded the second item, which gathered a collection of changes with a similar theme. Here, the names of the converted objects have been modified. This might be due to duplicate names that would result from names being shortened during the conversion to comply with Oracle naming standards, or there may be other characters that do not match Oracle naming standards. In these cases, the name changes are for information purposes, and no error exists. You may still want to adjust some of the names to comply with your company's or project's standards.

This is a good opportunity to review the changed names and make additional modifications to the objects before the DDL scripts are prepared.

Generating scripts

Once you have made the changes and updated the converted model, you are ready to generate the scripts that are executed against the target schema. You may have changed the name of the captured and converted models, but the DDL script creates the new target schema based on the details of the source schema. We recommend that you review this name before you generate the DDL.

In the example that follows, the default name created for the Northwind sample model is shown. To change this name, select the main folder in the converted model and invoke the context menu. Select **Rename Schema** and change it to a more appropriate name for your target database:

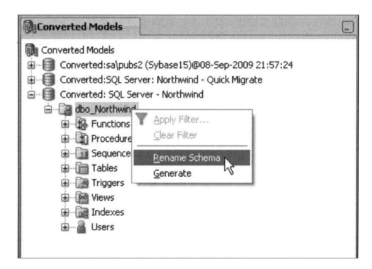

Once you're happy with all of the changes you have made, select **Generate** from the context menu. Close the dialog to reveal the complete script. In the example that follows, we have highlighted the Create User statement. This is the schema name that you may have changed:

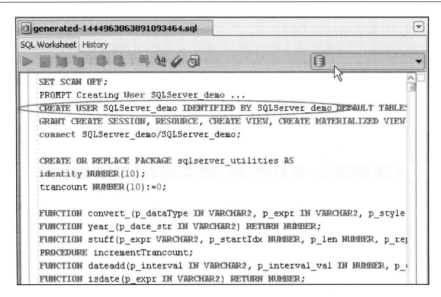

Migration reports

Once you have completed your migration, you can review the output of the various phases by reviewing reports that are run against the repository owner:

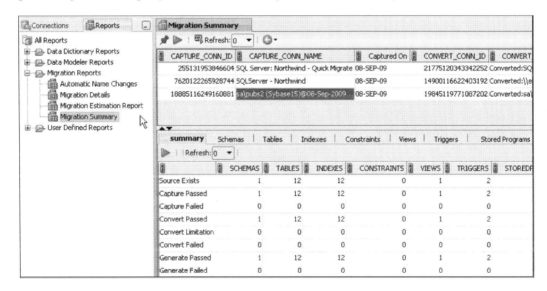

Migration reports are a useful addition to the migration process. These reports have the following functions:

- Help you determine the size of the project by outlining the number of objects you have
- Show the number of objects that failed to migrate, and in doing so, they help determine what and how much needs to be handled manually
- Display the automatic changes made to names

SQL Developer provides three reports that detail the success and failure points of the migration. An example of one of these reports is displayed in the previous screenshot. The set of reports also includes **Migration Estimation Report**.

Summary

In this chapter, we showed you how to prepare a migration repository, set up the database drivers, and create connections to non-Oracle databases. For further information on preparing for a database migration, refer to the *Migration Technology Center* on the *Oracle Technology Network*.

13
Oracle Data Miner 4.1

The data mining process just means extracting relevant information from the tons of available data in the database. The relevance of data is with respect to the problem statement of any particular project. Data miner in SQL Developer 4.1 has enhanced features, and though it is significant to touch upon the new features that can be useful for emerging technologies and the users, in this chapter we will be discussing all the new features provided with the **Data Miner** tool and also the general enhancements in and around the tool. One of the most relevant and significant additions to the data mining capability is the growing popularity of JSON data and its use in **Big Data** configuration. Data Miner now provides an easy-to-use JSON Query node. In this chapter, we will start off with data source node preparation.

Data source node

As a first step, to invoke the data miner tool within SQL Developer, the next screenshot explains the data miner architecture diagrammatically. Data Miner by default is integrated into SQL Developer since version 2.0 and when invoked from **Tools | Data Miner**, it checks for the Data Miner repository.

As a prerequisite, **Oracle Enterprise Edition** is required to hold the **Data Miner Repository** under the schema called ODMRS.

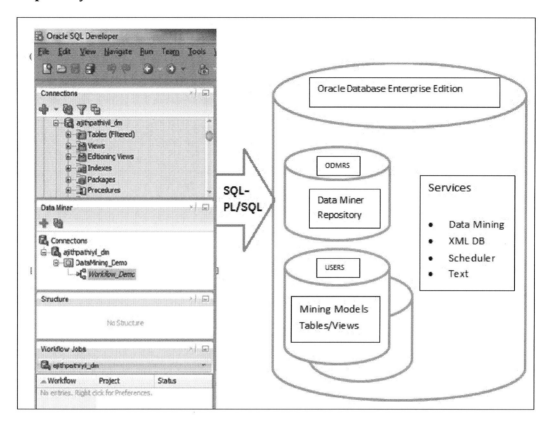

- Oracle Database Enterprise Edition will have all the services required to support Oracle Data Miner.

- Oracle Data Miner is a part of Oracle Advanced Analytics option to Oracle Database EE. Oracle Data Miner helps us in model building, testing, and scoring capabilities for Data Miner.

- Oracle XML DB provides services to manage the Data Miner repository metadata, such as the details of the workflow specifications.

- Oracle Scheduler provides the engine for scheduling the Data Miner workflows.

- Oracle Text provides the necessary services required to support Text Mining.

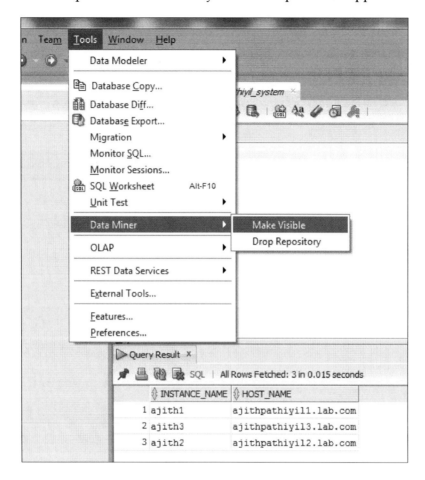

If the **Data Miner** tab is not visible, you can dock it in Oracle SQL Developer window.

When invoked, SQL Developer prompts for the installation of the **Data Miner** repository, if the repository is not already built. In my case, my database did not have a repository and I was prompted to create one, as shown in the following screenshot:

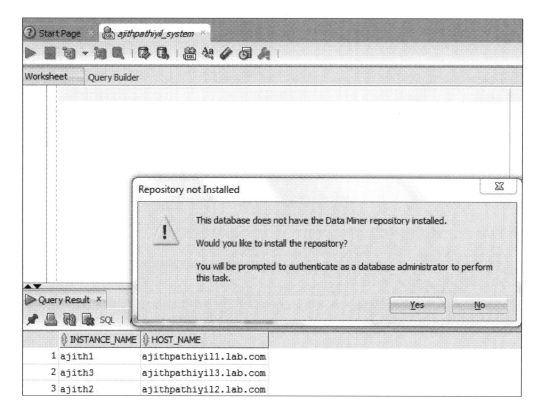

A Data Source node becomes the source of data for the data mining project. A data source node specifies the build data for a model. We will use the examples that were installed during the installation of the **Data Miner** repository. The following is the sequence that we will follow to add the data source node:

- Create a new project
- Create a new workflow
- Add nodes to workflows
- Link nodes
- Run the nodes
- View reports

Creating a new project

We can have the **Workflow Jobs** tab also open while we start creating our first project. To do this, go to **View** | **Data Miner** | **Workflow Jobs**.

Before you begin working on a **Data Miner** workflow, you need to create a **Data Miner** project, which serves as a container for one or more workflows. We created the data mining user during the installation; the user name is DM user. In the **Data Miner** tab, right-click on the data mining user connection that you previously created and select **New Project**, as shown in the following screenshot:

My new project name will be `DataMining_Demo`

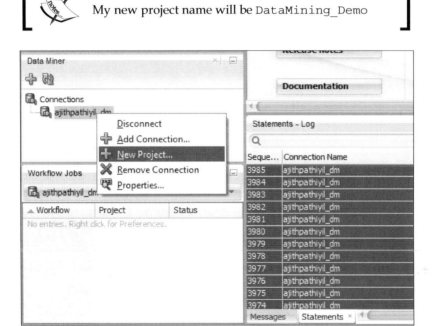

Creating a new workflow

A **Data Miner** workflow is a collection of connected nodes that describe data mining processes and provide directions for the **Data Mining** server. The workflow actually emulates all phases of a process designed to solve a particular business problem.

The workflow enables us to interactively build, analyze, and test a data mining process within a graphical environment, as shown in the following screenshot:

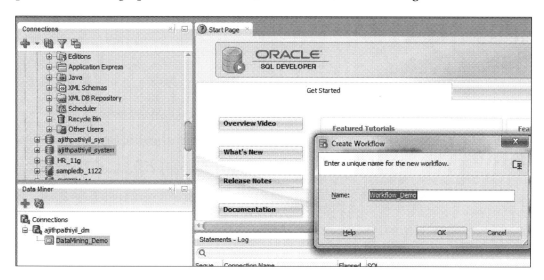

Addition of nodes to the workflow

Immediately after creating a new workflow, we will be able to see a blank workflow screen ready to build the workflow. The graphical representation for the workflow can be built by dragging and dropping into the workflow area. The components pane will give us all the nodes that we wish to add to the workflow.

> Each element that we drag and drop from the components pane will become a node in our workflow. To begin with the workflow, the first element is always the data source.

The components palette shows all the available types of nodes that we can use to build our workflow, but we will only use a couple of nodes as examples in this chapter.

The following table shows all the available types of nodes, only for reference purposes.

Type	Description
Model Nodes	They specify models to build or models to add to a workflow.
Evaluate and Apply Nodes	They evaluate and apply models.
Data Nodes	They specify data for mining operation, data transformation or to save data to a table.
Transforms Nodes	They perform one or more transformation on the table or tables identified in a Data node.
Predictive Query Nodes	They create predictive results without the need to build models. The predictive queries automatically generate refined predictions based on data partitions.
Text Nodes	They prepare data sources that contain one or more text columns so that the data can be used to Build and Apply models.
Link Nodes	They provide a way to link or connect nodes.

Remember, we had installed the sample data along with the data miner repository. For the rest of the chapter, we will use the sample tables from the sample to show the data miner concepts. As shown in the following screenshot, we will be using the table called INSUR_CUST_LTV_SAMPLE owned by the DM user to mine the data and exhibit the analytics capability of **Data Miner**:

In the **Define Data source** dialog box, select the said table, click on **Next** and then finish to have the data source created. **Explore Data** is another node that will be added, which can help us validate the data source. For this, just right-click on the **Data Source** node and select **Connect**, drag the arrow up to the **Explore Data** node, and we have completed the step.

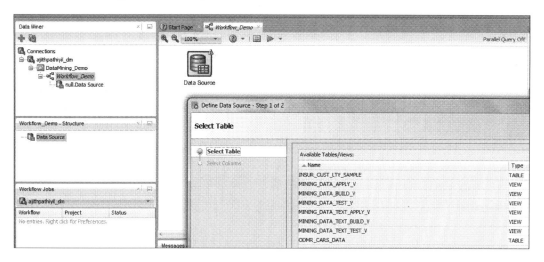

Link nodes

Once all the nodes are placed in the required order, the next step would be to link the nodes in a meaningful and correct way. In the following example, you can see how the **Data Source** node is connected to the **Explore Data** node by right-clicking and selecting the **Connect** option.

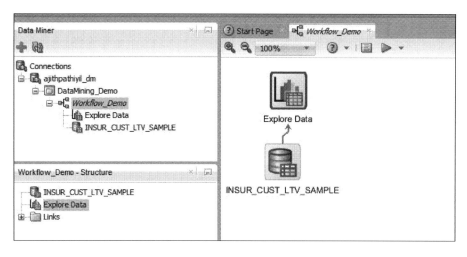

Run nodes

After connecting the nodes in a meaningful fashion, we will be able to run the node and submit a workflow job related to it. Right-click on the **Explore Data** node and select the **Run** option to submit the workflow job. The status of the related workflow job will be displayed in runtime on the **Workflow Jobs** pane.

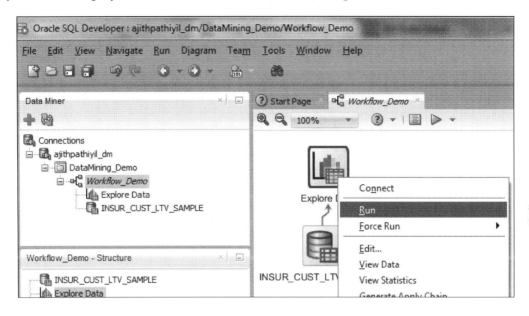

Once the nodes are defined, we are ready to run the nodes, which in turn submits the workflow job. The workflow job pane displays the submitted job and its status. A completed job is shown with a green tick (√) under the status column. We are now ready to generate the statistics report for the **Explore Data** node.

View reports

By clicking on **View Data**, **Data Miner** creates statistics based on a lot of information about each attribute in the dataset including a histogram, distinct values, mode, average, min and max value, standard deviation, variance, skewness, and kurtosis.

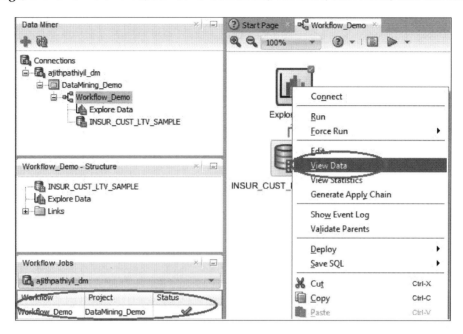

The display enables you to visualize and validate the data, and also to manually inspect the data for patterns or structure.

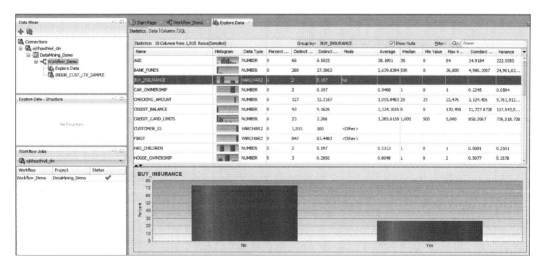

JSON data type

The growing popularity of JSON data and its easy implementation and use in mobile apps for the GET and POST methods of data transfer prompted Oracle to include the capability in **Data Miner**, which now provides an easy-to-use **JSON Query** node. The **JSON Query** node allows select and aggregate JSON data without entering any SQL commands. The **JSON Query** node opens, using all of the existing **Data Miner** features with JSON data. The enhancements include the following:

- Data Source node:
    - Identifies all the columns containing JSON data by referring to the IS_JSON constraint
    - Generates JSON schema for any selected column that contains JSON data in XML format
    - Imports JSON schema for a given column in XML format
    - Using the JSON schema viewer, the data is displayed

- Create Table node:
    - Ability to select a column to be typed as JSON
    - Generates JSON schema in the same manner as the data source node

JSON data from a 12c native table can be recreated over to **Data Miner** via the new **JSON Query** node. Once the data is projected to a relational format, **Data Miner** uses the data for processes such as graphing, data analysis, text processing, transformation, and modeling, as it is for any normal table without the JSON data column.

JSON Query node

This new node is automatically identified when connected to a 12c table with a column that contains data in the JSON format, which can be dragged and dropped into our workflow builder screen. Once the **JSON Query** node is added, we can link them to the **Data Source** node and the **Explore Data** node.

The data will start flowing from **Data Source | JSON Query | Explore Data**, as shown in the following figure. Apart from this, we can add the data classification to other nodes as we need.

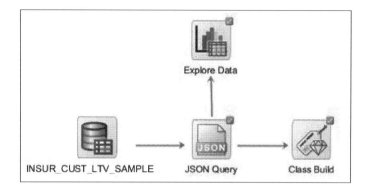

The APIs for data mining

The PL/SQL interface to Oracle Data Mining is implemented mainly using the following three packages:

- DBMS_DATA_MINING: This is the primary interface to Oracle Data Mining
- DBMS_DATA_MINING_TRANSFORM: This enables us to make use of convenient routines for data transformation
- DBMS_PREDICTIVE_ANALYTICS: This is a predictive analytics package

Using the available SQL and PL/SQL APIs, we can perform all following actions in the data miner:

- Run a workflow
- Cancel a running workflow
- Rename a workflow
- Delete a workflow
- Import a workflow
- Export a workflow
- Create a project
- Delete one or more projects
- Rename a project

Summary

In this chapter, we reviewed the many aspects of using Data Miner that is integrated with SQL Developer 4.1 and briefly went through its 12c support for the JSON data type. Using this easy-to-use data miner extension, we can quickly create a BI solution by mining out meaningful business intelligence data from a large volume of data. Though the data mining topic is, in itself, a complete source for another book, we are restricting the information provided in this book to the minimal concepts related to data mining that can be explored using SQL Developer 4.1.

The next and final chapter is about working with REST data services and REST development.

14

REST Data Services and REST Development

Oracle REST Data Services is based on Java EE and was developed as a substitute for other normally used web services options. Since REST Data Services is built on the Java EE, it provides many features by default, among which RESTful web services is the feature we will be concentrating on for this chapter. Oracle REST Data Services can also support deployments using Oracle WebLogic Server, GlassFish Server, Apache Tomcat, and a run in a standalone mode.

The Oracle Application Express installed in our database satisfies some of the requirements for implementing REST Data Services. Oracle REST Data Services simplifies the deployment process because there is no Oracle home required and connectivity is provided using an embedded JDBC driver.

About Oracle REST Data Services

This chapter is written with the assumption that you already have Oracle Apex installed in your machine. The setup steps provided are provided next to create an example that you can delete later on.

The latest release of REST Data Services can be downloaded from `http://www.oracle.com/technetwork/developer-tools/rest-data-services/downloads/index.html`. Oracle REST Data Services 3.0.2 is the latest release available for you to download and the filename is `ords.3.0.2.294.08.40.zip`.

If you are new to Application Express, you can refer to *Chapter 11, Working with Application Express.*

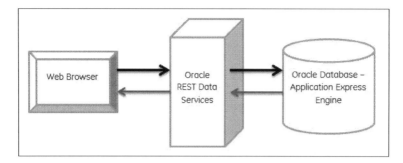

The preceding diagram briefly shows how a middle tier isolates the database server from the web browser access directly by creating a proxy layer. The middle tier can be a standalone REST Data Service on top of a Tomcat server, which would not require the help of a PL/SQL embedded gateway or mod_plsql. RESTful services connections are made through the APEX_REST_PUBLIC_USER user, while invoking PL/SQL Gateway operations, and for the database user APEX_LISTENER, which is used to query RESTful services definitions stored in Oracle Application Express.

SQL Developer gives us an easy way to install and run REST Data Services. The navigation you need to follow to install REST Data Services is **Tools | REST Data Services | Install**. The installation wizard takes us through four steps for having the connection creation. The **ORDS (Oracle REST Data Service)** ords.war file is used for the installation. In step 2 of the installation process, we will be choosing the option of using the ords.war file that comes with SQL Developer for installation.

 For Oracle REST Data Services there is no need of an Oracle home and the connectivity between the web tier and the database tier is provided using an embedded JDBC driver.

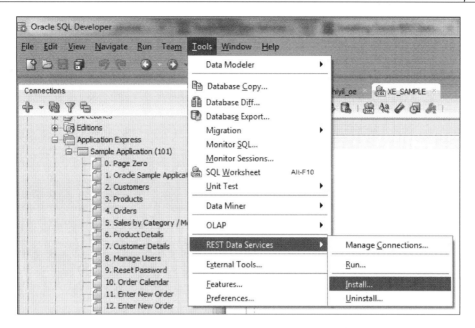

There are a few main ORDS configuration files that require a location for storage, we can specify any available space for keeping all the configuration files in one place.

For example, since we have SQL Developer installed on Windows, we can create a `c:\ORDS` directory to place all the configuration files during the installation.

Some of the major configuration files and the directory structure are shown in the following:

```
./
|
+-defaults.xml
+-apex.properties*
+-url-mapping.xml
|
+conf/
|
+-apex.xml
+-apex_al.xml
+-apex_rt.xml
+-apex_pu.xml
```

```
|
...
+-(db-name).xml
+-(db-name)_al.xml
+-(db-name)_rt.xml
+-(db-name)_pu.xml
```

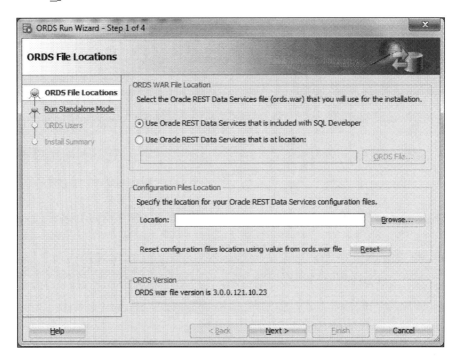

Oracle REST Data Services includes a web server that enables you to run in standalone mode. Standalone mode is designed for use only in development and test environments, and is not supported for use in production environments. We need to fill in a few details such as **HTTP Port**, **Static Resources Location**, **Database Connection** details, and **ORDS Users**.

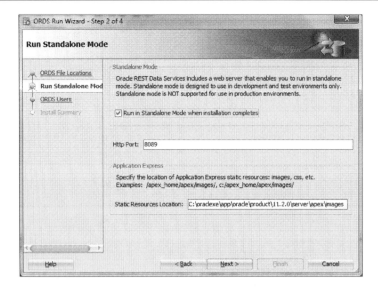

 Run in Standalone Mode when installation completes: This causes Oracle REST Data Services to run in standalone mode when the installation completes.

Step 2 of the ORDS installation wizard prompts us for the static resources location and also an option to run ORDS in standalone mode after installation, basically the standalone mode is the production mode where the ORDS services are not in editable mode, which is desirable for the production environments.

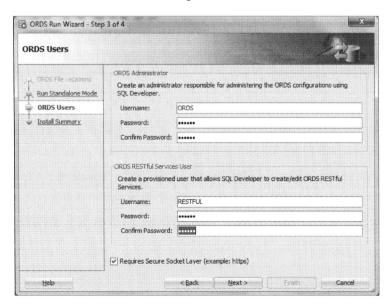

Before we proceed with the installation, the summary of the options selected in the wizard screens are displayed and when we click on the **Finish** button, ORDS progresses. The sample summary of my installation is shown in the following screenshot:

Once the installation of ORDS is complete, we can have two options under the **View** menu, which are as follows:

1. Open the **Administration** window for ORDS.
2. Open the development pane for the ORDS web service creation.

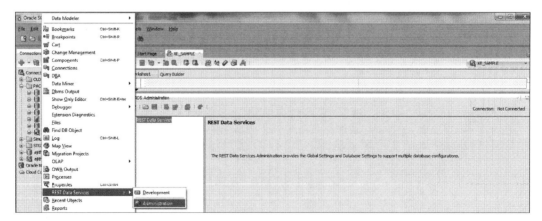

If **Administration** is selected, the **REST Data Services Administration** window opens, which enables us to add or edit new ORDS connections. How to create new connections is explained in the upcoming sections of this chapter.

The Oracle REST Data Services Administration toolbar and context menu

The Oracle REST Data Services **Administration** window has a toolbar with icons at the top, and a context menu when you right-click on the **REST Data Services** navigator. The toolbar and context menu let you perform the following actions:

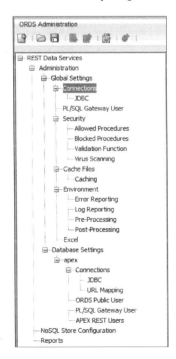

- A new administration **Create REST Data Services Administration** window is displayed.

- Global and database settings nodes are shown in the ORDS **Administration** pane.

- **Open File**: Any saved admin settings can be opened using this menu icon and if administration settings are already displayed, you will be warned if you want to overwrite the existing settings.

- **Save As**: This saves the current global and database settings to a .zip file.

- **Retrieve Settings**: This obtains the administration settings from REST Data Services.

- **Upload Settings**: This uploads the administration settings to REST Data Services. The database settings will be validated before they are uploaded. If any settings are invalid or if required settings are missing, the administration settings will not be uploaded.

- **Test Settings**: This validates the database settings and displays informational messages for incorrect settings or required settings that are missing. If errors are not found during validation, a message will be displayed that validation is completed successfully.

- **Launch URL**: This displays the home page in your browser, for example, `http://host:port/apex`.

- **Connect** (context menu only): This connects to Oracle REST Data Services (see *Connecting to Oracle REST Data Services*).

- **Disconnect** (context menu only): This disconnects from Oracle REST Data Services.

 Retrieve Settings, **Upload Settings**, and **Launch URL** are enabled when you connect to Oracle REST Data Services.

Once all the settings are done, we can verify the administration settings by clicking on the **Test Settings** icon which will display the errors in our settings; if there are no errors, then it will show a successful message.

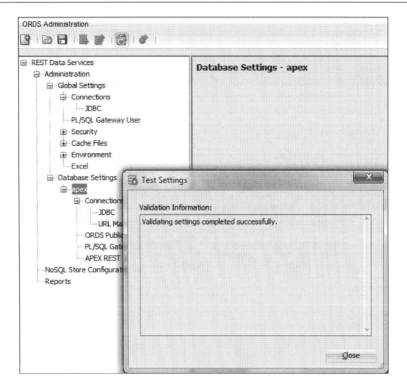

Connecting to Oracle REST Data Services

Oracle REST Data Services Administration connects to Oracle REST Data Services to retrieve or upload the administration settings. Right-click on the **REST Data Services** navigator to display the context-menu and select **Connect**. In the **Connection** dialog box, you can select an existing connection.

When you select a connection and click on **OK**, we will be prompted for the APEX_PUBLIC_USER password to connect to the database. The information we provide while creating the new connection are listed here:

- **Connection Name**: Any identifiable name to identify the REST Data Services that you are connecting to, we can have unique names for our own identification purpose.

- **Username**: REST Data Services Administrator username that you provided during REST Data Services installation. In our case it would be the APEX_PUBLIC_USER user, since we are using direct the PL/SQL Gateway for database connections.

- **Http or https**: Select the protocol that you want to use. For SSL based secured connections we will be using https.

- **Hostname**: DNS name or IP address of REST Data Services. This is the host where our database with APEX is up and running.

- **Port**: Port on which REST Data Services is listening for requests.

- **Server Path**: Location at which REST Data Services is deployed on the application server. Default: `/ords`.

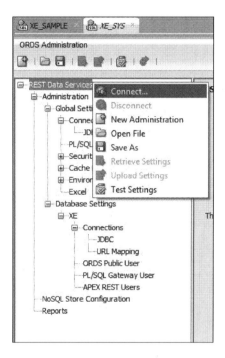

REST Data Services navigator – global and database settings

The **REST Data Services Administration** settings consist of the global settings and database settings for one or more databases. The settings are displayed in the following navigator hierarchy:

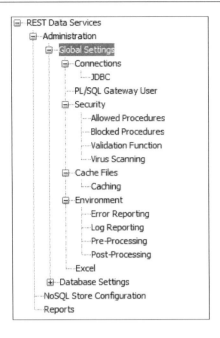

- **Connections**
    - ° **Username**: The database user used when invoking PL/SQL Gateway operations, for example, all Oracle Application Express operations. In our case it's APEX_PUBLIC_USER.
    - ° **Password**: The password for APEX_PUBLIC_USER database user.

- **Security**
    - ° **Verify Secure Socket Layer Requests**: Enable this option if HTTPS is a requirement.
    - ° **Maximum Cache Entries**: Maximum cache size.
    - ° **Allowed Procedures**: Specify procedures, packages, or schema names that can be executed using web services.
    - ° **Blocked Procedures**: Specify procedures, packages, or schema names that cannot be executed using web services.
    - ° **Validation Function**: Specify a Validation Function to determine if the requested procedure in the URL can be executed.

- **Cache Files**
  - ○ **Keep most recently used files**: Files that are most recently used will remain in the cache.
  - ○ **Keep files for the specified duration**: If selected, files that are cached expire after the specified number of days, hours, or minutes.
  - ○ **Total Cache Entries**: Maximum cache size.
  - ○ **Clear Cache**: Deletes the current cache entries.
  - ○ **Cache File Location**: Directory for the cache files.

- **Environment**
  - ○ **Error Reporting**: You can specify to show debug messages on the console, or to show error messages in a browser, or to do both or neither. In production systems, you should leave both options unselected (disabled).
  - ○ **Show debug messages on console**: If selected, displays debug messages on the console. This may help with problem diagnosis and is appended to the REST Data Services log output. However, you should not enable this option on production systems due to the performance impact of outputting large amounts of data to the log.
  - ○ **Show error messages on browser**: If selected, displays error responses in the browser, including for each a detailed error message and a stack trace. However, do not enable this option on productions systems due to the risk of sensitive information being revealed.

- **Log Reporting**
  - ○ **Logging**: Specifies whether to make entries in the Oracle REST Data Services log. The log includes activities such as adding a procedure to the cache, finding a procedure in the cache, or reloading a procedure. The log displays the database time and processing time in milliseconds for that procedure.
  - ○ **Keep most recent log messages**: If selected, entries that are most recent will remain in the log. Specify the maximum number of log messages to cache. When the maximum entries have been reached, the older log messages are removed from the cache when a new log message is added.

- **Excel**: If you are using Oracle Application Express, you have the option of placing your Excel files into an Application Express collection.

About RESTful services

Representational State Transfer (REST) is a new technology that suits the requirements of flashing the requested contents from a database on to the web browser screen. A service is described as RESTful when it conforms to the tenets of REST Data Services implemented.

Web services enable applications to interact with one another over the web browser or any similar platform independent environment. In a typical web services scenario, a business application sends a request to a service at a given URL by using the protocol over HTTP. The service receives the request, processes it, and returns a response. The web services is found in the URI format and method of the service is described by the HTTP method like GET, POST, PUT, and DELETE.

RESTful services terminology

The following are some major terms related to RESTful services:

- **RESTful service**: An HTTP web service based on the RESTful architecture.

- **Resource template:** An individual RESTful service that is able to service requests for some set of URIs.

- **Resource module**: A group of related resource templates.

- **URI template**: A URL that is formed for doing a particular action using the bind variable attached to it. For example, the pattern employees/{id} will match any URI whose path begins with employees/, such as employees/301.

- **Resource handler**: This is a query or an anonymous PL/SQL block that handles a particular HTTP method. Only one resource handler per HTTP method can be used.

  ```
  select empno, ename, dept from emp where empno = :id
  ```

- **HTTP operation**: Standard methods that can be performed on resources: GET (retrieve the resource contents), POST (store a new resource), PUT (update an existing resource), and DELETE (remove a resource).

RESTful services requirements and setup

For you to use the RESTful services features in SQL Developer, Oracle REST Data Services 3.0 must be installed and running.

You can use the **Oracle REST Data Services Install** wizard to install and run ORDS in standalone mode. This method is well explained in the initial sections of this chapter.

We can run the Oracle REST Data Services installer from the command line too.

Summary

In this chapter, we reviewed the many aspects of REST Data Services as an extension of SQL Developer 4.1. You learned how using SQL Developer installation of REST Data Services is made easy for web services developers. You also learned how to access and develop RESTful services based on the REST Data Services which you have implemented.

Index

exporting 84
folders, creating 71, 72
general reports, creating 73
importing 84
master-detail reports 78
running 18, 19
sharing, through user defined
extensions 84, 85
storing 72, 73
repository
associating, with user 270
creating 269, 270
managing 268
owner, setting up 269
**Representational State Transfer
(REST) 307**
resource consumer group 130
resource manager
about 129
issues 129
resource plan 130
RESTful services
about 307
HTTP operation 307
requirements 308
resource handler 307
resource module 307
resource template 307
setup 308
terminology 307
URI template 307
restore points
about 121
creating 121
guaranteed restore point 121
normal restore point 121
View Database Feature Usage option 121
reverse engineering
about 211, 212
models 213
RMAN backup/recovery
about 127
backup jobs 127
backup sets 127
image copies 128

RMAN settings 128
scheduled RMAN actions 128
roles 134
Rollback Segments option 135

S

sample schemas
installing 13
scene
setting 241, 242
setting up, in Application Express 242
scheduler 131, 132
screen magnifiers
using 143
screen reader readability
about 137
setting up 138
technologies 137
script runner
about 42-44
Autotrace pane 46, 47
DBMS Output pane 48-50
execution plan 44, 45, 46
Oracle Web Agent (OWA) pane 50, 51
Query Builder 51
scripts
running 42-44
snapshots (filtered)
about 123
creating 123
source editor
line number, reading 145
SQL Developer
applications, browsing 245-247
applications, managing 257
connection, creating 245
customizing 146, 147
Data Modeler 191
extensibility 219, 220
reports 56
schema objects, browsing 245
schema objects, working 245
used, for reporting on applications 260
used, for tuning PL/SQL code 250, 251
used, for tuning SQL 250, 251

Thank you for buying

Oracle SQL Developer

About Packt Publishing

Packt, pronounced 'packed', published its first book, *Mastering phpMyAdmin for Effective MySQL Management*, in April 2004, and subsequently continued to specialize in publishing highly focused books on specific technologies and solutions.

Our books and publications share the experiences of your fellow IT professionals in adapting and customizing today's systems, applications, and frameworks. Our solution-based books give you the knowledge and power to customize the software and technologies you're using to get the job done. Packt books are more specific and less general than the IT books you have seen in the past. Our unique business model allows us to bring you more focused information, giving you more of what you need to know, and less of what you don't.

Packt is a modern yet unique publishing company that focuses on producing quality, cutting-edge books for communities of developers, administrators, and newbies alike. For more information, please visit our website at www.packtpub.com.

About Packt Enterprise

In 2010, Packt launched two new brands, Packt Enterprise and Packt Open Source, in order to continue its focus on specialization. This book is part of the Packt Enterprise brand, home to books published on enterprise software – software created by major vendors, including (but not limited to) IBM, Microsoft, and Oracle, often for use in other corporations. Its titles will offer information relevant to a range of users of this software, including administrators, developers, architects, and end users.

Writing for Packt

We welcome all inquiries from people who are interested in authoring. Book proposals should be sent to author@packtpub.com. If your book idea is still at an early stage and you would like to discuss it first before writing a formal book proposal, then please contact us; one of our commissioning editors will get in touch with you.

We're not just looking for published authors; if you have strong technical skills but no writing experience, our experienced editors can help you develop a writing career, or simply get some additional reward for your expertise.

Getting Started with Oracle SOA B2B Integration: A Hands-On Tutorial

ISBN: 978-1-84968-886-4 Paperback: 332 pages

Implement Oracle B2B solutions effortlessly with the help of one of the most knowledgeable Oracle author teams ever assembled

1. Design, implement and monitor B2B transactions quickly using this clear, detailed and practical guide.

2. Wide coverage and detailed discussion of Oracle B2B functionality and features for the new and advanced users.

Getting Started with Oracle SOA B2B Integration: A Hands-On Tutorial

Implement Oracle B2B solutions effortlessly with the help of one of the most knowledgeable Oracle author teams ever assembled

Krishnaprem Bhatia   Alan Perlovsky
Scott Haaland

Oracle SOA Suite 11g Developer's Cookbook

ISBN: 978-1-84968-388-3 Paperback: 346 pages

Over 65 high-level recipes for extending your Oracle SOA applications and enhancing your skills with expert tips and tricks for developers

1. Extend and enhance the tricks in your Oracle SOA Suite developer arsenal with expert tips and best practices.

2. Get to grips with Java integration, OSB message patterns, SOA Clusters and much more in this book and e-book.

3. A practical Cookbook packed with recipes for achieving the most important SOA Suite tasks for developers.

Oracle SOA Suite 11g Developer's Cookbook

Over 65 high-level recipes for extending your Oracle SOA applications and enhancing your skills with expert tips and tricks for developers

Antony Reynolds   Matt Wright

Please check **www.PacktPub.com** for information on our titles

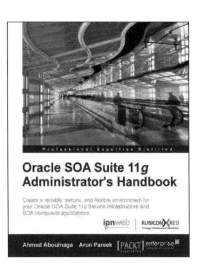

Oracle SOA Suite 11g
Administrator's Handbook

ISBN: 978-1-84968-608-2   Paperback: 380 pages

Create a reliable, secure, and flexible environment for
your Oracle SOA Suite 11g Service Infrastructure and
SOA composite applications

1. Monitor your Oracle SOA Suite environment
   and fine tune the performance of your Oracle
   SOA Suite services and applications.

2. Manage the underlying WebLogic server,
   threads and timeouts, file systems, and
   composite applications.

Oracle SOA Suite 11g R1
Developer's Guide

ISBN: 978-1-84968-018-9   Paperback: 720 pages

Develop Service-Oriented Architecture Solutions
with the Oracle SOA Suite

1. A hands-on, best-practice guide to using and
   applying the Oracle SOA Suite in the delivery
   of real-world SOA applications.

2. Detailed coverage of the Oracle Service Bus,
   BPEL PM, Rules, Human Workflow, Event
   Delivery Network, and Business Activity
   Monitoring.

3. Master the best way to use and combine
   each of these different components in the
   implementation of a SOA solution.

Please check **www.PacktPub.com** for information on our titles

Printed in Great Britain
by Amazon